CHARACTERS OF WOMEN IN NARRATIVE LITERATURE

By the same author

ALDOUS HUXLEY
OUT OF THE MAELSTROM : Psychology and the Novel in
the Twentieth Century

CHARACTERS OF WOMEN IN NARRATIVE LITERATURE

Keith M. May

.

St. Martin's Press   New York

All rights reserved. For information, write:
St. Martin's Press, Inc., 175 Fifth Avenue, New York, NY 10010
Printed in Hong Kong
First published in the United States of America in 1981

ISBN 0–312–12993–9

Library of Congress Cataloging in Publication Data

May, Keith M
    Characters of women in narrative literature.

    Bibliography: p. 176
    Includes index.
    1. Women in literature.   I.   Title.
PN56.5.W64M38 1981   809′.93352042   80–26237
ISBN 0–312–12993–9

Nothing so true as what you once let fall:
'Most women have no characters at all.'

Pope, *Moral Essays,* Epistle II
'Of the Characters of Women'

When they elevate *themselves* as 'woman in
herself', as 'higher woman', as 'idealist'
woman, they want to *lower* the general level
of rank of woman . . .

Nietzsche, *Ecce Homo*

Contents

1 Creative Myths

> Humanity does not pass through phases as a train passes through stations: being alive, it has the privilege of always moving yet never leaving anything behind. Whatever we have been, in some sort we are still.
>
> C. S. Lewis

The nature of the relationship between fictional characters and the development of character in everyday life seems always to have been taken for granted rather than thoroughly studied, yet the subject is neither simple nor unimportant. Faced with this question many people are likely to point out that writers in their works offer interpretations of individuals they have met, or produce composites of observed traits in accordance with their deliberate or unwitting purposes. In other words, the first assumption would be that art inexactly copies life.

The inexactness, it will be said, is due in the first instance to the mere need and function of art: to impose order upon what is 'in itself' a jumble. Thus even the most fully developed fictional character, say Joyce's Leopold Bloom, has more shape than an actual human being. Then, over and above this basic requirement of art, is the author's desire to make a particular personal order, to express himself through characters and actions. Further elaborations arise at this point. The author must work within a convention, and the convention itself dictates, or at all events limits, the range and quality of character portrayed. Moreover, literary characters themselves often have forebears or progeny, so that once a figure has been presented to the world many subsequent figures owe at least as much to him as to their creators' observations of life.

However, all these familiar points do nothing more than qualify the first assumption, that art imitates life. But what of the reverse process? People also assume, and rightly, that life imitates art in some degree. We gather, for instance, from the novels of Jane Austen as well as from other sources that in the late eighteenth and early nineteenth centuries some women emulated the heroines of the novels of sensibility. Some of these women tried in vain to be more fervent and more sentimental than they would otherwise have been, while others presumably discovered or created in themselves a genuine propensity to acute feeling. Many more illustrations of this sort of process could be provided, so that in the end it would seem certain that fiction is liable to modify character in the social world. Nor, as I have suggested, is this necessarily a matter of the individual's having one sort of character to begin with and subsequently changing under the influence of literature: rather it may sometimes be that the person's real potentialities are fostered through acquaintance with literary models. Conversely, of course, potentialities might be blocked, as when sensibilities are blunted or distorted by literature. These and similar possibilities have been recognized from the time of Plato at least, yet there are phases in literary criticism (and ours is one of them) when the question of the influence of literature upon character is rarely a serious subject for discussion.

It is clear enough that the whole topic, for all the numerous scattered assertions and (more commonly) tacit assumptions down the ages, still requires systematic investigation. One thing no one knows is whether there are characters of the utmost verisimilitude in literature who are actually impossible. The psychologist R. B. Cattell suggests as much in his *The Scientific Analysis of Personality*,[1] but what Cattell does not consider is the possibility that an author may give one of his characters a remarkable combination of personality traits to such potent effect that a similar combination subsequently appears for the first time in the real world. Is this merely fanciful? What is certain is that there are types of character in fiction who seem at first unbelievable and are later to be found, so to speak, living next door.

I raise these questions not of course to answer them but to explain the position taken in this book. Clearly the position cannot here be 'justified' in the careful manner of a philosopher, but at least it can be roughly expounded. I assume straightforwardly that the groundwork of a character, in life and literature, consists of the socio-historical circumstances in which the character appears. Plainly there are always ambitious people, envious people, courageous people and so forth, but of course it is the precise varieties of these dispositions that we shall be dealing with. The social circumstances, then, are the soil which germinates the general aspects of character. Thus, while there have perhaps always been questioning men, no period before the Renaissance produced the species of perplexity which unfolded into the character of Hamlet. Hamlet was a new man.

However, character does not grow, or does not regularly grow, entirely of its own accord from specific conditions: its cultivation is assisted by artists of one sort or another, mainly writers. The writer does not select from or distort character features he has encountered merely in the interests of his private vision: however eccentric his vision, it is a vision of something that is actually there. He is not alone. Commonly certain modes of thought and feeling are stirring in the soil and are dimly apprehended by perhaps only a few people. Among these people are writers who, unlike their fellows in this percipient minority, have the ability to raise the stirrings to full consciousness and if they are writers of fiction to embody them in characters. When this has been done (the Hamlet-character, say, has been developed in a play) at first a few and then a good many people begin to discern in themselves the possibilities of such a character. It is not that they necessarily model themselves on the personality but that they find the values of the personality congenial, and incorporate them, with modifications, into their own attitudes and behaviour. In this way writers in part imitate and in part beget real-life character.

On the basis of this brief outline I wish to emphasize two points: first, that writers have a legislative function, however far removed their works may be from polemic or didacticism, and secondly that character is evolutionary. When Shelley said, 'Poets are the unacknowledged legislators of the world', he meant that literature is the source of moral attitudes and creeds; and this observation, in its full profundity, would be hard to refute. Shelley might have added that when the 'poet' or writer invents characters these are charged with his notions of value; they are elements in his criticism of life. In the main characters will be examined from this point of view.

We are concerned with characterizations of women in literature and if writers are seen partly (though far from exclusively) as legislators there will be little temptation to worry about the truth, or to belittle the influence, of their models of women. It will be understood that fictional women, whether they are naturalistic or fabulous, whether they are presented as descriptive or prescriptive, convey some sort of exemplary effect.

This is the right emphasis because it directs our attention to more or less answerable questions and helps to fend off suppositions that some writers disinterestedly portray real women while others, perhaps no less talented, just make propaganda. Distinctions of this kind can and will be drawn, but they will be allowed through the barrier only after careful inspection. We cannot sensibly mark off a body of real-life perceptions and compound them into an image-cluster labelled 'real women'. People often fancy that they have such a criterion but actually they have only a hotch-potch of observations, cultural models, fantasies, prejudices and (to accommodate the Jungian 'anima') images derived from mother-figures. In any event, the verisimilitude of a woman in literature does not depend on how closely she corresponds with either one's experience or one's preconceptions.

Neither of course does the verisimilitude of a man, and part of the reason for addressing oneself to this topic is that until fairly recent times women were predominantly portrayed by men, so there is the suspicion that the portraits were not drawn rightly. Certainly there is truth in this but, as will be seen, it is a complicated truth. However, the chief question is not about truth and falsity but about legislative force.

In other words, how and to what effect have women down the ages been depicted in literature? Always there has been purpose; always there has been advocacy. Women should be this or that, and since writers are unacknowledged legislators their representations have affected social being. However, we should not contemplate past models of women merely out of curiosity and in the secure knowledge that a number of quaint notions have now been discarded in favour of the truth. Contemporary women are in some degree an accretion of past beliefs about the nature of women. If a modern woman rebels against her inheritance, putting forward not indeed the 'truth' but her own model, she does so with a consciousness substantially formed by her inheritance. So we are faced with the usual paradox of historical activities: the attempt to see the past with eyes that the past has to a degree created. Nevertheless, if anything stands apart from the evolutionary process we shall be considering it is not some aboriginal core of womanliness but just the measured attitude involved in trying to trace the phases of such evolution. Since our attention will be confined not merely to literature but to narrative and dramatic literature, there is no difficulty in knowing where to begin : we begin of course with Homer.

As most commentators have recognized, Homer's work is realistic, though not in the nineteenth- or twentieth-century sense. The point is partly that he is an accurate, unillusioned observer of behaviour and partly, as E. M. W. Tillyard has pointed out, that his characters are characters, not symbols.[2] Homer's people may be typical, and even in many instances prototypical, but they scarcely represent general forces or ideas. They do, however, reflect a wide range of social and psychological reality. At that period, whatever Homer's dates and whatever the distance between him and the age which he celebrated, there was a society in which the women, with a tiny number of exceptions, were in bondage to their menfolk. The culture was predominantly heroic and its zenith was the *Iliad,* a poem recounting fifty days of a ten-year war.

The values of the *Iliad* are transmitted most clearly through the figure of Achilles, whose behaviour until his final act of decency towards Priam, king of Troy, is less than admirable. Hector, the Trojan hero, is plainly a nobler figure than Achilles, but the latter is the man whose actions, for good or ill, illustrate the Homeric standards. Achilles is badly treated by Agamemnon over the captive girl, Briseis, but he himself then behaves badly in withdrawing from the fighting. His return, after the killing of his friend, Patroclus, is triumphant but merciless, for while he is justified in killing Hector, he is wrong to abuse Hector's corpse. In short, Achilles' actions emphasize the mores which the poem celebrates. At the same time the reader or audience is expected on the whole to sympathize with the 'swift and excellent Achilles' and certainly not to loathe him or be disappointed that he does not suffer some nemesis in the poem itself. (Of course he is a fated man and this fact partly explains his nature and our sympathy.) Certainly judgements from a humanitarian standpoint, such as the judgement in Auden's phrase, 'Iron-hearted, man-slaying Achilles',[3] can only be made by standing outside the world of the poem.

The world of the poem naturally and prominently includes sorrow, but the sorrow is part of a necessary ambivalence. Homer seems to feel that many of the situations are terrible, but without the bad things there would be no honour. Such, then, is the ethos in which the women must play their part. It is an ancillary part, yet the women, mortal or immortal, are vivid, congruent and believable. Even Hera, the consort of Zeus, is an excellent copy of a pugnacious wife who knows that in open disagreement her husband can always get his own way. Her only chance is to fool Zeus through beauty and love, as she does in Book 14, when, decked out by Aphrodite, she arouses in him greater desire than he has ever felt before. Such Olympian comedy must have been a reasonably faithful reflection of social being in that Hera has every bit as much force of character as Zeus but lacks his power.

In general the women of the *Iliad* exist to aid or lament over the warriors. Achilles naturally receives the unquestioning (though fatalistic) support of Thetis, his mother : he is also helped by Iris, the messenger of the gods, and by Athene who at the beginning checks his move to commit the great crime of killing Agamemnon. Among the Trojan nobles Paris is the favourite of Aphrodite, while Hector has a devoted wife in Andromache, and his death is lamented by Andromache, Hecabe and Helen in turn. Helen in fact regards Hector as the finest of her Trojan 'brothers', the only man in Troy to treat her with courtesy and kindness.

Andromache and Helen, the most notable women of the *Iliad,* make only brief appearances amid the copious scenes of battle and male transactions, but each is impressive. Andromache is the prototype of all the fictional wives who seek to restrain their men from fatal encounters and are left at the end bereft of protection for themselves and their children. After Hector's death she knows prophetically that Troy will eventually be sacked and the women and children 'carried off in the hollow ships', taken as slaves. All the Trojans are in mourning for Hector, but, says Andromache, 'Mine is the bitterest regret of all, because you did not die in bed and stretching out your arms to me give me some tender word that I might have treasured in my tears by night and day'.[4]

Helen is a more complex figure. She retains her beauty and sensuality but is now repentant. Paris still fascinates her sexually but she has a poor opinion of his character : in effect she thinks, 'I have exiled myself and brought about all this destruction on account of a mediocre fellow whom, nevertheless, I still can't resist.' Throughout the years in Troy she has had little occupation except to weave a web depicting the events of the war, and she is torn at times between a desire to see again her real husband, Menelaus, and a certain acceptance of her acquired Trojan identity.

If the women of the *Iliad* have the function of highlighting the heroic ethos (though as personalities they are not merely functional), this is more emphatically the case with the women of the *Odyssey*. Women may detain or threaten Odysseus but eventually all except the Sirens speed him on his way to Ithaca, reunion with Penelope and a proper end to his struggles.

What matters most in this poem is the character of Odysseus. He is the most imitable of ancient heroes, the paragon of his pre-Platonic and pre-Christian age. In terms of instruction, as opposed to delight, we glean from the *Odyssey* the values of resource, wisdom, expertise, steadfastness and bravery. In these qualities Penelope, wife of Odysseus, is almost his equal. (In steadfastness she is fully his equal.) Beauty is a value, but a lesser one. Beauty, in the persons of Calypso, Nausicaa, Circe and the Sirens, seeks to detain Odysseus from his journey home, yet also serves to support or heighten him.

In Book I it is Athene (one of Achilles' divine helpers) who takes compassion on Odysseus, because he had been languishing on Calypso's isle of Oxygia for seven years, making love to Calypso at night and weeping on the sea-shore by day. At her own request Athene departs from the halls of Zeus to Ithaca, there to guide Telemachus, son of Oydsseus. Meanwhile Hermes is despatched to Oxygia to help Odysseus himself. In Book IV Helen, now at home with Menelaus, uses a drug and persuasion to enlist the aid of her husband (since Odysseus' plight is ultimately her fault and she is regretful). Calypso, though she loves Odysseus, is quickly persuaded to give him up and soon provides him with a raft, a fair wind, clothing and sumptuous victuals. After that, in Phaeacia the princess Nausicaa wishes to marry Odysseus who in a wretched state has been cast up on her shore, but she too is willing to let him go, with only the request that he remember her from time to time. Circe is perhaps the most noteworthy. Having tried and failed to turn Odysseus into one of her hapless swine, she soon becomes yet another of the hero's helpers. Odysseus defeats Circe and, terrifying her with his sword, makes her promise to commit no further mischief. From that moment Circe gives Odysseus exactly the guidance he needs: on how to conduct himself in Hades, how to parley with Teirisias and how to evade the Sirens, Scylla and Charybdis and the isle of Helios. While Odysseus is undergoing these and other adventures Penelope in Ithaca wards off the suitors by her device of weaving and unpicking a web for Laertes.

Penelope is the perfect wife for Odysseus : comely, enduring, faithful, intelligent and almost excessively wary, so that she is only with
the greatest difficulty persuaded at the end that the disguised
Odysseus is indeed he.

In Homer's world there are of course destructive women though
they chiefly serve to highlight the qualities of heroes. The man who
counts is not brought down by women. Men die directly or in-
directly through the devices of women, but the great men are
untouched by these devices or profit from them. Odysseus, for
example, learns from the shade of Agamemnon of Agamemnon's
murder by Clytemnestra and this serves to increase Odysseus'
caution when he arrives at Ithaca. In fact the women generally
enhance the heroic values and most of the women are positively
likeable. The values remain intact, beyond question. The sorrow-
ing of women is not anti-war but an inescapable part of war.
Things are as they are. Though Helen sparks off the dreadful
conflict, she is not blamed for this, except by individuals in
moments of bitterness. Circe with her wand, her beauty and her
lovely voice is invaluable to the man, favoured by the gods, who
can master her.

How sound, therefore, is the belief of some modern commentators that many major female characters of ancient literature
should be classified as either 'good mothers' or 'terrible mothers',
the former category consisting of nurturing, supportive women and
the latter of sorceresses, betrayers, murderesses and *femmes fatales*?
It is further conjectured that well before Homer there existed, if
not a matriarchy, at least a pantheon of goddesses whose over-
throw by the Hellenes explains an insecurely aggressive posture
towards women in Greek literature.[5] Leaving aside the anthropological speculation, for which there seems to be no evidence,
the classification as such is acceptable, provided it is tempered by
an appreciation that in Homer at least, the terrible mothers are
not finally terrible. They are more correctly viewed as enchanting
women whose power to sap a man of his valour proves his
(possibly only slight) inferiority. 'Terrible mothers' such as Helen
and Circe are less a threat to male excellence than a confirmation
of it. Nor does it seem reasonable to read into Homer a marked
fear that goddesses, which is to say anti-heroic values, might regain
strength and sack the present dispensation.

But it must be remembered that as yet human life has no goal
and no one is conducting a searching criticism of moral values.

The journey of the *Odyssey* (unlike some later journeys such as those of the *Aeneid* and *A Pilgrim's Progress*) is a journey home. The combatants of the *Iliad* too just want to end the war or, like Achilles, to keep on winning trophies. There is no probing examination of justice, no heaven to which mortals can aspire and no assumption that a better life can be built on earth. By the time of the Athenian dramatists an examination of justice at least was in progress and the dramatists themselves, often and strikingly through their female characters, were among the moral pioneers. In this phase some of the women may be firmly classed as 'terrible mothers', though even here one is forced to add qualifications.

Gilbert Murray has remarked that Greek plays are plays of ideas, so that concomitantly with the dramatic splendour of some of them, the feats of characterization, the poetry and the structural features which Aristotle discusses in the *Poetics* the authors were questioning customs and laws, not merely portraying them.[6] Aeschylus, Sophocles and Euripedes as well as some of the comic writers, were more interested in concepts than Shakespeare can be held to have been. In this most questioning of ancient periods, the fifth century, the dramatists embodied in their plays some of the moral questions which the philosophers were discussing. From the point of view which excludes the idea of goodness as a state, moral problems can perhaps be reduced to problems of justice. Right action is just action towards others. Which laws are satisfactory and which need changing? When, if ever, is it right for a woman to kill her husband or a son to kill his mother? Should a man discard his wife for the sake of self-advancement or sacrifice his offspring to appease the gods? Can a wife be reasonably expected to die for her husband? Behind all such considerations lies nemesis, meaning not justifiable retribution in human terms but simply the unchallengeable penalties imposed by the gods. Naturally these matters have to be explored from the standpoint of sufferers, and while tragic heroes are commonly victims of the gods, heroines are victims of men, or of masculine proclivities. Is this not the main reason why there are so many splendid women in the tragedies and why the wickedest are worthy of respect?

The wickedest, in the sense that their names have been bywords for evil, are Clytemnestra and Medea, but in the tragedies they do not appear in such an unequivocal light. A plain recital of Clytemnestra's deeds in the *Agamemnon* of Aeschylus would leave her almost no redeeming features, yet she is magnificent. The triumphant Agamemnon returns from the war, bringing with him Cassandra, daughter of Priam, as part of his spoils. Clytemnestra gives him greetings which though ostensibly suitable are designed to make him feel uneasy. She goes on to demonstrate her mastery over this leader of men by persuading him against his will into the hubristic act of walking upon a purple carpet. Then, as she has plotted in advance, she kills him and Cassandra : the palace doors open to reveal an exultant Clytemnestra standing over the two bodies as they lie in a silver bath. However, after this climax come interchanges between Clytemnestra and the Chorus of Elders in which she confidently and jubilantly argues that Agamemnon, a rather weak and conceited man whose authority always exceeded his merits, has been rightly killed because he sacrificed their daughter, Iphigenia, in order to gain a favourable wind for the Trojan expedition. Helen didn't cause the war : she simply gave an excuse to these fools of men to go away fighting and whoring for ten years. And Clytemnestra has never been able to forgive that moment before the Argive fleet set sail when 'on my virgin daughter his savage sword descended'.

Clytemnestra is evil in her total bloodthirsty elation (and there are the complications that she has a lover, Aegisthus, and no acceptable reason for killing Cassandra), but her argument leaves even the hostile male Chorus unable to tell right from wrong. This is the point : Aeschylus, the earliest and most conservative of the three great tragic dramatists, was already unsure of traditional moral judgements. This becomes even more apparent in the other two plays of the Oresteian triology. In *The Libation-Bearers* Clytemnestra is hopelessly corrupt but her entreaties to her son, Orestes, to spare her life are entirely reasonable, and in the *Eumenides* when Orestes is brought to trial he is only narrowly acquitted of the murder. Apollo, who caused Orestes to kill his murderess mother, acts as counsel for Orestes but produces palpably weak 'male' arguments. In the end Athene gives the casting vote in favour of Orestes, so that a verdict of 'justifiable matricide' is reached; but it is made plain that the moral and legal problems involved are beyond human capacity.

Euripedes' Medea is an even more strikingly ambiguous characterization. She is a beautiful homicidal maniac and yet, if anything, members of the audience identify themselves with her, even as she sends a poisoned robe to Jason's innocent bride and kills her own innocent children. Medea is the complete wronged woman in that she, a barbarian beauty who once saved Jason's life, has been proudly brought by him to Corinth as his wife but is now to be cast off and parted from her children so that her husband might enhance his social standing. Accordingly, before the beginning of the play Jason has made preparations to marry a princess and Medea is sleepless with grief. Jason comforts Medea with politic arguments, while she in return rails against him and all men. Interestingly enough, when the killings of the innocents are over and the mob are in pursuit to tear Medea to pieces, she escapes in a dragon-drawn chariot (the equivalent in this play of a *deus ex machina*). So one of the worst of legendary women in a sense gets away with it because while she is certainly a 'fiend' and a 'foul tigress', she is also a victim of attitudes which Euripedes felt compelled to question.

This is not the constant function of the women in the plays but it is one of the most common. It is possible to detect in the tragedies a series of propitiatory acts towards women or, Jungianly speaking, towards the 'female' components of the psyche. That is one way of looking at the matter. What is certain, however, is that the plays reveal intellectual curiosity, realistic observation, erosion of myths and an access of moral uncertainty. The mythical personages change shape, doing the same deeds for different motives, doing different deeds altogether, assuming forms appropriate to fifth-century Athens. Jason can be self-seeking, Achilles a faint-heart, Electra a whining housewife, Theseus a tragic blunderer. Clytemnestra and Medea have their partial justifications. The dramatists in their legislative role focused their gaze upon women especially, transforming them from embellishments of the action into dynamic agents. Antigone, as the protagonist of Sophocles' third Theban play, is an outstanding example.

According to one critic, Herbert Marder, Virginia Woolf saw the *Antigone* of Sophocles as 'a primer of resistance to masculine tyranny', but this is far from Sophocles' whole story.[7] Another writer, Sven Armens, refers to the character of Antigone as representing 'the humanistic principle of the matriachal world with its emphasis on man's goodness and dignity'.[8] In fact Antigone is a brave fanatic, who is realistically capable of spite towards her less ardent sister and who defies Creon, the king, partly out of love for her dead brother, Polynices, and partly from principle. I doubt if there is much more feeling for 'man's greatness and dignity' in Antigone's attitude than in Creon's, since each of them has respectable motives. Creon orders that the body of Polynices should be left to rot because he wishes to warn the populace against any further treason and his desire is for a stable city. Nevertheless, Antigone has our sympathy and admiration in her resolute defiance. The play is about the incompatibility of two loves : love for the state and love for an individual. In the end it is Creon's tragedy as well as Antigone's, since his son kills himself for love of Antigone, and the attitude of the play as a whole, expressed through the Chorus, is an even-handed sense of loss and of man's powerlessness before the gods.

The *Antigone* may be used as a primer of resistance to men but it was not written as such. Greek tragedies, especially some of the plays of Euripedes, exhibit compassion for suffering women and often it is shown that they suffer because they are women. But what is in question is the law, human or divine, rather than a harshness which is supposed to belong to male nature as such. There seems to be no suggestion that inherent masculine qualities tend to authoritarian strictness while female qualities are emotional and lenient. It is simply that the men are in power, on earth and therefore on Olympus. Euripedes indeed, much more than his two great predecessors, regularly deflates the heroic outlook, but he does so in consequence of his realistic concern with justice. He seems to ask what people in these situations would actually do and how they would feel. Euripedes' unfortunate women are not necessarily nice, though some of them are. His Electra is a peasant's drab wife who urges Orestes to kill their mother, Clytemnestra, out of vindictiveness. Clytemnestra herself is a commonplace woman who doesn't deserve to be killed. Euripedes' *The Trojan Women* is filled with the lamentations of women because it is a thoroughgoing anti-war play. (It should be added that this play includes the piteous parting scene between Andromache and her little boy; a portrait, that is, of the event which Homer's Andromache foresees but which it was not part of Homer's purpose to include.) The same dramatist's *Iphigenia in Tauris* and *Iphigenia in Aulis* give us, by and large, women (especially Iphigenia herself) who are notably more reasonable and more sensible than the men. And we should not overlook the *Alcestis* of Euripedes, which is an attack on the assumption that a wife might fairly be expected to die for her husband.

Over and above these Euripedean revaluations of women (which some critics regard as precursers of those Athenian comedies, notably Aristophanes' *Lysistrata,* in which women rebel against their men) it may well be that Euripedes' chief contribution lay in the *Hippolytus.* This play is presumably the first complete love-tragedy, announcing the theme which is so prominent in Western literature down to modern times. Phaedra, the heroine, is the ancestor not only of other dramatists' Phaedras but of such a modern figure as Anna Karenina. Here indeed was a new role, giving rise to immense and varied consequences.

It will be convenient briefly to recall the plot of this play. Phaedra, wife of Theseus, has fallen hopelessly in love with Hippolytus, the illegitimate son whom Theseus begot twenty-odd years earlier when he raped the Queen of the Amazons. Phaedra has told no one of her feelings and is starving herself to death. Eventually she is persuaded to tell her nurse who, after promising to keep the secret, nevertheless informs Hippolytus. On learning about this betrayal Phaedra writes a note making false accusations against Hippolytus and then hangs herself. When Theseus learns the contents of the suicide note he exiles Hippolytus who, as he is departing, receives fatal injuries in a chariot accident engineered by the god Poseidon. Finally, Theseus learns the truth.

There are several points germane to our purpose to make about the *Hippolytus.* First, Euripedes' innovation (for it does seem to have been his) was to make an entire play out of the kind of story which had formerly been subordinate. Phaedra's love is not related to such 'larger' spheres as war, justice, heroic enterprise. It is of itself and for itself. The only alternative way of reading the play is to fasten on Theseus' final despair or on Hippolytus' dying lament: 'Would that the human race might bring a curse on the gods!' But to look at the story in this way is, once again, to stress the importance of human emotions, upon which the gods so readily trample.

The second point is that Phaedra insensately loves not Theseus, the virile adventurer and wise lawgiver, but his conspicuously less virile son. Hippolytus reveres Artemis, goddess of chastity: he loathes sex and shuns women. Arising from this is the third point, that Aphrodite contrives the whole tragedy out of jealousy and wounded pride. In the distant past Aphrodite had been largely responsible for the immense upheaval of the Trojan War, because it was she who brought Paris and Helen together, but from now on she will be responsible for merely personal tragedies – and sometimes, of course, for personal joys. In other words, while the poetry of adventure and the poetry of justice continue (though the former suffers some abatement), they are joined by the poetry of sexual love.

These categories of poetry are not of course meant to be comprehensive (celebratory verse for instance is omitted) and they are too broad to satisfy a scholar of the classics. Such a scholar would also point out that I am in danger of giving the impression that the poetry of sexual love arose after Athenian tragedy, whereas any historian of the subject would begin in the seventh century with Sappho. Here, however, we must so far as possible confine ourselves to portraits of women occurring in some sort of narrative, and therefore mention lyric poetry only in passing.

It seems true to say that the Roman centuries produced fresh and influential attitudes to women in lyric and satiric verse, while in narrative form older attitudes were merely – though in at least one instance powerfully – elaborated. Thus it is necessary to recall, without dwelling on the matter, that some of the odes of Catullus express for the first time the feelings of a man obsessed with a beautiful woman whom he knows to be vicious. Those scattered odes addressed to Lesbia (actually Clodia, a consul's wife) form a rudimentary story-structure and Lesbia emerges for us as virtually a literary character, certainly a type of woman not earlier represented in any detail by poets. From the fifth ode, which rings with joy and success ('Let us live, my Lesbia, and love') to the seventy-second in which Catullus explains that he loves her even more but likes her less (he is 'more of a lover but less of a friend') it is as if we encounter the fragments of a drama and of a dramatic female character.

In Ovid's works especially, the attitude towards women amounts to supplying them with new possibilities. The lady Corinna of the *Amores,* the verse-letters of the *Heroides* and in particular the mock-guidance on seduction of the *Ars Amatoria* do not merely offer a picture of Rome : they also imply and sometimes go so far as to fashion, changed varieties of womanhood – in literature and no doubt in life. In Ovid's *Metamorphoses,* on the other hand, any fresh colouring of the Hellenic myths, and hence of the female characters in those myths, seems simply bound up with the process of latinization.

Naturally there are changes when the Latin author has re-worked ancient fictions whose forms and characters were never in any event fixed. But the changes are not new departures, not advances. Seneca's Medea and his Phaedra are in some ways different people from the characters of Euripedes, but chiefly in the sense that they are cruder. The Roman Medea is actually more of a witch, in other words a more primitive conception. There is in Seneca an emphasis upon Medea's use of the supernatural for her evil ends and, while some excuse for the deeds is implied, there is monotonous stress on her cunning, insanity and sheer blood-thirstiness. In Seneca's *Hippolytus* (alternatively *Phaedra*) the heroine kills herself solely and straightforwardly because she has caused Hippolytus' death. Her motive is less complex, more obvious (and also more 'Roman') than the motive Euripedes gave to Phaedra. Then, in Seneca's *Agamemnon* Clytemnestra is not without some justification for murder but she lacks the grandeur of her Aeschylean predecessor. In short, Seneca's treatment of these tragic women lacks the sympathy and psychological inventiveness of the major Greek dramatists.

However it was in the *Aeneid* that an earlier type of characterization was reproduced with increased psychological subtlety. Dido, Queen of Carthage, as she appears in the fourth book of Virgil's poem, belongs in essentials to the same class as Medea and Phaedra, that is the class of woman driven out of her mind by love. Whatever the differences in behaviour among literary women of this kind, no matter how varied their stories, there is the constant feature that they are true votaries of love while the men, basely or nobly, have additional concerns.

Aeneas, of course, has the overwhelming mission of reaching Italy and there founding the city of Rome. According to the legend with which Virgil worked Aeneas was the son of Anchises of Troy and the goddess Venus. He escaped from the smouldering ruins of Troy and led a band of refugees through many adventures to the fulfilment of his destiny. Thus Rome and the great men of Rome (especially Augustus Caesar) had resplendent origins. In other words Virgil's purpose was to celebrate Rome with all its manly virtues, yet even to contemporaries, such as Ovid and Augustus himself, the finest of all twelve books appeared to be Book 4, which tells the story of Dido's love for Aeneas. Renaissance poets were most impressed with this small part of the work and almost any modern reader makes the same response.

Perhaps this is partly a matter of superior technical accomplishment, but it may also be an indication of how far the poetry of love had even then ousted older interests. Furthermore, there is now, in Virgil, something approaching a modern concentration on the woman's mental processes. As Book 4 begins Dido is already (like Phaedra before her) 'unlawfully' infatuated. Following the death of her husband she made a vow (a binding promise, attested by the gods) never to marry again. But Aeneas is of noble birth and, further she is besotted with 'the manhood of the man', his sheer body. Consequently Dido rationalizes her love : Carthage needs a king; she needs a protector against foreign enemies. She asks the gods to let her rescind her vow but when they refuse, she proceeds without their approval to throw herself at Aeneas, accompanying him on his tours of the city, until the whole business becomes a scandal. Now the goddess Juno, with the compliance of Venus, contrives a consummation by producing a great storm during which Aeneas and Dido find themselves sheltering in the same cave. After that Dido, but not Aeneas, regards their liaison as a marriage.

But Mercury is despatched to Carthage to remind Aeneas of his mission and Aeneas presently, with keen regrets, goes to Dido to announce his departure. Dido blazes at him, grovels for pity, will not accept his priorities. He for his part cannot understand her lack of understanding : surely she appreciates that great public enterprises come before private affections.

The final part of the Book is extraordinarily impressive, not least in Virgil's portrait of a woman moving towards suicide in an emotional state compounded of despair, vindictiveness and wishful thinking. Dido orders the construction of a pyre in the courtyard of her palace on top of which are to be placed some of Aeneas' clothes and armour and their 'bridal' bed. So far as anyone else knows the object is to burn away all relics of Aeneas and to send up curses, with the flames, to heaven. But as Aeneas and his band set sail Dido mounts the pyre, throws herself on the bed and stabs herself with Aeneas' sword.

Dido's story, which has often been held to rival anything in Homer, is a perfect tragedy incorporated into an epic poem. The theme of the poem, the fulfilment of Aeneas's destiny, is the occasion of the tragedy. Everything fits, yet it was the tragic tale regarded in isolation that became the most fertile source for future generations. Time and again, in Medieval poets, in Renaissance dramatists, and in eighteenth- and nineteenth-century novelists, the tragic woman owes her main features to Virgil's Dido. Such a woman loves with the fine, immoral recklessness, the disregard of qualifications and bolt-holes, of an epic hero in battle. It is her form of heroism. Yet in the nature of things she must be degraded in the process. She must lie, cheat, murder perhaps and (as the Christian centuries would have it) be defiled in the flesh. Moreover, because of the ultimate futility of her desire and its defiance of social rules, she is curiously built out of shame.

For our purposes, with the development of the tragic heroine in Virgil we end our survey of the classical authors. It is desirable to pause here to re-emphasize the function of these fictional women : they are figures composed by men as part of an attempt to give coherence to the world. To say this is not to deny the mimetic groundwork of narrative and dramatic literature but only to stress its legislative intent. In other words, if the politically dominant sex, including almost all the poets, wishes to make an order through heroic values, the invented women consolidate those values, even if by tortuous and paradoxical methods. If the male poets share a tragic vision but wish also to question customary attitudes, women are fashioned to serve that purpose. And when sexual love becomes the adventure (entailing its own hazards, prizes, bereavements, nemeses) women characters are shaped by men to play their reckless or sublime roles. To some extent this must mean that the woman's own vision was misrepresented : the fragments of Sappho, however extraordinary a woman she might have been, can be taken to confirm this suspicion. At the same time the poets we have considered were beyond question excellent observers and among the foremost 'legislators of the world'. The result, whatever the ratio of misrepresentation to objective accuracy, is that these fictional women have entered into the make-up of women everywhere in the West. Women are now in part what Homer and Euripedes and Virgil have, without women's permission, made them. In this restricted sense, bearing in mind absolute biological constraints and some elementary psychological laws, human nature is continually being created.

It is now necessary to discuss a creative myth of extraordinary potency which had no basis whatever in reality. Up to this point, the close of the classical ages and the beginnings of Christianity, characterizations of women were, as we have seen, fairly closely related to social circumstances so that each female figure has required no commentary in the terms of magic, religion or primordial disposition. Certainly, supernatural conceptions – personifications of psychic experience or natural events – lie behind the characters of early literature, but readers mainly encounter recognizable human beings in whom there are mere vestiges of primitive beliefs. Homer's Circe, for example, is apprehended pretty much as a real woman despite her magic powers, though she is plainly descended from some barely imaginable witch-figure. Circe's origins are of anthropological rather than literary interest.

But Christianity brought into Western literature, along with its shatteringly new ethics, a fresh variation of an age-old attitude to women which rationalistic Greeks and Romans tended (but only tended) to suppress. The woman had always been seen as intimately connected with the processes of nature from which the man stood apart, superior yet baffled. Now, everything depends on how nature is valued; on whether it is accepted (albeit in the tragic spirit) as man's proper element or whether it is viewed as a wretched sphere to which mankind has been banished.

The attitude which links woman with non-human nature was subdued, sublimated and surpassed by Greek and Roman authors. (Of course, they did not lose it altogether; nor have we in the twentieth century.) But in Christian belief the woman's fecundity and also her power of attraction caused her once again to be seen as more inescapably part of nature than the man.

Despite the spirit within her she was an agent of 'idolatry' in St Paul's sense; that is, she invited distraction from God and the veneration of earthly things. For the flesh was sinful: Jesus came 'in the likeness of sinful flesh'. More precisely, the flesh was the contaminated medium through which sin entered mankind. It follows that while men were great sinners and the author of evil was male, women had a peculiar burden of guilt thrust upon them. Karl Vossler, an historian of medieval culture, puts the matter as follows:

> Taught by Aristotle, Ovid and the Church, they [philosopher-clerics] beheld in woman 'only a fickle unaccountable creature, incapable of education, controlled by evil impulses, who must be subordinated to man, for whose sake alone she exists. They saw in her only the Eve of the Old Testament, through whom man had become a sinner, without whom Adam would always have remained a saint, and the Atonement would never have been needed'.[9]

It should be pointed out that Aristotle and Ovid had a low opinion of women, but not in the same sense or to the same degree as some clerics of the Middle Ages. To these later denigrators of women the emphasis was on the woman's association with nature, with life itself. It was Eve whom the serpent tempted since women had long before had a certain affiliation with the serpent of fertility in the Canaanite agrarian rituals against which the ancient Hebrew prophets had tried to warn their people. Toil, sensuality, child-bearing, death: these were the consequences of eating from the Tree of Knowledge of Good and Evil, and while in *Genesis* Adam and Eve are blamed equally for their transgression, Eve is never-theless the first transgressor. The serpent tempted Eve and she tempted Adam: this was the inevitable order in the eyes of a priesthood to whom the flesh was corrupt. Morbidity of exactly this kind is absent from Classical writings, along with its creative fruits, but from the Middle Ages onwards it rarely disappears com-pletely. In a sense woman acquired a new and vicious quality: she was lower than the man, not merely in social station but in her very nature.

However, this debasement of women eventually gave rise to an entirely novel attitude, infinitely more flattering but equally monstrous. It seems likely (in the absence of records we cannot be sure) that German knights of the twelfth century resisted Church teachings and continued living their rumbustious lives as best they could. They valued women, along with other objects of secular desire, and were unintentionally pioneers of women's emancipa-tion. Something of their rough and ready attitude flowered into elegant consciousness among the knights and troubadours of twelfth-century Provence, or else the Provencal development took place independently. This is now a very familiar, though rather disputed, story. What seems beyond dispute, however, is that a religion of love grew up alongside the religion of the Church. In some ways the former imitated or parodied the latter; certainly there was conscious rivalry.

At all events there was a movement over the centuries (not of course a simple, unbroken progression) from the worshipful, obedient, self-abnegating posture of the male lover to expressions of frank though rhapsodical sensuality. To begin with, the real aim was not to elevate the woman but to improve the man. Of course the lady was venerated beyond reason and her wishes, however capricious, were so far as possible carried out, but it was her lover's state of mind, *his* spiritual progression that mattered. In this earlier poetry the lady is an exalted image or idea 'based upon' some real or imagined woman. Cavalcanti in the thirteenth century tends to mention not so much his lady's actual features as those things of nature such as roses and rich green bushes with which she is to be compared. But she is scarcely an individual physical presence; rather, she bears the likeness of an angel ('angelica sembianzi') and it is his feelings upon which the poems dwell. Similarly, Petrarch's Laura has no discernible human nature : she is simply the loved one, the yearned-for. Typically Petrarch wanders in the woods or over the hills seeing her (undescribed) face in his mind's eye. But in some other poets of the fourteenth century and more markedly of the fifteenth there was a greater concentration on the woman's physical features, though these were still idealized. For example, Uberti (a contemporary of Petrarch) straightforwardly enthuses over his mistress's neck, arms and breasts, but she has no special characteristics – of body or, needless to say, of personality. Even a hundred years later in the openly lascivious passages of Ariosto a lady will remain an object of desire rather than a complex individual.

The denigration of women and the concomitant elevation of them were aspects of Christian idealism, the belief that earthly things are at best imperfect manifestations of a higher order of being. Eve's characteristic action led us into this burdensome world and all women share her weakness and guilt. On the other hand a woman might bring some deserving man to a distant prospect of paradise. Each point of view assigned women to a point on the boundary of the merely human.

However, the overwhelming majority of women characters in medieval narrative literature are human enough, though quite often the extreme views we have been considering lurk behind the more or less realistic presentations. Naturally the great characters such as Jean de Meun's Duenna and Chaucer's Wife of Bath and his Criseyde approximate more to the standards of ecclesiastical anti-feminism than to the sublimities of the love-religion, which are by definition unreal. Such striking feats of characterization chiefly exhibit advances in literary technique rather than new attitudes to women, but in so far as they offer a general view of womankind (and medieval portraiture is grounded in generalities), it is a low view. The woman is coarse and sensual, she is calculating or self-willed or morally frail. This tendency cannot be explained just by saying that it is always easier to portray bad qualities than good ones, since earlier and later writers alike managed to produce higher proportions of credibly engaging women. But amid this scene of tawdriness a small number of excellent faces appear; for example, the 'stedfast countenaunce' of Blanche in Chaucer's *Book of the Duchess* and pre-eminently the face of Dante's Beatrice. As a rule when the woman is a full literary 'character' she is at least mildly deplorable, but whenever she is admirable she has little or no character.

It is not appropriate to speak of the 'personality' of Beatrice : she is beyond personality, even in the *Vita Nuova* where she is a real Florentine girl, while in the *Divine Comedy* she is of course a pure vision. Dante tells us at the beginning of the *Vita Nuova* that he first set eyes on Beatrice when he was nearly nine and she a little over eight. From then on he was ruled by Love, a powerful god who commanded him time and again to frequent places where Beatrice might be glimpsed. Everything in her demeanour convinced him that she was praiseworthy and noble, so that despite her mortality she seemed the daughter of a god. Apparently in this childhood phase Dante never became acquainted with Beatrice, but one day when he was eighteen she greeted him in the street where she was walking with two older ladies. The relationship never developed much beyond the stage of salutations and acknowledgements in public places. Just the same Dante was presumably of some importance to Beatrice because she snubbed him on one occasion, as a result of a scheme Dante had devised, out of delicacy, to convince society that he was in love with another woman. Nothing of note in the ordinary sense occurred between Dante and this girl (who was probably a certain Beatrice Portinari) and the *Vita Nuova* is a record of feelings rather than of incidents. She died at the age of twenty-four and at the conclusion of the *Vita Nuova* Dante included a sonnet in which he imagines Beatrice in heaven, a 'soul in glory'.

In the later parts of the *Divine Comedy* Beatrice is a soul in glory cast in the form of a woman. In Canto 28 of the *Purgatorio* Dante and Virgil make their leisurely way into the sacred wood of the earthly paradise, the Garden of Eden. Here their progress is blocked by the River Lethe, immersion in which produces forgetfulness of one's sins and vivid recollection of one's good deeds. On the opposite bank appears a beautiful lady called Matilda. She explains to the poets the phenomena of paradise and the functions of Lethe. She also shows them a heavenly pageant at the conclusion of which Beatrice appears, veiled, wearing a

green cloak and an olive crown. Dante is transported back to his
youth, but in terror not in joy. He turns for support to Virgil, but
Virgil has vanished (for Dante must now proceed without support).
Well might Dante be afraid, for Beatrice is fierce in accusation of
him : he has not lived up to the high standards of which he seemed
capable. He must now repent utterly in order to be fit to enter the
waters of Lethe. Beatrice unveils and her eyes are as a blinding
light, so that when Dante turns his gaze away from her he cannot
for a while see anything else. Even so Dante has not yet perceived
the true, the heavenly Beatrice and it is not until the final canto
when Dante's purification has been completed that he is able to
apprehend her unutterable perfection.

Beatrice in the *Purgatorio,* especially at the very end, is both a
woman and not a woman. She is the height of imaginable felicity;
she is goodness and beauty and joyousness to the extent that these
qualities can be distilled from moments of experience and con-
densed into one image. In particular this is the meaning of Beatrice
in the *Paradiso* where she shows Dante the perfected universe that
now enfolds them, and finally fades away to be replaced by Mary.

There is a sense, therefore, in which Beatrice is not a character
ascribed by men to women, a sense in which she cannot be compared to Helen or Phaedra or Dido. What mattered to Dante was
the image of which the actual Beatrice was the source. At the same
time Beatrice remains a completely physical presence : she is always
realized and is never allegorical. It is clear that she represents – or
from a secular point of view that she positively *is* – the pinnacle of
man's spiritual aspirations, arrived at by a process of sifting the
purities from sexual love and love of beauty. The image of Beatrice
was not achieved by embodying abstract ideas, but rather by sub-
tracting grossness and imperfection from reality. This at least is
our materialistic and post-Freudian way of looking at the matter.
To the people of the Middle Ages, the vision or dream was
primordial and the coarseness of everyday life was added later.
We see, almost inescapably, a sublimation of sexual desire, not so
much in Freud's sense but in the strict dictionary sense of exalta-
tion and purification. Beatrice is passion and beauty refined to the
last degree, so that every touch of physical and mental imperfection
has melted away. Take hold of any moment of love such as we
actually experience; normal physical, affectionate love (with no
admixture of sado-masochism), intensify it and imagine it as
unalterable, and that is Beatrice. She is not 'ethereal' but carnal :

she has lovely limbs and radiant eyes. Intellectually she is perfection too, because she is incarnate Reason. She does not utter a word that is untrue and her every gesture is morally flawless.

Looked at from another point of view Beatrice is the resolution of conflicts in men and amongst men. Heroism, adventure, justice, sexual love : these normal themes of poetry reflecting the struggles of life are transcended in Beatrice. Likewise desire and duty are no longer opposed. Aeneas needed to leave Dido, but the Beatrician image is exactly what any man should go towards. Charles Williams in his book, *The Figure of Beatrice,* explains this point as follows :

> The image of the woman was not new in him [Dante] nor even the mode in which he treated it. What was new was the intensity of his treatment and the extent to which he carried it. In his master's great poem – in Virgil's *Aeneid* – the image of the woman and the image of the city had both existed, but opposed. Dido had been the enemy of Rome, and morality had carried the hero away from Dido to Rome. But in Dante they are reconciled; the appearance of Virgil at the opening of the *Commedia* has about it this emphasis also.[10]

Thus by presenting the figure of Beatrice Dante solved an ancient problem : morality and beauty are at one in her. He also fused the religion of love and the religion of the Church. But these were temporary integrations dependent on time and place in socio-cultural history and almost at once the dream began to fade or tarnish. Of course the dream has been a long time dying and it still lingers on, but it is inconceivable that it should ever be re-invigorated. The reason for this is not our modern materialism, which is unlikely to be irreversible, but that women will never again be set apart as intrinsically either baser or nobler than men. Surely that phase is over. It follows that if beauty and morality should once more flow together, this will not come about through the image of a woman.

Dante has normally been seen as the culmination of a tradition, a goal to which important features of the two preceding centuries had aspired. An antithetical movement began at once, or rather it began to gather force, since it had existed long before Dante. A part of this opposing process, the long, slow advance towards 'bourgeois realism', entailed the literary emancipation of women because it consisted generally of the emergence of the individual from types and categories.

It is impossible to point to two adjacent periods of history in the first of which type-structures predominate in literary characterization while in the second individual traits are primary. There is no dividing line but only a confused and fitful progress. For example there is plainly more bourgeois realism in Chaucer than in Spenser, more in Shakespeare than in Dryden. However, we can discern a pattern of increasing individualization. Consider the following remarks by a recent critic :

> Nevertheless, the more deeply one inquires into a medieval or Renaissance character, the more universal his nature becomes; he is a version of Everyman sharing Everyman's universe, and he draws his vitality from this deep common source. The alien quantity of experience is known and felt by all. In nineteenth- and twentieth-century fiction, on the other hand, characters draw together at their surfaces but in their depths each lives apart; the alien quantity is the private predicament.[11]

This seems to be true. To take examples, Chaucer's Wife of Bath is a markedly different personality from his Prioress, but they both belong, and know they belong, to a common world and are specimens of something general called 'human nature', or something only a little less general called 'womankind'. In contrast modern characters are often less idiosyncratic but feel estranged and unique : it is as if they can acknowledge their common qualities only in theory. They (not merely the avowed 'outsiders' but other characters as well) do not fully apprehend themselves as members of a class, even when they are proclaiming solidarity with others. Each is, or imagines himself to be *sui generis*.

Now, the passing from the old collectivity to the modern individuality was, as I have said, a desultory as well as an immensely long process. The Middle Ages were merely an episode in this history but in late medieval times the movement gathered strength. Specifically, if we compare Chaucer's Criseyde as a character belonging to the 'Matter of Troy' with Homer's portraits of women we can see how far the process had developed by the fourteenth century, and how successfully Chaucer himself furthered its development.

Modern critics properly warn their readers against reading too much realism or modernity into Chaucer. Thus Charles Muscatine writes of Chaucer that

> He does not announce the Renaissance, at least not more than do medieval humanism and Gothic realism generally. He is not 'modern': nowhere does he assert the primacy of realism in art or the primacy of man and matter in the universe. He is medieval.[12]

Bearing in mind this kind of corrective, it is still possible to support the assumption of many readers that in *Troilus and Criseyde* they encounter a heroine who resembles the heroines of realistic novels. Indeed the portrait of Criseyde goes beyond some esteemed later feats of characterization in the direction of mundane reality, because she evades narrow definition while remaining coherent. Attempts to explain her nature in the terms of psychology, of social forces, or of both combined have usually been well-founded, but never comprehensive. Thus the argument of C. S. Lewis[13] that Criseyde's ruling passion is fear (she is the 'ferfulleste wight'[14]) is borne out by the text: nevertheless the reduction of her to a diagnosis is scarcely more satisfactory than the reduction of an actual acquaintance. For the same reason Criseyde's behaviour cannot be accounted for by her vulnerable situation, though this is of great importance and is carefully established by Chaucer (through his narrator) at the outset. She is an unprotected widow who has never before needed to fend for herself and her father has run away to the Greek camp; but these facts even taken together with her timidity leave the essential Criseyde standing free.

Or, rather, one might almost speak of the 'existential' Criseyde, for her only essential quality is her mutability, which she shares with the rest of nature. It is as if Chaucer allowed his heroine to flow towards her destiny of her own accord. This doesn't mean that she lacks definition, but rather that she defines herself by the choices she makes, and of course by the attitudes she has formed for herself in the past. She is hemmed in as everyone is hemmed in, and free as all are free. At all events, this is the impression Chaucer triumphantly manages to convey.

In this way Criseyde's nature (her entire self, the sum of her mental states and actions) consolidates the moral point of the poem, which concerns the variability, the sheer 'shiftiness' of worldly things. Nothing in nature can be relied upon; our faith should be in God alone. There is no moral in the poem apart from this. Criseyde is not condemned by the author; nor indeed is Pandarus, or Diomede, or Calchas. Chaucer is wholly sympathetic towards his main characters and objective about the minor figures, so that he is a moralist purely in the grand sense of depicting (with conviction but without melancholy) an imperfect world.

With no precedents in English Literature to guide him (and no adequate model in his immediate source, Boccaccio's *Il Filostrato*) Chaucer managed to accommodate some contemporary prejudices about women while showing up the absurdity of all such prejudices. Criseyde is false not because she is a woman, or as the result of any kind of predetermination, but a hidebound person could contrive so to interpret the poem. However Criseyde is representative not of a segment of humanity but of humanity as a whole. By dramatizing such a large proportion of the story (Troilus' initial contempt for love and his instant infatuation with Criseyde; the character and the machinations of Pandarus; Criseyde's fears, self-deceptions, vacillations, moments of joy; the consummation at Deiphebus' house; the thoughts and actions of the lovers before and after their separation) Chaucer asserted a religious attitude by precise observation rather than by argument. Until the very end the idea or belief of the poem is concealed beneath a stream of graphic detail, but the detail bears out the idea. All along it is shown and finally it is stated that instability is the one sure attribute not of women but of the world.

Criseyde is a woman in a woman's situation, but she does not bear out notions about female nature as such. From now on, in this chapter but more particularly in later chapters, it will be fruitful to notice how far and with what apparent justification authors apprehend their women characters as having an inherently different psychological constitution from men. We shall wish to observe and explore writers' tendencies to think, implicitly or explicity, in terms of 'masculine' and 'feminine' qualities. We shall need, further, to give special consideration to those authors who evidently discern a mystical, as opposed to a merely biological polarity in nature; authors to whom sexual distinctions are of overwhelming – one might say of religious – significance.

I say that it will be profitable to notice these matters from now on because it seems that such differentiations began to inform the works of some writers (not the majority by any means) from the

Middle Ages onwards. If the ancients were impressed by sexual polarities the fact is not explicit in literature and is not stated in philosophy. (Plato and Aristotle assume that women are basically similar to men, though inferior, and that this distinction may not be inevitable.)

In the next great phase of narrative literature, the phase of Renaissance drama, there is, certainly, an extraordinary amount of reference to women's qualities, an unprecedented assertion of womanhood; but this should not mislead us, for the playwrights were making social rather than psychological points. If in the Elizabethan and Jacobean dramatists especially (though the tendency persists down to eighteenth-century drama) it seems as though a woman character could scarcely appear on the stage without pointed comment upon her womanly qualities or circumstances, this was not because the authors regarded women as different from themselves.

The real reasons may well be those emphasized in a recent study, *Shakespeare and the Nature of Women* by Juliet Dusinberre.[15] This critic maintains that most English Renaissance playwrights were feminist in inclination, partly in accordance with radical puritan arguments and partly from a sense of identification with fellow victims of conventionality. In particular women suffered from the double standards of sexual morality while the dramatists (like the actors) were welcomed as entertainers though distrusted for their manner of life. It was necessary also for the playwright to please the many women members of his audience, some of whom would have been the 'liberated' women of the day. In addition there was the technical problem of boy actors playing female parts : since femininity could not be effortlessly displayed it needed to be emphasized in dialogue. The same problem presumably fostered the frequent productions of scenes in which women characters disguise themselves as men; scenes, that is, where the playwright's skill has been employed to depict the less stereotyped features of womanliness. Somehow the 'woman' must remain a woman, and assert as much to the audience, while comporting herself like a young man. It is likely (Juliet Dusinberre has no doubts about the matter) that this theatrical convention helped the playwrights to do what they wanted to do anyway : to moderate some extravagant notions of personality differences between the sexes and in this way (it is not the only way) to assert the equality of women.

What is sure, and has often been remarked upon, is that women characters in Renaissance drama are assertive, resourceful and gratifyingly diverse. In particular, a Shakespearean woman can be almost anything under the sun, though she is rarely a flaccid victim or mere focus of her situation. Even Shakespeare's innocents generally possess some kind of initiative and are not inhibited in personality.

Miranda, for instance, is as innocent as could be imagined and is unavoidably controlled by Prospero, her father (though she is capable of defiance when her affections and her ready compassion are aroused): nevertheless, she is vivacious, forthcoming and guilessly determined. The sexual modesty of Miranda, which she refers to as 'the jewel in my dower', is the opposite of sullen inhibition. Similar things may be said of Perdita in *The Winter's Tale,* who nevertheless has a different personality. Perdita's gifts of flowers to the disguised Polixenes and Camillo are accompanied by phrases conveying natural sexuality (the sexuality of mating and reproduction with not a twinge of lewdness), so that she is erotic and modest at the same time. Marina in *Pericles* is likewise totally innocent in every sense, not merely the sexual. 'I never killed a mouse, nor hurt a fly', she says. In the brothel at Mytiline, Marina impresses, as she has previously impressed the pirates who captured her, by her wit as well as by her resolution. This is one of the interesting points about Shakespeare's innocent girls: their chastity is accompanied by felicitous, even witty, assertiveness, and they thus possess a combination of qualities which later writers have rarely managed to depict. They also bear out George Eliot's contention that 'Shakespeare's women almost always *make love,* in opposition to the conventional notion of what is fitting for woman'.[16] Shakespeare's Juliet makes love as spontaneously and ardently as Romeo, and can speak as flamboyantly as anyone else in the play, except Mercutio. There are few dully passive figures in this category of Shakespearean woman: there is poor Ophelia, certainly, who is meant to be mediocre, and such a character as Katherine in *Henry V,* who has little English and exists chiefly to illustrate the soldier Henry's skill at wooing.

If Shakespeare's innocent girls are far from social nullities, how much truer is this of his guiltless older women. Lack of vitality is not the basis of their goodness. Such a woman in Shakespeare is beset by male trickery and stupidity, and whether she triumphs or dies she is remembered as a bright spot in a predominantly dark or grotesque picture. Imogen is the striking figure of *Cymbeline,* honourable, candid, scornful, loving; a faithful woman (she calls herself 'Fidele' when disguised) in the midst of knaves and fools. Hermione in *The Winter's Tale* remains intelligent and dignified in the face of Leontes' unjust imbecilities. The pattern, of course, in the tragedies and elsewhere is for this kind of woman to be misjudged as a result of someone's craftiness or someone's folly. She is in the power of men inferior to her, so that whatever Shakespeare's personal attitudes might have been, we receive an impression of feminist sympathies.

No one deceives Lear about Cordelia, and his own vanity coupled with her scrupulosity is enough to secure her fate. The important point here is that Lear's misjudgement and susceptibility to professions of love rest not so much on kingship as such but on power over territory and people. Cordelia, like other good women of Shakespeare, is in the hands of moral and intellectual inferiors, but she is also at the mercy of a power-system which demands from women only spurious virtue – protestations of affection, obedience and chastity. However, the Shakespearean heroine such as Cordelia is not in revolt against patrimony itself, since she would prefer to be obedient to an intelligent and honourable man : rather she stands firm against the falsehoods which patrimony is liable to exact.

One such falsehood is the pretence of chastity. The good woman is genuinely chaste (or faithful, according to circumstances), though not from want of vigour. In *Measure for Measure* Isabella's adamant chastity is part of a robust personality which seems to include a strong sexual element. Isabella's 'coldness' in the face of her brother's pleas, no less than her refusal to yield to Angelo, constitutes a turning of the tables on the men, though of course that is not Isabella's motive. It is Shakespeare who is conducting a satirical attack on common male standards. In this light Isabella can be seen as one who takes men at their word, who accepts as an absolute moral law what men commonly regard as a convenient social rule. In this respect Isabella is like some other heroines : that is, she relentlessly practices a kind of honour which men, for their welfare or self-aggrandizement, practice selectively. Similarly, in *Othello* Desdemona has listened often enough to tales of masculine honour and bravery, but she carried such notions 'to an extreme' by marrying a valiant Moor. At once in the eyes of Brabantio, her father, she has passed (under the influence of drugs, he supposes) from being 'a maid so tender, fair and happy', to complete whoredom. Othello himself is not amazed when Iago suggests to him that as a general rule only a whoreish white woman marries a black man. It should be added that Desdemona is certainly no ennervated creature but one whose healthy libidinousness has been taken up into admiration for male valour and nobility.

These, then, are some of the more notable good women in Shakespeare. They are distinctive and strong. In the main their traits are not ascribed by Shakespeare to female nature but are virtues that may arise in certain social circumstances. Lacking power these women are obedient to goodness, and defiant (whenever they have a chance) in the face of evil or stupidity. If there is a quality which Shakespeare attributes to the true woman it is compassion or mercy. A good man as opposed to his female counterpart may need to be reminded of his duty to be merciful. In Shakespeare's world Portia's paean to mercy would not come well from the lips of a man, though it comes admirably from a woman who is not merely disguised as a man but displays exactly the superior qualities of mind and character that men claim for themselves. Conversely, of course, the bad woman, or the woman who develops 'masculine' designs, must often be without mercy. The woman's tendency to protect suffering or vulnerable creatures is what Lady Macbeth has to obliterate; it is what Goneril and Regan have never possessed. Volumnia in the early scenes of *Coriolanus* so far accepts the heroic code that she would rather have her son die in battle than live a life of ease. 'The breasts of Hecuba,' she says, 'when she did suckle Hector, look'd not lovelier / than Hector's forehead when it spit forth blood.'

Of course this is absurd and Volumnia is deceiving herself somewhat as Lady Macbeth deceives herself about her capacity to annihilate sympathetic feelings. In Shakespeare the genuinely merciless women, in particular Goneril and Regan, have no need to make passionate speeches (that is, to fantasize) about their hardness. They are viewed as aberrations from nature. Positive gloating cruelty is sometimes another matter, since this can proceed from a woman whose womanliness has been perverted rather than negated, as for example when Queen Margaret torments the captured Duke of York in the third part of *Henry VI*. However there is only a thin dividing line between characters such as Margaret and Goneril : each is regarded as less than human (an animal, a 'she-wolf'), while a base man is at least allowed to retain his humanity.

In Shakespeare, it seems, for all his assertion of equality between the sexes there is one important and traditional distinction which usually favours the woman. Her natural tenderness is a disadvantage in certain circumstances, but generally it is to her credit. When Cleopatra decides to kill herself she has to summon up a 'masculine' or 'Roman' courage; yet even then she refers to the asp as the 'baby at my breast'. Cleopatra's suicide (which is performed with the same histrionic sincerity as all her other actions) unites the male mode of honourable death with the sort of maternal tenderness which Lady Macbeth thwarts in herself. Joan of Arc in *Henry VI Part III* is presented as transcending rather than denying her femininity in that her former occupation as a shepherdess watching anxiously over the lambs is not trampled out of mind or distorted into cruelty as she prepares to make war. Her combativeness is viewed as a surpassing of nature : 'My courage try in combat,' she says, 'And thou shalt find that I exceed my sex.'

Apparently there is a right and a wrong way for a woman to 'exceed her sex'. The truly superior woman in Shakespeare is not perhaps Cordelia but rather the woman who can act the man almost to perfection and is only caught out, if at all, by some looming trial of arms or physical stamina. In respect of our theme Shakespeare's chief contribution lay in the creation of such characters as Portia, Imogen, Julia, Beatrice, Rosalind and Viola. Whether the matter is light or serious these women display a kind of roundedness of personality, a flexibility and power of adaptation which has nothing to do with politic calculation. Certainly they are shrewd and make calculations, but not for the sake of power. It would be wrong to think of them as 'androgynous' because this term relies on an assumption of eternal male and female qualities. Rather they are human beings who have not developed lopsidedly as a result of social expectations or for any other reason. They manage to be both rational and emotional, imaginative and practical, sympathetic and tough. They have moral sense rather than principles and are able in the main (not invariably) to assess the world around them in a realistic fashion.

No man in Shakespeare quite matches these characters as an exemplar of fully developed humanity, for they are not the female equivalent of such ordinary decent fellows as Horatio or Enobarbus, and whenever there is a male partner in the play (Benedict, for instance, as partner to Beatrice) he is, if only slightly, her inferior. What this tells us, I presume, is not that Shakespeare necessarily had a higher view of women's potentialities than of men's, but that he took advantage of theatrical necessities to produce models of sane development.

For all the affirmations of womanliness in Shakespeare, for all the assertion of the 'woman's point of view', he in common with other Renaissance playwrights pointed the way to an ultimate break-down of unnecessary or factitious differences between the sexes. It was not Shakespeare alone but most of the dramatists after Marlowe (despite his pioneering, no pioneer in this respect) who revelled in presenting women of striking character. The main women on stage were not figures of passivity, endurance, com-pliance, sullen resistance, but on the contrary were distinct and potent individuals. The same must be said about the Restoration stage. The whole point about a Restoration heroine is that she claims and wins effective equality with the hero. She uses her charms of course but does not retreat into helplessness if the man shows signs of worsting her. Indeed the distinction between the heroine and other women is that she has cavalier audacity; she is the peer in terms both of intelligence and social nerve of the rakish hero. This is true, outstandingly, of Congreve's Millament in *The Way of the World* and of Etherege's Harriet in *The Man of Mode*. The woman now is valued not appreciably for her virtue and not only for her beauty but for other qualities which she shares with the man.

From now on what we shall be noticing in the centuries after the Restoration, chiefly through an examination of characters in novels and plays, will be a slight tendency for women's behaviour to be attributed to social circumstances. Of course we shall find challenges to such assumptions some of which (especially in nineteenth- and twentieth-century authors) are dialectical rather than simply reactionary, and express a desire to enlarge notions not of womanhood alone but of human being. However, in the eighteenth-century novel, the subject of the next chapter, the emphasis is on behaviour in relation to customs, laws and institutions.

2 The Eighteenth Century

The attitudes towards women of the three novelists with whom we shall be most concerned in this chapter may usefully be summarized at the outset. Defoe thought that men and women were alike, except that women had livelier minds and potentially better abilities. Richardson also regarded men and women as 'brothers and sisters', as he put it, akin but for circumstances and education. He however relished certain social and sexual roles which through his genius he so powerfully reinforced that the results of his influence can be felt to the present day. Fielding's attitude might be described as one of disappointed chivalry. He seems to have believed that men should be able to look to women for moral guidance, but that they rarely could because many women either aped men or exploited their own positions for selfish purposes.

If *Moll Flanders* and *Roxana* were not enough to convince us of Defoe's high opinion of women's abilities, we have his words in the essay, 'An Academy for Women'.

> The Capacities of Women are suppos'd to be greater, and their Senses quicker than those of Men; and what they might be capable of being bred to, is plain from some instances of Female-Wit, which this Age is not without; which upbraids us with Injustice, and looks as if we deni'd Women the advantage of Education, for fear they should *vye* with Men in their Improvements.[1]

It is not clear how widely this opinion of women's capacities was held, and perhaps we should take Defoe to mean that he shared the view with other sensible people. He and others had been impressed by women's powers of quick understanding, by their awareness and responsiveness. 'The whole Sex are generally Quick and Sharp,' he writes, and as children they rarely display the sheer cloddishness of many boys. Defoe is here valuing the qualities he gives his women in the novels : nimbleness, manoeuvrability, practical intelligence not weighed down by dullness of the senses or some unwieldy structure of ideas and principles.

These last words are not a euphemism for 'immoral'. Of course Moll and Roxana are immoral and it is not enough to say that they are forced into their ways of life by poverty. In fact both heroines embody a view of human nature which is sufficiently different from modern views to warrant a brief exposition before we proceed to an examination of individual characters.

What can be gathered from Defoe's writings in general is an undismayed assessment of human nature as 'fallen', an assumption that man's very being lies in his concrete social existence, which of necessity makes him gravely imperfect. In life people have not even a touch of the angelic in their composition. Goodness as a state is merely a dream because one's day-to-day transactions prevent it. Nor for that matter should one strive for goodness as such : it is not in man's God-given nature to be good, though he can and should repent of his misdeeds before death. There is no need to repent of one's entire flawed life, but only one's *unnecessary* misdeeds. The facts of life should certainly not encourage an automatic acceptance of any vice or scoundrelism, but they dictate a great deal of what pious, self-deceiving folk regard as wickedness.

Defoe appears to have agreed with Hobbes that self-preservation is a fundamental requirement : in fact he went further than Hobbes in suggesting that 'dishonour' is to be preferred to death or to any form of devastating personal defeat. In the poem, *Jure Divino* he writes :

The Laws of God, as I can understand,
Do never Laws of Nature countermand;
Nature Commands, and 'tis Prescribed to Sense
For all Men to adhere to *Self-Defence:*
Self-Preservation is the only Law,
That does *Involuntary Duty* Draw;
It serves for Reason and Authority,
And they'll defend themselves, that know not why.[2]

The idea in these lines is that man's imperfect nature is prescribed by God so that whatever a person does as a *rational* response to his or her situation is completely in accord with God's will. The laws of nature are the laws of God: there is no distinction. Self-preservation is instinctual and *therefore* it is rational. Here lies the root difference between Defoe's attitudes and those of later (and earlier) periods which opposed reason to instinct. One might say that for Defoe, as for Freud a century and a half later, right reason (an ego-faculty) intelligently guides the instincts rather than holding them down.

What, then, is bad behaviour? It is unreasonable, uninstinctual and foolish behaviour. Self-interest, or 'Self-love' as Defoe calls it, is actually good, so that people act wrongly when through habitual vice, stupidity or misconceived notions they 'oppose themselves'.

Men may sometimes by Subtilty and Slight
Oppose themselves, and Sacrifice their Right;
But all's a Blast, the empty Fraud's in vain,
Int'rest Instructs, and all's restor'd again;
Self-Love's the Ground of all the things we do,
Which they *that talk on't least* do must pursue.[3]

The 'Right' which Defoe refers to here is a God-given right to act reasonably in furtherance of one's self-interest. Such action is also right in the sense of correct. Apparently the usual ways of opposing oneself are through 'subtilty', or elaborate thinking, and 'slight', meaning heedlessness. Positively bad behaviour (the sort of behaviour for which repentance is mandatory) is not instinctual, does not further self-interest and is bound up with the wrong sort of thinking or with carelessness.

With this general attitude in mind (an attitude which perhaps seems wholesome enough but scarcely the last word in moral philosophy) we can begin to consider the personalities and careers of Defoe's heroines in relation to a society which signally failed to distinguish between self-love and wickedness.

Moll Flanders is presented as a creature of her situations, to say which is not of course to deny her a vast amount of free choice. Her very being consists of her responses to circumstances, even though some of her activities (a number of thefts, for example) are addictive rather than self-expressive. Insofar as Moll is presumed to have an existence outside her situations, this lies in her talents as an autobiographer. She can compose a story of her life (which in itself makes her an exceptional criminal or adventuress) and relate it in vigorous, inelegant prose. Nevertheless, to a large extent Moll is what she does and a high proportion of what she does (not the whole by any means) is made up of self-loving reactions to circumstances.

I do not suggest that Moll is a narrow conception of woman-kind, the result of either irony or incapacity on Defoe's part. On the contrary, Moll's style represents her in the same way and to the same extent as the style of many an autobiographer represents him. We are all familiar with the memoirs of men and women of affairs, practical people of striking character, perhaps, but little complexity and little in the way of personal vision. Often enough such memoirs read like a bald summary of experiences because they are largely confined to facts interspersed with readily compre-hensible emotions and trite sentiments; yet they are in fact a fair reflection of the author's felt experiences. He simply did whatever he did and absorbed from the world around him roughly the im-pressions he now records, so that it is probably an error to ascribe to him an extra 'area' of subjectivity which he thinks unimportant or for which he cannot find the words. Such a writer seems to have no 'inside', however marvellous his career and creditable his deeds. Moll is to be imagined as belonging to this category, though she is given an exceptional skill with language, not very different from Defoe's style.

It seems likely that Moll is a reduced version of Defoe himself, placed of course in entirely different circumstances, with the result that the distance between the fictional character and her creator is not appreciably ironic or condemnatory. Ian Watt in his *The Rise of the Novel* goes so far as to say that 'Defoe's identification with Moll Flanders was so complete that, despite a few feminine traits, he created a personality that was in essence his own'.[4] This is one point of view in a copious debate about Defoe's attitude towards his heroine which has raged over the years. I share the view, since the ironic touches within the novel are proportionately few and hardly affect the general tone. In addition Defoe's manner of life together with his writings (not excepting the manifestly ironic works such as *The Shortest-Way with the Dissenters*) suggest that he would have gone beyond mere sympathy with Moll to the point of identification. For Ian Watt, however, Defoe's projecting himself into the character of Moll entailed a deficiency. Professor Watt writes,

For Moll Flanders is suspiciously like her author, even in matters where we would expect striking and obvious differences. The facts show that she is a woman and a criminal, for example; but neither of these roles determine her personality as Defoe has drawn it.[5]

Is Moll, then, a 'masculine' woman or possibly no woman at all? Is she furthermore an improbable criminal in that her criminality leaves her psychologically unscathed? Certainly her consciousness is thin and dry: there is a marked absence of imagination and sensuousness, and Moll's emotions are subordinate to her practical intelligence. Consider, for instance, the celebrated Newgate passages. Moll recalls her first impressions of Newgate in the following words:

> I was now fix'd indeed, 'tis impossible to describe the terror of my mind, when I was first brought in, and when I look'd round upon all the horrors of that dismal Place: I look'd on myself as lost, and that I had nothing to think of, but of going out of the World, and that with the utmost Infamy; the hellish Noise, the Roaring, Swearing and Clamour, the Stench and Nastiness, and all the crowd of Afflicting things that I saw there; joyn'd together to make the Place seem an Emblem of Hell itself, and a kind of Entrance into it.[6]

Here is a situation in which Moll, for once, is robbed of initiative and can do nothing but observe and feel. Years later, at the time of writing the memoir, she could in theory have contemplated her recollections, bringing out the exact features of the prison and the exact quality of her emotions. But she finds it impossible to describe her terror and Newgate itself is reported only in general terms. Defoe of course was well acquainted with Newgate, but it is doubtful whether he minutely noticed the noises, the smells and 'all the crowd of Afflicting things'.

Moll's perceptions, external and internal, are always of this limited order. We gain only bare information about her husbands or other persons with whom she is intimate; about places, incidents, sensations and feelings. For the most part the tale is told in functional terms: it is a story of what people did and why, though neither the doings nor the motives are intricately explained. The dialogue is uniform, which surely means that Defoe himself could not catch the peculiarities of speech. Actions are reported rather than fully described, so that precise movements, gestures, facial expressions, styles of walking and so on (the features in which Dickens, for example, luxuriated) are omitted.

On the voyage to Virginia with her third husband Moll undergoes great storms and a pirate attack but, since Moll did not keep a journal, as she informs us, she can do no more than mention these dire experiences in passing. When in Virginia Moll meets her mother-in-law who turns out to be her mother, this important lady is first described simply as a 'mighty chearful, good humour'd old Woman'. Moll's love-making is perfunctorily conveyed in such terms as 'there was no more resisting him'. Even the accounts of thefts and swindles, which take up a not inconsiderable proportion of the second half of the book, are notable as social or criminal history rather than for their vividness. For all this Moll Flanders is rightly reckoned to be a feat of characterization, and Moll is probably the most discussed character in English fiction.

The truth is, it seems, that an aspect of Defoe's genius lay in his capacity to select narrators who could plausibly possess approximately his own mental make-up. Defoe's cast of mind was factual, literal, unambiguous, prosaic, and Moll is similarly endowed. If he had no aptitude for imagery, neither has she. In character too there are obvious resemblances, as Ian Watt points out. Defoe was energetic, somewhat unscrupulous, a questing individual with regular goals in mind, a man who lived by his wits and his will rather than at the dictates of either emotion or principle. All these things are of course true of Moll as well.

The mistake is to assume that a woman could not be like that, unless she was unrepresentative of her sex. Moll is unusual certainly, but not specifically in the sense that she departs from some female norm. Defoe surely knew what he was about; he was aware, for example, through simple observation that women do not necessarily have receptive rather than assertive minds. Women's capacities for feeling and sensation are not invariably, or even normally, greater than man's. Some women, it is true, are minutely aware of colours, smells, variations in temperature, the texture of materials, the precise features of houses, furniture, clothing, and so on, but other women are not. Similarly, a preoccupation with emotions and a corresponding cultivation of emotional life are not so much feminine traits as tendencies which are liable to grow to the extent that powers of effective action are curtailed. If for one reason or another (as a result of customs, laws, imposed ethical principles, natural timidity) people cannot find drama in their outer or public lives, they sometimes make an inner drama. Plainly women have been thus constrained far more often than men, but many a woman has found channels for direct, purposive action. So it is with Moll. Furthermore it is relevant to point out that only the gift of forming strong sensory images, especially visual images ('pictures in the head'), enables a writer to recreate the very texture of things he has observed. Moll lacks such a gift because Defoe lacked it, and this fact is unimportant since the gift is not, so far as one can judge, a property more of one sex than the other.

For these reasons we must attribute to Defoe one important achievement which, unlike his other achievements, has not been sufficiently recognized. He aided the liberation of women by ignoring stereotypes altogether (indeed he seems scarcely to have been aware of them) and by his unprecedentedly thorough portraits of some of the deplorable circumstances in which a woman could be placed. In other words, Defoe's procedure of imagining himself in a woman's situations both illuminated the situations and helped to break down the notion of a fixed or proper female character.

In this respect *Roxana the Fortunate Mistress* is quite as valuable as *Moll Flanders,* though it has usually been accounted a less impressive novel. One of the reasons for this judgement is that Roxana is regarded as more blameworthy than Moll, a truly vicious woman. Certainly Roxana is a figure of guilt and self-reproach beside whom Moll is little more than a conventional penitent. At the confused and abrupt end of her story Roxana tells us that she subsequently 'fell into a dreadful Course of Calamity' and these words put us in mind of tragic potentialities. A tragedian would have shifted Roxana's story onwards in time, beginning at the point where she has reached the heights of wealthy independence. Then he would have introduced the importunate daughter, making a climax of the daughter's murder and a denouement out of Roxana's nemesis – whatever it might have been.

But Defoe of course had an ambivalent attitude towards this heroine. He obviously realized that the murder of the daughter would haunt Roxana, despite the fact that it was none of her doing, because her whole career had led up to this crime. Just the same, Defoe implicitly approves of Roxana, of her ambitions and designs: what he resents is the need for endless secrecies and machinations. Roxana, living at the time of the Restoration, has a modern woman's aspirations. Consider the arguments between Roxana and her Dutch merchant, when they are lodging in the same (London) house and he is trying to persuade her to marry him. After a good deal of considerate courtship (by one who has earlier saved Roxana's life) the merchant finally gets her to bed, but he does so with the express purpose of making it impossible for her to refuse his proposal of marriage. The good-humoured debate which follows is all but the *raison d'être* of the novel. This, the question of women's independence, was what interested Defoe to whom the agonies of tragic guilt meant almost nothing.

Roxana's point, against which her honourable suitor finds he cannot prevail, is that a mistress with money of her own is in a far better position than a wife. Even when the merchant assures her that he will not touch her money, she insists that her independence is too valuable to give up.

I told him [Roxana recalls], I had, perhaps, differing Notions of Matrimony, from what the receiv'd Custom had given us of it; that I thought a Woman was a free Agent, as well as a Man, and was born free, and cou'd she manage herself suitably, might enjoy that Liberty to as much Purpose as the Men do; that the Laws of Matrimony were indeed, otherwise, and Mankind at this time, acted quite upon other Principles, and those such, that a Woman gave herself entirely away from herself, in Marriage, and capitulated only to be, at best, but *an Upper-Servant,* and from the time she took the Man, she was no better or worse than the Servant among the *Israelites,* who had his ears bor'd, *that is,* nail'd to the Door-Post; who by this Act, gave himself to be a Servant during Life.[7]

In writing words such as these (there are several similar passages) Defoe was not detachedly creating a character but placing himself, with all his zest for freedom, in Roxana's position. Roxana goes too far, and Defoe knew that he would have been tempted to do the same. So highly does she rate her liberty that she continues to refuse the Dutch merchant even though his marriage terms would give her the maximum independence consistent with security. She knows she is imprudent; she knows she is violating the great principle of self-love. Thus Roxana falls (though her fall is only beginning at the end of the book), and in this way Defoe expressed his own temptations and weakness. If he had anything resembling a tragic sense it arose from his fear that the individual cannot finally evade the clutches of society.

Whether we view Defoe's individualism, his way of espousing the rights of the individual at the expense of any conceivable society, as good or bad, we must concede that he extended the same rights to other people, notably to women. In total contrast Samuel Richardson had no wish to live freely. Not that he invariably respected society, for some of his admired characters flout social customs, but that he savoured the intricacies of tied personal relationships in which he found all the drama and excitement (including intellectual excitement) he could have desired. Instead of freedom he sought to be shackled to others – as the man of power is shackled to his subjects.

However, there seems to be no doubt that Richardson regarded the sexes as basically alike. It is not only one of his characters, Harriet Byron in *Sir Charles Grandison* who proclaims men and women to be 'brothers and sisters',[8] for Richardson said the same in a letter to his Dutch translator, Johannes Stinstra.

Men and women are brothers and sisters; they are not of different species; and what need be obtained to know both, but to allow for different modes of education, for situation and constitution, or perhaps I should rather say, for habits, whether good or bad.[9]

A number of similar remarks can be found : for example, Richardson wrote to a Miss Grainger that women should be educated at least to the point where they may be 'Companions and Friends, not Slaves and Servants to Men'.[10] Such egalitarian views are the same as Defoe's, but whereas Defoe's fiction plainly bears out his general pronouncements, the novels of Richardson support his letters in complex and paradoxical ways.

The first thing to note about Richardson's art of characterization is his way of placing side by side figures of fancy and figures based on observation. Hazlitt was shrewd to comment that Richardson was not 'an observer of the characters of life' but 'seemed to spin his materials entirely out of his own brain, as if there had been nothing existing in the world beyond the little room in which he sat writing.' Hazlitt continued : 'There is an artificial reality about his works, which is nowhere else to be met with. They have the romantic air of a pure fiction, with the literal minuteness of a common diary'.[11]

As a matter of fact Richardson told various correspondents about the provenance of some of his characters and his remarks tend to bear out the thrust, if not the precise detail, of Hazlitt's comments.[12] They also bear out one's impressions that Richardson's principal characters were spun out of his own brain while some of the satellite figures in all three books are 'characters of life'. Then, we can surely agree with Hazlitt about the aspect of 'pure fiction' in the novels: in particular the plots have not matured sufficiently beyond their origins in wish-fulfilment. Finally Hazlitt's point about the combination of pure fiction with 'literal minuteness' is valuable. That is one of the peculiar Richardson qualities.

To understand these contradictions it is necessary first to acknowledge that Richardson's zeal for virtue (his genuine zeal, it may still be necessary to add) made him unable to grasp and represent the mixed nature of virtue as it actually exists. His moralistic fervour led him to fantasies of perfection – of a kind of perfection, moreover, which (as Fielding was the first to point out in *Shamela*) is not necessarily likeable or admirable. On the other hand he had a sharp eye for ordinary imperfections of character, with the result that his technique of surrounding paragons by morally lower figures produces part of the strange combination that Hazlitt commented upon. It is clear that Richardson firmly grasped his social world – the world of family tyrannies, marriage-able daughters, dowries, rakes, interminable gossip, sententious comment – then placed against it notions of faultless conduct which were for him the mainstay of life. The social world was right; the notions of conduct were psychologically wrong.

For whatever the assertions of sympathetic critics and of Richardson himself (for instance, in the Preface to *Clarissa* and in the concluding Note to *Sir Charles Grandison*) the heroines and the one hero, Grandison are pretty well unblemished. It is not enough to point to their moments of self-criticism, because these are only tiny, somewhat factitious stains on otherwise immaculate portraits. In other words these characters are alleged to slip up occasionally, but 'naive' readers (who surely provide the test in such matters) do not take the slips seriously. In all probability neither did Richardson, though he may have been mildly and sporadically concerned over his own pride, which is reflected in the pride of his admired characters.

Pamela's excellencies are emphasized, venerated indeed through-out both parts of her story, so it makes little difference (in fact it only highlights what is seen by Richardson as her goodness) when at one point she wonders whether God has put her to various trials in order to encourage her to overcome the 'lurking vileness' of her heart. Certainly Pamela is supposed to be proud, and she has her moment of near-despair, but Richardson gives no force to such flaws. Clarissa's saintliness is a state to which she grows, but she does not grow from real inferiority. In the first letter of Clarissa the heroine is spoken of, without undue partiality, as excelling all her sex: so she continues to her dying gasp. In *Sir Charles Grandison* Harriet Byron is fulsomely praised almost from first to last, though she, admittedly, is a promising character with interesting thought-processes at least up to the point when Grandison rescues her from abduction, and later she has her phase of understandable jealousy. But the incipient complexities in Harriet are not allowed to grow.

What Richardson evidently did was to take the faults he so discriminatingly saw around him and compose figures, women especially, as the antithesis of those faults. In addition, or as part of the same process, he gave each of the heroines a false coherence. Whatever contradictions they display are muted, merged too smoothly into the dominant pattern of their thoughts and feelings, and they lack idiosyncrancies. In other words Richardson could not manage, did not wish to contemplate, the life-like kind of moral superiority (transcending but not always displacing common-place pieces of bad or foolish behaviour) which Tolstoy, for example, includes in his novels. Richardson saw goodness as a symmetrical or monochrome condition. He was obviously interested in quirks of personality, but he showed them in characters who support, surround or affront the heroine, not in the heroine herself.

At the same time Richardson was in his curious way a man of the world. He was a fussy perfectionist in regard to social conduct and he disliked vice but it does not seem that he wholeheartedly wished it away. This is not to point out what is indeed obvious, that there was a vice-loving underside to his nature, a Shadow-component (to use Jung's terminology) which could express itself in the shape of a Lovelace: I mean instead that he revelled in the fight against vice. Richardson's dream was not like the dream of the Middle Ages, an image quite offset against the world. His heroines need the corruption as something to combat: it provides the pungency of life. He evidently relished the sphere of pure *domestic* suffering, in which what gives meaning to life amidst the necessary trivia is beleaguered heroism. He wanted the trivia as well, the daily preoccupations, courtesies, insults, but as the circumstances of heroic action. His novels are in part moralistic and in part a domestication, even at times an interiorization, of heroic enterprise.

So while it is easy, for example, to make fun of Pamela's father for his exhortation to his daughter, 'Resolve to lose your life sooner than your virtue',[13] this is of course a stance of heroism for a girl of the period, friendless or ineffectually befriended in her master's house. The stance may be regarded as ridiculous but Richardson must have inwardly thrilled over such daring defiance. Surely he was able to *be* Pamela, as Defoe could be Moll Flanders and Roxana. He wished to stand like her, upright and defiant in a soiled and muddled world. He wished also to endure the thrills of being assailed, but above all, perhaps, he desired mastery, as Pamela achieves mastery even over her social betters such as Lady Davers and her nominal master Mr B.

This reading of Richardson doesn't preclude the possibility (the near-certainty in fact) that he also stood apart from his heroines seeing them as their violators see them. In *Pamela* this sadistic viewpoint is implicit in the position of the author rather than included within the novel, for Richardson did not enter into the mind of Mr B. (which is why B. is such a perfunctorily drawn character). In *Clarissa* however, Richardson is alternately Clarissa and Lovelace. Clarissa is a feminized version of his own ego-ideal, irreproachable (despite the minor self-reproaches), assaulted, martyred and yet, in the end, somehow the victor. (Clarissa's posthumous letters, letters 127 to 131 of the final volume, beg forgiveness of the members of her family who have badly treated her and so ensure that these members will, deservedly, feel wretched for evermore.) And of course Clarissa conquers Lovelace; that is, the rake of rakes is brought to veneration of her, to raving and to death. This is one aspect of Richardson's attitude to Lovelace and his sort; they are the lusty unprincipled swaggerers of the age who ought to be brought down by Richardsonian virtues, so mild and despised, yet so unbending.

We recognize now that Richardson sought and enjoyed dominance and that he probably agreed with the remarks of Anna Howe in *Clarissa* that '*Men,* no more than *women,* know how to make a moderate use of power . . . All the animals in the creation are more or less in a state of hostility with each other'.[14] It is clear, too, that his notion of how to make moderate use of power, thus raising onself far above not only the animals but also other human beings is chiefly exemplified in the behaviour of Sir Charles Grandison. At the same time we should realize that he was readily capable of imagining himself as a victim – a victim precisely of those such as Lovelace whose power-urges are unrestrained. But he of course, would have wished to be a victim like Clarissa, who resists and in the way of a martyr wins. Richardson's life was one of personal struggle against odds : he admired effort and endurance. Clarissa, a young woman, comes to the conclusion that her creator must have come to at some point in his career :

> Upon my word, I am sometimes tempted to think that we may make the world allow for and respect us as we please, if we can but be sturdy in our wills, and set out accordingly.[15]

Accordingly, as Richardson devised for Clarissa a complete, inter-locking set of snares and an infinitely extended rape he no doubt identified himself with her, in her fears, her stalwartness, her over-weening charity, her capacity to make at least some of her persecutors worship her. It is not much of an exaggeration to say that, discounting her friends, chiefly Anna Howe and her avenger Colonel Morden, Clarissa is in a manner raped by human society as a whole. She is besieged by vice, selfishness, envy, misunder-standing to such a degree and with such 'literal minuteness' that it is no wonder that any latent disbelief in her is liable to be over-powered by sympathy. Moreover, Richardson so wanted a Clarissa in the world, so wanted to be like her in a way, that his fervour can easily overwhelm the reader.

But Richardson is also Lovelace. It is true that he hated Love-lace and grew angry when lady readers were tempted to see good in such a villain; it is also true, as I have said, that he wished to defeat the Lovelace-type, the actual London rakes who bore some very rough resemblance to this fantastic character. Just the same, Lovelace's designs, imaginings, talents, wit, cruelty, deliriums, sharp observations and all his other heterogeneous features were spun out of the author's own brain. They were not copied. It is there-fore correct to understand Lovelace as Richardson's 'Shadow' in the Jungian sense of a composite of those qualities which one inwardly possesses but disowns. This doesn't mean that Richardson was a hypocrite or a self-deceiver: it means, on the contrary, that he was unusually aware of his Shadow-side and genuinely, though perhaps pathologically, wanted to overcome it. Thus Richardson was both rapist and victim, the seeker after virtue and its would-be destroyer. Nevertheless virtue was lovely in his eyes (as it is in the eyes of Lovelace) and there is no doubt that he desired avidly to promote it in society.

He was also in love with absolutes despite his careful attention to variegated particulars. Lovelace, he insisted, was an absolute villain, thoroughly evil, and if any correspondent pointed to Lovelace's 'good' attributes he angrily pushed such attributes to one side. This further illustrates his tendency to regard evil as essentially mixed, but goodness as uniform. What additionally emerges from this consideration of Richardson is that he, in contrast to Defoe, loved the tribulations and triumphs of entrapment. In his novels scarcely anyone flits about from place to place, from group to group, from lover to lover. His plots are the reverse of the picaresque and are in fact claustrophobic. It is no wonder that, despite his awareness of social injustices (the Harlowe family, probably the vilest in fiction, are able to persecute Clarissa because of various unjust customs and laws), he seems to have had little desire for social reform. For reform could have brought to women in particular enough independence to obviate the domestic heroism he admired. In his vision people had to be chained to one another (to be literally in bondage if necessary) so as to savour their loves and hatreds, and in order to develop their virtues and vices.

Therefore those women in Richardson's novels who hanker after independence are interesting but 'inferior'. Anna Howe is quite the most promising of his women, the one who was bound to lead to further studies in later novelists. This happened in due course, for Anna is of the class of 'real' women membership of which increased from Jane Austen's novels onwards. Nevertheless the image of Clarissa took hold: weakened or debased versions of her abound in Gothic and sentimental fiction and her influence is richly apparent in American fiction, as Leslie Fiedler has so thoroughly demonstrated.[16] This happened in spite of the fact that Richardson himself moved some way beyond the Clarissa-image of perfect womanhood when in the earlier parts of *Sir Charles Grandison* especially, he gave to his last heroine, Harriet, many passages of shrewd reflection upon the real social world.

But Harriet is mastered by the goodness and sagacity of Grandison : she is not allowed to develop properly in her own right. Accordingly, it is the lesser female figures in the novels, mainly Anna Howe and Charlotte Grandison, who stand behind the more intricate and engaging women characters of subsequent writers. More precisely, when later realistic authors wish to produce a good woman they, at their best, build upon the foundation Richardson provided in the portrait of Harriet Byron but add something of the spirit, the perversity, the outgoing energy, the capability of wrong-headedness discovered in Richardson's 'inferior' women.

For it must be admitted that Richardson did succeed in bringing out the less appealing features of these spirited girls. Lady Davers in *Pamela,* a passionate and (in Part 1 at least) a coarsely domineering woman, is clearly inferior. Richardson put her in the novel chiefly in order to show how such a commanding person, even when she is high on the social scale, can be subdued by virtue and stronger will-power. One of the features of the Richardson heroine is that she obtains the love and acquiescence of lesser women, even when these women are anything but servile. So it is that Anna Howe is not merely an admirer and champion of Clarissa but also something of a lover. Anna is obviously a curious and complex girl, witty, percipient, pugnacious, capable both of cruelty and of great loyalty. We are also allowed to sense her eroticism, mainly in relation to Clarissa. In short she is very much a living creature, 'fitter', as she says to Clarissa, 'for this world than you'. Indeed she is of this world, whereas Clarissa herself is not. Something similar may be said of the relationship between Charlotte Grandison and Harriet Byron. Here again the heroine is offset against a lively, irreverent girl who rails against many conventions, in particular the convention of marriage. A few days after her wedding Charlotte writes to Harriet: 'Well, but enough of this husband – HUSBAND ! What a word !'

But it is clear that Anna and Charlotte are, in their different ways, nuisances and mischief-makers as well as charmers. Both are potentially destructive, as well they might be, since they are set in circumstances that invite derision and rebellion. A modern woman of independent mind, let alone an ardent liberationist, is likely to identify herself with these women and to feel that Richardson in his conception and presentation of them threw away certain opportunities. Behind each can be imagined another, more unambiguously sympathetic figure whom Richardson could in theory have created. But how could he, given his values and objectives? An even finer Anna Howe would have diminished Clarissa herself, despite the grandeur of Clarissa's suffering. More precisely, a superior Anna would have let in enough fresh air, enough sanity, enough perceptive and witty analysis, to upset the heroic tenor of the novel. Similarly, if Charlotte Grandison were less irritating the pretensions of both Grandison and Harriet Byron would be punctured. As it is, the portrayals of these (and some other, less important characters) are kept to precisely the pitch that Richardson wanted. They help to verify the fantasy-plots, to provide that optimum quota of intelligent ridicule which lends credibility to preposterous situations without undermining Richardson's whole enterprise.

Most significantly they promote the author's legislation for women in society. Here is Anna Howe, a woman of fine impulses, but by a narrow margin second-rate. She is believable and she adores Clarissa. If she sees Clarissa as a higher type of womanhood, how can we do otherwise? This is how the trick is played. In the same way, though Charlotte Grandison vigorously argues with Harriet Byron (about men, about marriage, about good behaviour), she accepts Harriet as her superior. Therefore the reader is further encouraged to accept Harriet as a model.

In this way Richardson, who knew that men and women are alike except 'for habits, whether good or bad', helped to preserve the sexual roles he enjoyed. The questioners of those roles are given some rein (since Richardson, a proud man, knew that in their positions he too would have been tempted to revolt) but not enough to let them move ahead of the heroines in the reader's esteem. Richardson clearly understood the merits of some of Anna's attitudes, and some of Charlotte's, but could not allow his understanding to chip away at the beliefs which sustained him. He needed to believe in a sort of utter nobility of soul and he realized that a woman like Anna or Charlotte who questions her social function must fall short of such nobility, because of the feelings of anger, bitterness and contempt produced by her struggles. Consequently Richardson, the champion and counsellor of women, actually aimed to keep women 'in their place', in the supreme cause of virtue and in order to savour (from both the masculine and the feminine standpoints) the ordeals which virtue is obliged to face.

From the very beginning, of course, Richardson's notion of feminine virtue was attacked; was attacked, moreover, by a man whom lady readers came to regard as nowhere near Richardson's equal in his understanding of their sex. Fielding's authorship of *Shamela* and *Joseph Andrews* was unforgivable to Richardson. Yet later Fielding enthused over *Clarissa* in his magazine, 'The Jacobite's Journal', and wrote a laudatory letter to Richardson about that novel. The fact is that Fielding was moved to tears by the plight of Clarissa Harlowe when he had been moved only to ridicule by Pamela Andrews. What this testifies to, I think, is a quality in Fielding which has a strong bearing on our theme, namely his chivalry. Unlike Richardson he wished not to dominate over vulnerable women but to protect them. Apparently he was one of the many readers who wanted *Clarissa* to end happily.

This should not be taken to suggest that Fielding was in some way less able than Richardson to face harsh realities: it means on the contrary that he never even tried to find a means of positively enjoying the pains and injustices with which his novels deal. No doubt Fielding's mockery in his novels softens eighteenth-century scurrilities and misfortunes but it also unequivocally attacks them. Perhaps it could be argued that Fielding's comic mode is more evasive than Richardsonian tragedy, but a truer way of comparing these authors would be to emphasize Fielding's compassion and sense of outrage. It was the manly Fielding, after all, who cried over the rape of Clarissa, whereas it was the less manly Richardson who devised her ordeal.

One of the many differences between these two authors forms a neat, unexceptional paradox. Richardson, a nervous, and in some respects a timid, man saw social life as conflict and shaped for himself an heroic ideal. Fielding who was genuinely daring entertained an ideal of domestic peace. Partly as a concomitant of this, Fielding's notion of an admirable woman included her ready sympathies, her common sense and her moral superiority. His attitude in fact was absolutely 'normal' in that he assumed a good man to be tougher but less responsible and less nice than a good woman. Such a woman needs a man to watch over her, but the man needs the woman to keep him fully sensible and decent.

Fielding nowhere argues *in propria persona* for the existence of any intrinsic psychological differences between the sexes but it seems likely from the novels that he believed in such differences. Certainly he thought in terms of sexual norms and disliked sexual confusions. The approved woman in Fielding is not in the least mannish. She is sweet-natured, morally firm and passive, except when the situation absolutely requires her to be otherwise. She asserts not herself but, when necessary, her principles or the interests of those she loves. She is generally grave and any light-hearted mood is the result of happiness rather than frivolity. The good woman is more prudent than adventurous, though not from petty calculation. Another important feature is that she is psychologically harmonious, so that her conflicts, if any, are liable to be about practical matters alone.

As an ideal or as a norm of womanhood this is obviously a limiting set of qualities, acceptable to many men in all ages and few women in our own age. Furthermore, Fielding never makes clear how the qualities arise in a tiny fraction of the population of his novels, or how they are sustained in the teeth of all sorts of adversities. Fanny in *Joseph Andrews,* Sophia Western in *Tom Jones* and Amelia Booth in her novel shine forth from the general foolishness or depravity. But their resplendence is a kind of magic lacking explanation. These heroines are enchanted creatures, not heroic as are the 'best' women in Richardson but consistently without malice and only occasionally misguided – through innocence. Yet Fielding was as close an observer as anyone could be of everyday weaknesses, of spite, irresponsibility and bad faith. The point may be that he didn't expect his first two heroines at least to be taken altogether seriously as literary creations: they are simply and candidly an expression of his generous wishes. It is true that he declared Sophia to be an expression of the worth of his own wife, Charlotte, but perhaps this remark should be taken literally: Sophia is a tribute to Charlotte's *worth* rather than a faithful representation. *Joseph Andrews* and *Tom Jones* are comedies in the popular sense as well as satires on the age, so that the point of these novels is to portray the bad things, offsetting against them not so much a lifelike kind of decency as stylized images of good nature. Viewed in this light Fanny and Sophia should invite scarcely more critical analysis than the heroines of fairy tales or romances.

To put the matter more precisely, there is an ascending scale of realism in the presentation of Fielding's three main heroines. To begin with, Fanny is merely a young, illiterate woman of great beauty, amiability and perfect virtue. None of her adventures, notably her attempted abduction by the wretched squire, Beau Didapper, brings out any complication in her character.

Sophia Western is slightly more interesting, for various reasons. First, her virtues (pretty well the same as those of Fanny) are laid before us by more dramatic means. We see and hear her in action. In particular she is given a kind of demureness and precision in conversation and this lends her a certain colour. Next, she falls into scrapes which at times rob her, quite agreeably but not excessively, of her dignity. Finally, the most important feature is her naivety about which Fielding's tone is not completely clear. It is likely, for instance, that Fielding intended us to smile at Sophia when at the close of the seventh chapter of Book 11 of *Tom Jones*, Sophia appears to think that any lady who marries an Irishman ensures a tragic destiny. The point is of course that Sophia combines her capacity for fellow-feeling with a tendency to grasp situations according to fixed rules, like a model Sunday-school child. She *knows* that Irishmen are wild and feckless. At the same time this kind of childlike certainty in Sophia contributes to a pattern of ironies in which the persons of fixed rules, of generalizing certainties, are sometimes right and sometimes wrong, while the characters who accommodate their principles to their impulses are always wrong.

One strand of this pattern is brought to a culmination in the penultimate chapter when Jones and Sophia mention the differences between men and women. Tom, no doubt speaking on behalf of the author, declares that 'The delicacy of your sex cannot conceive the grossness of ours, nor how little one sort of amour has to do with the heart.' 'I will never marry a man,' Sophia replies, 'who shall not learn refinement enough to be as incapable as I am myself of making such a distinction'.[17]

Here in a nutshell is Fielding's notion of the proper, almost the ordained, difference between men and women. Any man who is true to his nature (not effeminate, not unduly restrained) is in some degree gross. Whatever his merits the masculine coarseness remains. But the true woman, uncorrupted by fashion or false education, is delicate. It seems at a guess that Fielding, like Tom Jones, regarded women as having inherent delicacy which should be fostered or at least sustained by an appropriate upbringing. On the other hand a man's sexual excitability can only be suppressed, or even deformed, by teaching and example. He must be gross if he is not to be unnatural, while grossness in a woman is always in some degree a perversion of her basic nature.

From this purely sexual foundation, it may be deduced, arises the man's general inferiority. In alliance somehow with his capacity for instant, unloving desire the man has greater assertiveness than the woman and is therefore more prone to error of many kinds. He and she may have an equal share of what Fielding calls 'good nature', a tendency to fellow-feeling, but she surpasses this shared virtue through her natural passiveness. She hangs back until it is necessary to do good, to help someone, while he must rush forward for no sufficient reason.

All this is made very clear in the character of Amelia Booth, Fielding's least unrealistic heroine. Amelia's life is devoted to looking after her well-disposed but rather irresponsible husband and to bringing up her children (a task which she undertakes more or less single-handedly) on the principle of associating evil with fear and shame in their minds. Arrayed against Amelia are, first, some legal and social iniquities, and secondly the bad characters, notably Miss Matthews, an appealing whore, and Colonel James who is out to wrest Amelia from her husband. At one point this heroine is brought to such a pitch of misery that she becomes convinced of Original Sin, and here her adviser, the good Dr Harrison, counsels her as follows :

> Do not make a conclusion so much to the dishonour of the great Creator. The nature of man is far from being in itself evil; it abounds with benevolence, charity, and pity, coveting praise and honour, and shunning shame and disgrace. Bad education, bad habits, and bad customs, debauch our nature, and drive it headlong as it were into vice. The governors of the world, and I am afraid the priesthood, are answerable for the badness of it.[18]

Such is the presentation of Dr Harrison (an honourable, intelligent man, though not without his comic points) that we can be sure that these Socratic, or even Rousseauesque sentiments are Fielding's. The nature of man is good until he is corrupted by the world, whose governors are themselves inevitably bad. Thus, such decent fellows as Tom Jones and Booth retain their natural benevolence. Nevertheless, each cannot avoid the snares of life without the help, the constant presence indeed, of a woman finer than himself.

Unfortunately, the great majority of women, as well as men, are drawn into debauchery of one sort or another, and a sure sign that a woman has relinquished her proper nature is a display of personality, opinions or desires. In other words, as soon as a woman in Fielding's novels asserts herself beyond the level strictly required by the situation she is to be marked down as some sort of scallywag or fool. She may be anything from a likable jade, such as Mrs Waters in *Tom Jones,* to a completely vicious woman such as Lady Bellaston in the same novel, but she cannot approach the standards of a Fielding heroine.

As a matter of fact the chatterer in Fielding, the vividly self-expressive person of either sex always turns out to be faulty in one way or another (though the fault may be slight and comic), but in a man such behaviour seems at times to be inescapable. The point is that only a few characters in the novels attain the heights of excellence, and these characters are all women. (Good and grave men such as Parson Adams, Squire Allworthy and Dr Harrison have their foolishness or their foibles.)

At all events the inferior woman may be charming, full of life, superficially sensible, but gradually her inferiority emerges. Like Mrs Fitzpatrick in *Tom Jones* she may tell her story in the manner of one who has learned the lessons of her mistakes, yet it is apparent that she will hurtle into the same errors time and again. Like Mrs Waters who seduces Jones a few hours after Jones has rescued her from rape, she will continue to batter her promiscuous way through life. Like Miss Matthews in *Amelia* she will go on affirming her spiritedness and her sensitivity while looking out for the main chance. Such women as these (let alone the obvious intriguers or harridans) have, in Fielding's evident view, exchanged their true female role for a spurious one. Whether they are delightfully feminine in the way of Miss Matthews or masculinely opinionated after the fashion of Sophia Western's Aunt Harriet, they have mistakenly adopted a man's thrusting ways. They impose themselves, they initiate actions, instead of allowing actions begun by others to flow around them.

So far was Fielding from desiring 'unisex' manifestations of any kind that he emphasized, after the manner of the Middle Ages, the sort of utterly feminine loveliness that few women have ever possessed, and wrote slightingly of bold features in a woman. In appearance, though not in character, Sophia Western is a courtly lady, a very Criseyde. On the other hand, Molly Seagrim, the gamekeeper's sluttish daughter who seduces Tom Jones before he has begun seriously to notice Sophia, is also beautiful, esteemed as 'one of the handsomest girls in the whole country', but her attractions are of a different order.

> Now though Molly was, as we have said, generally thought a very fine girl, and in reality she was so, yet her beauty was not of the amiable kind. It had indeed very little of feminine in it, and would at least have become a man as well as a woman; for, to say the truth, youth and florid health had a very considerable share in the composition.[19]

In other words, Molly's looks are of the sort that will early deteriorate as a result of sex, childbearing, hard work and stupidity; yet at sixteen her face has exactly the healthy lustfulness that is more fashionable today than the sweetness of a Sophia Western. You could easily disguise her as a man but it would be difficult to do the same with Sophia. Molly's very dirtiness (she works in the fields) is an attraction and Fielding shows that he feels this himself, but he is recommending a standard above his own feelings and conduct.

For, of course, while Fielding scarcely resembled Tom Jones or Booth, his behaviour in relation to his wife, Charlotte, was such as could well be reflected in the behaviour of these characters. He too had his Molly Seagrims and his London mistresses; he too ran fearfully into debt; he too had all the masculine coarseness and thrust. In short, Fielding was an open advocate of double standards. He was anything but hypocritical but he obviously felt that double standards were quite inevitable. There *was* one law for men and one for women, not for men's convenience, but because some people had to stand aloof from the general depravity and these people could only be women – and perhaps men well past their prime.

So far as Fielding was concerned herein lay the sadness as well as the comedy of life. One avenue of improvement was the reform of laws and customs so as to maximize the natural benevolence of mankind. In one's writings it was necessary to highlight this benevolence, to show up the tainted customs, but it was also desirable to bring home to women that they alone could behave with perfect decency. It was not only unnecessary but also a kind of treason to their sex for women to emulate men, because the potentially higher should never adopt the standards of the intrinsically lower.

In the ways we have considered Defoe, Richardson and Fielding promulgated more powerfully than other English writers of the eighteenth century certain possibilities for women. Defoe alone widened their possibilities virtually to the extent enjoyed by men, but partly perhaps because of the immorality of his women and partly for the very reason that people then, as now, seek defined roles, we can deduce that his advocacy was heeded least. Certainly there are few successors in literature to Moll and Roxana: in English fiction there is Thackeray's Becky Sharpe and in French literature there are the courtesans of Balzac, but these characters are ostensibly condemned by their authors as well as admired for their vitality. Indeed they are unpleasant in varying degrees. The mere fact that the liberation of women from specific roles or stereotypes has taken such a long time (I do not suggest that it has been completed) tells us that Defoe's attitudes have not been taken very seriously, even by women. Virginia Woolf was enthusiastic about Moll Flanders but how many other women writers have shared her enthusiasm? Perhaps Moll is coming into her own to-day, though one is more struck by the praises still being lavished on Clarissa Harlowe, and even – by male critics at least – on Pamela Andrews. Of course this tendency is due in part to the determination of critics to be so novel as to take Richardson at something like his valuation of himself; or, in other words, to avoid repeating familiar anti-Richardson sentiments. Nevertheless the admiration which Richardson's genius undoubtedly deserves (and which even such an antipathetic contemporary as Fielding accorded) should not spill over into tacit acceptance of his assumptions about human nature in general or sex-relationships in particular.

As a consequence of Richardson's influence four things (excluding the use of the epistolary form) principally happened. First, the Clarissa-model was disseminated in Gothic fiction. Secondly, apart from authors in the Gothic mode, as narrowly defined, some talented writers as well as some minor ones explored the possibilities of a male-female polarity of a sort which they found in Richardson, for all his professed views. Thirdly, women authors of novels of sentiment tried to minimize sex-differences, not by giving their heroines more initiative but by giving their heroes less. Finally there occurred, mainly in these same women novelists, the sensible development of acute observations made by Richardson.

In short, his influence took varied and sometimes contradictory forms.

In Gothic fiction the Clarissa-figure was weakened into an inert girl whose *métier* was to be put upon (not usually to the point of seduction) by villainy. Since Clarissa Harlowe, for all the gifts that went into her composition, was herself a dream, and a dream of a particular phase of social history, it was perhaps a deserved fate that she should foster for a limited time such lesser fantasy-figures as the Gothic heroines. Thus Ann Radcliffe's Adeline (in *The Romance of the Forest*), as a child cruelly pent up in a convent, then undergoing a series of adventures until she settles with the hero in a pleasant house beside Lake Geneva, is perfectly representative. This pattern of imprisonment, escape, alarming vicissitudes, ending in a picturesque haven is fairly constant in the earlier Gothic romances. More important though is Adeline's unuttered vehemence: she is regularly fanciful, 'appalled', 'pitying', 'trembling' – and sometimes calmly steadfast. So it is, most famously, with Emily St Aubert in *The Mysteries of Udolpho*. Mrs Radcliffe's lady paragons are enfeebled, non-tragic descendants of Clarissa.

The second influence was more far-reaching. Some novelists who 'darkened', as it were, made more symbolical and more occult, a sexual polarization which they detected in Richardson, we shall consider in later chapters. For the moment it is enough to say that, building upon Richardsonian foundations, or 'acting upon suggestions received from Richardson' (contrary to his explicit intentions), they began to manufacture carnal mysteries with which we are still plagued. The third and fourth legacies from Richardson were in line with his expressed opinions on the essential similarity of men and women. They amounted to a flowing-together, an intermingling, of the sexes, and this is a feature of many productions by women novelists after about 1770. For one aspect of the cultural role of these ladies was to smooth away the rough attitudes found in their male predecessors and contemporaries. The pioneer authoresses were constrained by the age to 'civilize' their readers, to counteract the coarseness of Fielding, Sterne, Smollett and even, though he was the ladies' mentor, of Richardson. Accordingly, in Clara Reeve, Charlotte Smith, Elizabeth Griffith and Maria Edgeworth heroes and heroines are remarkably alike. Their minds, in particular their feelings, are regularly in harmony and this amounts to a kinship of personalities. Naturally there are differences of emphasis, especially among the most talented writers, but even Fanny Burney's *Evelina* (in the Preface to which Miss Burney tells us she set out 'to draw characters from nature, though not from life') displays a contrast between the nicely accurate dialogue of the baser characters and the set-piece sentiments of Evelina and her Lord Orville. Once again hero and heroine are a matching pair placed artificially apart from the cursing, caddish, convincing people who in one way or another cause all the trouble. This again is Richardsonian. I think it is true to say that only in the novels of Mary Wollstonecraft, who was indebted to Rousseau and scarcely at all to Richardson, do we find implied (but only implied) another and more promising notion of radical kinship between the sexes. She seems to have believed that the differences are master-and-slave differences, quite remediable.

There is much less to be said about Fielding's influence than about Richardson's. Fielding's view of womanly excellence was age-old and it is possible that his model of Amelia Booth was healthily enough conceived to endure through changing fashions and improved knowledge. For Amelia is the paradigm of any amiable and sensible person, and despite her undoubted femininity, her qualities are not exclusive to her sex. Amelia and Sophia Western are members of a line stretching back to antiquity, back to Andromache in particular. In major nineteenth- and twentieth-century authors there are few women characters of this type, partly at least because such characters lack the fascination of pathology or cultural deformity. More often than not sterling girls have been attached to exceedingly masculine heroes in adventure fiction, though some important writers in the tradition of realism – Tolstoy and George Eliot for example – presented versions of the Andromache-figure.

By the close of the eighteenth century the stage was set for an unprecedentedly thorough examination of female nature, not least because the novel had become the dominant literary form and women had something approaching men's opportunities for writing novels. We should now turn our attention to developments that took place from the time of Jane Austen onwards.

3 The Early Nineteenth Century

In relation to our topic, though not necessarily for historians of the novel, Jane Austen claims first attention in this period. She, like Richardson, seems to have regarded men and women as 'brothers and sisters', since this assumption is implicit in her fiction. The signs suggest that she thought of women overwhelmingly in respect of their social situation and scarcely at all in terms of some differentiated psychological make-up. Despite her firm assertion of the woman's point of view, she prescribed heroines who think, act or dream in what are supposed to be specifically feminine ways only in phases of error. At the same time no one doubts the femininity of, say, Anne Elliot or the masculinity of Mr Knightley. In other words, Jane Austen managed to preserve a sense of vital differences between her men and women while ascribing superogatory differences to them only for purposes of censure and ridicule.

In fact it is chiefly some of the lesser women characters in the novels who are 'truly feminine' in the popular sense, and since these are commonly rivals of the heroines or trouble-makers, it is clear enough what Jane Austen's views on these matters were. She evidently thought that the sexes should enjoy frank comradeship based upon much similarity of interests and an absolute sameness of values. If the main thrust of all her attacks is directed against falsity, or any kind of misreading of oneself and others, an important secondary thrust is against cultivated sex-distinctions. In *Northanger Abbey*, for example, the attack on Gothic fiction includes an attack on the artificial femininity of Gothic heroines. Accordingly, Catherine Morland is a clumping tomboy beside her rival, Isabella Thorpe. Isabella's manner is often ardent; her interests are personal, not to say self-centred, and her logic, when it manifests itself at all, is mere rationalization of her whims. It was easy enough perhaps for Jane Austen to show up the falsity of such as Isabella (and so to imply that womanliness of this order is generally an imposture), but it must have been harder for her to make Catherine Morland into an acceptable young woman without giving her any of the traits widely regarded as womanly. Of course Catherine's story is largely taken up with her attempts to acquire the silliness not merely of a Gothic lady but also of a 'normal' girl, though she settles in the end for being her individual and worthwhile self.

No doubt Jane Austen's design for this novel was not carried out with complete success, partly because Catherine is rather dull, but the intention is clear. There is a similar strand in the structure of *Sense and Sensibility,* and a not entirely dissimilar failure. Here, intertwined with the assault on the cult of feeling (the assumption that emotions should guide or ride roughshod over observations, thoughts and moral choices) is a study of how a woman may deceive herself in accordance with fashionable attitudes and, alternatively, how a woman might stand aloof from such attitudes. Thus, Marianne Dashwood's ingenuous cultivation of her feelings actually brings her to the verge of death, while Elinor Dashwood governs her feelings in the light of reason and out of consideration for others. Again, neither the shortcomings in execution (the failure for instance to impart enough warmth to Elinor) nor the fact that one object of ridicule is a literary mode, the sentimental novel, should hinder our recognition that Jane Austen wished to show up some purely cultural and imitative elements in female character.

A comparable pattern is present in all the other novels, since the heroines, whether as likeable as Elizabeth Bennet or as colourlessly formidable as Fanny Price, sooner or later become merely reasonable beings in certain social situations. When they err their errors have nothing to do with 'female psychology', in the sense of some age-old body of propensities, but are based on misinterpretations of reality.

Although Jane Austen's resolve to be faithful to the everyday world of conduct and manners happily ruled out much in the way of schematization, it is as if she set out to give her heroines some of those qualities which it has often been thought no woman should possess, while investing her lesser women with traits it is supposed no woman should altogether lack. So Elizabeth Bennet's cleverness, candour and venial pride are offset by the deficiencies of her mother and sisters, which (except for Mary Bennet's penchant for theorizing) were close enough to certain cultural models. It is Mrs Bennet, Kitty and Lydia who are 'real women', so to speak, and Jane is a decently simple member of the same category. Likewise, in *Mansfield Park* the shy, severe and rational Fanny Price is the paragon (a Cinderella only in situation, not in character), while Lady Bertram, Maria and Julia take advantage of their sex for various shoddy purposes. The complication in this novel, that Fanny's rival, Mary Crawford, has manly dash and frankness, does not lessen the feminist aspect of Jane Austen's presentation, because Mary illustrates how the right attributes fall to the ground when they are not supported by moral principles.

But perhaps Jane Austen's most striking piece of perversity is the portrait of Emma Woodhouse because Emma ('a heroine whom nobody but myself will much like') displays the candour, the over-weening confidence, the cheerful exploitation of others and the crass attempts at guile we associate with a spoiled but not neces-sarily unpleasant man. The other chief young woman of *Emma*, Harriet Smith and Jane Fairfax, are in their different ways closer to the norm, of popular fiction if not of life. Finally, will it be said that Anne Elliot at least is a womanly heroine, produced when Jane Austen had to a degree overcome her fear of emotion and romance? But this would be to make too much of Anne's sad passivity, which is an aspect more of her situation than of her character (though obviously she will never grow strident). Anne is simply decent, intelligent and observant, and it is her rival, Louisa Musgrove, who in a manner reminiscent of earlier rivals entertains deliberate enthusiasms. Consequently Captain Wentworth deceives himself into supposing that the lively expression of feelings (pro-vided they are not ungenerous) is itself a token of value especially in a young woman. We, the readers, are meant to undergo a similar education away from wrong assumptions about the desirable or indispensable features of womanhood.

However, it may be said that Jane Austen's presentation of character is in the strict sense superficial, that her people are generally observed in action and that on those rare occasions when we glimpse their unshared thoughts (for example Fanny Price's solitary musings) the thoughts are exclusively relevant to the immediate situation. Behind the social behaviour of a real-life approximation to Elizabeth Bennet must there not lurk patterns of fantasy that are radically feminine? Then there is the familiar point that Jane Austen's men are never seen alone or with only male companions. Is it therefore all a sort of trick by which some important differences between the sexes are most plausibly spirited away?

Against conjectures of this kind must be set the fact that nineteenth-century writers of a very different stamp from Jane Austen were united in praise of her accuracy. Scott, for example, thought Jane Austen's characterization was limited only in its range of human types, not in respect of each type considered individually. 'That young lady', he wrote, 'had a talent for describing the involvement and feelings and characters of ordinary life which is to me the most wonderful I ever met with.'[1] In other words, when a reader of Jane Austen looks around him what he sees confirms her fictions: her characters can be checked and given full marks. But – to select one illustration of the opposite tendency – if a reader turns away from *Clarissa Harlowe,* no reasonable approximation to the heroine of that novel can be found. Either Clarissa is of great rarity or she is a piece of sleight of hand.

Similarly, Macaulay thought Jane Austen the nearest writer to Shakespeare in her capacity to create characters 'such as we meet every day'.[2] G. H. Lewes was of the same opinion: neither his studies of psychology nor his acquaintance with the great European realists of the mid-century prevented him from comparing Jane Austen with Shakespeare. Her characters, he wrote, 'become equal to actual experiences'.[3] Even D. H. Lawrence a century later thought Jane Austen was accurate enough, but he regarded her powers of observation as those of a cold-eyed detective: she practised 'sharp knowing in apartness'.[4] And this judgement resembles Charlotte Brontë's, since she too believed that Jane Austen was adept at detached observation of the surface of things but ignored 'what throbs fast and full, though hidden, what the blood rushes through, what is the unseen seat of Life and the sentient target of death.'[5]

It is clear that these well-known praises and animadversions rest upon temperamental differences. Charlotte Brontë and Lawrence each had a sense of barely describable modes of being, in the absence of which, they thought, no fictional character could come alive. These modes were of course sexual, but were not confined to manifest sexual desires or activities. They were elemental, lying beneath such activities and connecting man with the world of nature. Jane Austen's sphere was overwhelmingly social, with nature excluded or merely used from time to time, and it was therefore possible for her to conclude that beyond a limited point distinctions of personality between the sexes are purely social. Indeed, so far as she was concerned such distinctions are *always* (not occasionally, as everyone accepts) histrionic and self-serving.

Likewise Jane Austen's greatest British contemporary in the novel, practising what he called 'the Big Bow-wow strain'[6] in contrast to her miniaturism, did not state or imply the unavoidable existence of a distinctly female mode of being. Scott's chief women characters in his major novels – Meg Merrilies, Edie Ochiltree, Flora Mac-Ivor, Diana Vernon, Effie and Jeanie Deans – are surely developed, with varying degrees of success, in relation to their socio-historical circumstances. At all events no one is likely to maintain that Scott's women are memorable for displaying qualities antithetical to those of men – or of those considered masculine. In particular, Diana Vernon of *Rob Roy* became for much of the nineteenth century, in France as well as in Britain, the model romantic heroine. And yet what is notable about Diana is her combination of 'manly' spirit and sexual attractiveness. She is courageous, candid, somewhat mocking and utterly loyal. From the moment when Francis Osbaldistone, the hero-narrator, first glimpses her, a beauty in a man's riding habit urging her black horse through the glen, to the final moment of her (successful) defiance of her captors, she remains a dashing personality, the exact opposite of the sentimental or lachrymose heroine.

Diana Vernon had great influence in Victorian times: generations of youths dreamed of obtaining someone like her. In our day, however, some influential theorizing has been offered about two relatively unimpressive pieces of characterization in Scott, namely Rebecca and Rowena of *Ivanhoe*.[7] Roughly speaking, Rebecca has been seen as the type of dark, sensual beauty whom men both admire and lust after, but fear to embrace. She is potentially destructive of social and psychological equilibriums. On the other hand Rowena's beauty is fair and 'safe': consequently the knight of Ivanhoe is caused to marry her, even though it was Rebecca (A Jewess, an alien) who tended him in his sickness.

The characterization of these two women in *Ivanhoe* is not itself praiseworthy but they have been regarded as prime examples, if not the originals, of a recurring motif. It is a matter of common observation that many novels, not to mention the stage and the cinema, have presented a contrast between a darkly fascinating woman and a fair woman, a pseudo-heroine and a real heroine.

The dark girl is more libidinous than her rival and she is got out of the way (often through death, dishonour or some act of self-sacrifice) leaving the hero free to marry the comfortable heroine. But in *Ivanhoe* the matter is more complex and more revealing. Rebecca's dark body houses an enlightened spirit: for all her exoticism (of dress, for instance) she is an exemplary modern type placed amid the superstitions and rivalries of the twelfth century. She looks forward to an age when healing has become a science rather than a form of magic and when the brotherhood of man has become the governing – though scarcely practised – ideal. Rowena, on the other hand, is merely a proper lady of her time, an *amateur* with no accomplishments and no gifts except for her beauty. While Rowena will bring to Ivanhoe just the soft courtesy he will yearn for after hunting, tournament or battle, Rebecca with her 'apt and powerful mind' would take Ivanhoe away from his crude activities, away from 'glory' itself, into her more frightening sphere of integrity and reason. In her most interesting conversation with Ivanhoe (in Chapter 29) Rebecca pours scorn on his notion of glory declaring it to be 'the rusted mail which hangs as a hatchment over the champion's dim and mouldering tomb'. She despises the very spirit of her age, not because she is primitive but because she is, impossibly, a figure of the distant future. So Rebecca is feared (by the Templars who propose to burn her) on account of her sanity which unaggressively challenges, among other things, a patrimonial code of perfect imbecility.

In the portrait of Rebecca, therefore, Scott attempted something well nigh impossible, in his age and apparently in ours: he tried to combine sensual beauty with goodness and reason. I say that this particular combination seems to be impossible even in modern times because there are no reasonable parallels to Rebecca. Her descendants in fictions of varying merit are generally travesties, since little remains in them except beauty, a generous nature and a tendency to be rejected by the community of which the hero is a sterling representative. Above all, it is Rebecca's rationality which fails to reappear. Certainly we can discern a fantasy structure beneath all the manifestations of Rebecca, but in Scott himself the fantasy is a rare amalgam of intellect, spirit and flesh.

Scott's creation is, then, an ideal offset against an unimpressive rival; yet she is rejected, shuffled off the stage, because by definition she could not be enduringly accommodated within the social scheme. At the same time she is an acceptable ideal in the sense of a model towards which it would be practicable to work. She is not, after all, a goddess, or a Beatrician figure who must forever stand above and beyond the world. But what of other ideals who masquerade as women and are venerated not especially because they are good and beautiful but because they are the antithesis of life's disorder?

When an author presents such a figure he is perhaps bodying forth his 'anima', as the Jungians would have it, but are there not instances where the author is doing something more or other than that? I do not refer to female characters who are failed attempts at realism but rather to women who are unashamedly dreams. There is nothing deeply mysterious about the production of such characters for they constitute a protest against the conditions of life, and as such are to be distinguished from feeble characters whom an author is immature enough to believe in. It is one thing to dream up an impossible girl under the impression that she might exist, or ought to exist, and quite another to create a woman who is a deliberate challenge to worldly possibilities.

Surely Poe's women fall into this second, more impressive category. They die young because they must and their deaths are intended as a criticism of life. Thus we are told that Lenore in Poe's poem was rich and in some fashion proud, but she was also innocent. The world, or a number of worldly specimens, hated her and now she lies 'on yon drear and rigid bier' floating down the river of death. It seems unlikely that Lenore was utterly good, a candidate for sainthood; she was just of the noble sort whom the world finds hateful.

But it is wrong to speak of such figures as if they were characters in the usual sense, for they are mere emblems employed to express Poe's sense of life's everlasting uncouthness. Poe's Ulalume is not even glimpsed as a person : she has been dead for precisely a year when the narrator of the poem, together with Psyche, his soul, comes upon her vault in the woods. The narrator is trying to live zestfully, despite Psyche's forebodings. He has thrust out of mind the memory of his dead love, Ulalume, but is plunged back into desolation when he sees the forest tomb. Ulalume is not Poe's, or the narrator's, 'anima', for that Jungian function is represented by Psyche : she is instead the yearned-for antithesis of reality. Therefore Ulalume is youthfully and irrecoverably dead.

Ligeia in her story is a perfect beauty, raven-haired and ivory-complexioned, who returns from death in her shroud to seize the life of Rowena whom the narrator has in false hopes married. Rowena is little more than a fair, commonplace woman, fit for everyday life: for this reason she too must be caused to die – as a token of her inferiority to Ligeia. The lady Madeline in 'The Fall of the House of Usher' has contracted a disease that 'has long baffled the skill of her physicians'. She dies and is placed in the donjon, only to return in a blood-stained white robe to claim the life of her brother. The artist in the story, 'The Oval Portrait' paints so lifelike a picture of his lovely wife that, on its completion, the wife herself is dead.

In every instance Poe is not creating female characters at all but saying that life and what the soul longs for (beauty, not morality) are irreconcilable opposites. For Poe the notion of beautiful realism, an aesthetic ordering of probabilities, was a contradiction in terms. Only to the extent that one departs from the real can one approach beauty. To look at Poe in this way (his own way, as we gather from such critical essays as 'The Veil of the Soul' and 'On Imagination') makes more sense than to regard some of his works as significant contortions of the sex-instinct. At the same time a number of the stories indeed seem to be expressions of the 'death-instinct' in Freud's sense of an impulse which promotes 'the most universal endeavour of all living substance – namely to return to the quiescence of the inorganic world'.[8] But, assuming that it is sensible to see Poe in this way, we should also bear in mind that he was not exceptional in possessing a death instinct, which according to Freud is universal and is to a degree involved in every search for order: he was unusual only in the nakedness of his expression of that instinct. At all events, Poe's women are simply personifications of his ideal, an ideal of coherence and harmony. Simone de Beauvoir comments in *The Second Sex* that 'Man feminizes the ideal he sets up before him as the essential Other, because woman is the material representation of alterity'.[9] This remark applies to Poe because in his works woman is the Other; that is, the perfect shapeliness he could not find in his everyday self or in the world around him.

Poe was much respected in France well before he was luke-warmly accepted as a serious author in America: nevertheless, the leading French novelists of his day approached their work with quite different purposes from his. As social realists rather than aesthetes Stendhal and Balzac produced women characters who are tied to social circumstances in the way that Poe found uncongenial, not to say hateful. To further our aims it is necessary now to consider the attitudes to women of these two French writers, partly because in each of them we find what is lacking in their British and American contemporaries, that is, a body of theory about society, history and the development of character. Furthermore, their theories were thorough opposites and will serve as useful points of reference, not merely in the present chapter but in later chapters as well. For Stendhal and Balzac anticipate in their different ways the arguments with which we, in the 1980s, are still vehemently concerned.

Stendhal did not produce a gallery of women but instead offered minute studies of a limited number each of whom stands out against a rather blurred background. We are given to understand that in the background are stock creatures living out their mediocre lives. By proceeding in this way he was not, however, following the usual practice of highlighting heroes and heroines of the community – a community requiring leadership and virtuous examples. On the contrary Stendhal wished to study exceptional people whose behaviour, good or bad, indicates a more stimulating and promising response to contemporary history than that of the majority. But these noteworthy attitudes are not necessarily, or even normally, 'correct', let alone morally superior : they are attitudes which, like those of some classical heroes, may be wildly mistaken yet by contrast elucidate the spirit of the time.

Thus in *Le Rouge et le Noir* Madame de Rênal, Julien Sorel's first love, is thought dull by the women of the small town of Verrières because she doesn't gossip with them or make endless calculations for getting round her husband, the mayor. Of the ladies of the district it is only Madame de Rênal who concerns us and in fact we never meet any examples of the gossiping towns-women. Later in the novel when Julien moves to Paris, his second love, Mathilde de la Mole, is bored by the high society of which she is a rather distinguished young member. She seems to have no firm women friends and rich young men pursue her to no avail. Once again Julien's mistress is closely depicted, while her milieu is seen to a large extent in terms of her, and Julien's contempt for it. The point is that Julien and his two ladies, constitute a focus on French society in the 1830s. They are not confined psychological studies, even though the small-spirited folk who surround them are little more than glimpsed by the reader.

Julien's two mistresses can sensibly be regarded as joint heroines, though it is commoner – and tempting – to venerate the un-pretentious Madame de Rênal as against her Parisienne rival. Certainly we can see Madame de Rênal as the heroine of the novel and Mathilde (whom Julien in his final, 'authentic' phase rejects) as the pseudo-heroine; nevertheless what they have in common is more important for the theme of the novel than their marked differences. Each stands apart from contemporary pettiness, Madame de Rênal out of intelligent naivety and Mathilde through haughty idealism. Julien Sorel himself, a clever peasant, erratically engages in social climbing and in this respect, for all his unique qualities, he represents his post-Napoleonic period. At the same time Julien is proud and imaginative with the result that he cannot give to his ambitions the prosaic, grovelling single-mindedness they require. In particular it seems likely (Stendhal for once offers no explanation) that when Julien returns from Paris to Verrières with the object of murdering Madame de Rênal he does so as a gesture of pride. At the prompting of her confessor Madame de Rênal (who inwardly knows better) has depicted Julien in a letter as a typical young man on the make; consequently he attempts his desperate crime in full view of a church congregation, thus showing himself and everyone else that, whatever else he is, he is not a type.

Julien loathes his social superiors not because he is an envious peasant but because he thinks of himself as an incomparable fellow, a non-pareil. Even to be just another aristocrat, supposing that were possible, would be humiliating. Just the same for most of his story he tries, for want of clear vision, to make himself a standard *arriviste*. His two women are also marked out from the age in which they live. Madame de Rênal neither compares herself with others nor tries to live up to an ideal. She stumbles along the path of her own inclinations which are predominantly good and generous. The important feature of her character is that it is free and flowing within broad limits, though she has obstacles of shyness and self-doubt to overcome. She is womanly and yet falls into no standard pattern of womanliness.

Mathilde, on the other hand, sees herself as a latter-day Queen Marguerite of Navarre: despising the present age, she looks back with the eyes of a nineteen-year-old to the 'honourable' sixteenth century. One of her ancestors, a certain Boniface de la Mole, was a secret lover of Queen Marguerite and was beheaded for his part in a plot. The Queen arranged to have her lover's head removed from the place of execution and then, at midnight, buried it with her own hands in a chapel at the foot of the hill of Montmartre. After Julien's execution Mathilde acts out her fantasies, becomes what she has long dreamed of becoming, by taking his head and with strange ceremony burying it in a cave in the Jura mountains. As for Madame de Rênal, three days after Julien's death 'she gave her children a last embrace, and died'.

Stendhal's unsystematic theories which lie behind the production of these and other leading characters in his novels are scattered among his non-fictional writings, in particular his letters. They are mainly notions about the relationship between literature and life, especially life in early ninetenth-century Europe. It is well known that Stendhal believed that a novel should be like a mirror, an undistorted reflection of portions of reality. He thought, however, that the novelist can point his mirror at whatever he chooses and that he had better choose objects which the reader will find pleasing as well as enlightening. The truth, in other words, but not the whole truth. The novel must obviously falsify by selection, but for Stendhal it should not falsify in any other way. More precisely, the novelist is bound to be a liar but he should aim to lie as little as possible. Despite Stendhal's republicanism, a fair way to put the matter is to say that a novelist is better employed describing a palace than a hovel, though the palace should be neutrally observed and its defects exposed no less than its glories. A palace is at least intended to be a noble edifice and is therefore a suitable, if flawed, expression of the human spirit.

It follows of course that the heroes and heroines of Stendhal's fiction are remarkable people, 'above the average' in something resembling Aristotle's sense,[10] but are at the same time full of faults and absurdities. What Stendhal hated (again in spite of his republicanism) was any notion of social determinism and the idea that 'average' human nature is the healthy standard to which everyone should aspire. Therefore his leading women Clelia Conti and the Duchessa Sanseverina in *La Chartreuse de Parme,* Mme de Chasteller in *Lucien Leuwen* as well as the two ladies of *Le Rouge et le Noir* exceed the limitations of character which society seeks to impose upon them and seem to do so out of choice. Of course the choices are blind in some respects; they are only fitfully deliberate or calculating. Nevertheless as we follow the confused thoughts of a Madame de Rênal or a Mathilde de la Mole, it is clear that they are groping (or sometimes leaping) forward of their own volition and manifestly flouting the standards of their peers.

In theory and to some extent in practice Balzac's women are the opposite : whatever they do and however adroitly Balzac describes their actions or accounts for their motives, they are supposed to obey laws which hold good for all women of their class — courtesans, long-suffering wives, poor relations, and so on. But Balzac is so adept at depicting behaviour that if it were not for the little essays, the 'anatomies', which he inserts into his dramatic episodes, a reader might take him to be copying or creating fairly specific individuals. However, as the anatomies make clear, he thought of individuals in the old sense of the word, that is, as specimens of common types.

Balzac's procedure was to select from the countless observations he made in daily life those features that he regarded as significant for the social history of his time. For example, from the scores of pretty young Parisiennes who were then (in the 1830s and 1840s) engaged in finding rich protectors he took certain representative features and excluded whatever he deemed accidental or individually peculiar. A suitable assemblage of such features then formed a fictional courtesan who was in a manner 'truer' than almost any actual courtesan could have been. Presumably Balzac did not faithfully work in such a way, but this was his tendency and his creed as an 'historian' or 'secretary' of society.

In this author the woman is utterly determined : however much initiative she displays it is by a paradox a sort of mechanical initiative. She schemes or she languishes, she is histrionic or sincere; but all her activities are dictated by her geographical origins, by her race, by her parentage, by her present position in society. Thus her very scheming is a form not of freedom but of enslavement, rather as a mechanical doll must perform certain tricks or as a cat is liable to freeze before pouncing on a bird.

Certainly, in Balzac there are not only categories of women but sub-categories as well, but however many sub-categories he presents, he is careful always to generalize. Consider the following passage from *Cousin Bette*.

To stray from the path of virtue is for the married woman an inexcusable fault; but there are degrees of guilt. Some women, far from becoming depraved, conceal their frailty, and remain apparently worthy of respect . . . ; while certain others add to their disgrace the shame of deliberate investment in their dishonour. Madame Marneffe may be considered a type of the ambitious married courtesan who from the start accepts moral depravity and all that it implies, resolving to make her fortune and enjoy herself too, with no scruples about the means. Like Madame Marneffe, such women almost always have their husbands as their agents and accomplices.

Machiavellis in petticoats such as these are the most dangerous and the worst among all the evil kinds of women in Paris. A true courtesan . . . conveys in the unmistakable nature of her situation a warning as brightly shining as a prostitute's red lamp or the blazing lights of gambling dens. A man knows that he risks ruin in such company. But the sweetly prim respectability, the outer semblance of virtue, the hypocritical ways of a married woman . . . lead men to unsignposted unspectacular ruin, ruin all the stranger because the victim finds excuses and cannot find a cause for his disaster.[11]

Thus Valérie Marneffe, one of Balzac's most fascinating courtesans (despite the moralizing typified by the above passage, Taine rightly and celebratedly said, '*Balzac aime sa Valérie*'[12]) is essentially one of a class. She is not a specific person who for purposes of generalization may be compared in certain respects with other persons: on the contrary, she is like these others through and through. The interesting thing is that Valérie is very much a creature of will rather than of feeling, and she has but limited imagination. Just the same her will is entirely set in one, commonplace direction. She never digresses. Similarly, Lisbeth Fischer of the same novel, Cousin Bette herself, is described as a 'peasant girl from the Vosges, with everything that that implies: thin, dark, with glossy black hair, hoary eyebrows meeting across the nose in a tuft, long and powerful arms and broad solid feet, with some warts on her long, simian face: there is a quick sketch of the spinster'.[13] Balzac of course does not mean that the region of the Vosges is thickly peopled with Lisbeths but merely that she is the commonest type in that region, in relation to which other local girls (girls such as her fair, honourable cousin, Adeline) are aberrant. The point is that Lisbeth, no less than Valérie, is fixed, 'wound up' as it were, to run along certain lines – lines of craftiness, passion and jealousy.

Fundamentally the question raised by Balzac's novels, like those of Stendhal, is the question of will. This of course is the point on which these two novelists are so neatly opposed. Balzac's characters often display will as surely as Stendhal's, and sometimes more devilishly, but in Balzac the will itself is somehow predetermined, like the will of an animal. Thus his great schemers such as the criminal, Vautrin or the successful social climber, Rastignac follow the laws of their nature in relation to social forces, rather like animals in a certain habitat. If you put a tiger in a particular kind of enclosure he is presumably bound to do one of a severely limited number of things: the tiger cannot decide to do something altogether different, as if he were a human being capable of forming unpredictable self-images and ideals.

Balzac in fact makes his assumption plain in the Preface to the *Human Comedy*. He develops the argument that society can and should be studied as the zoologist studies the animal kingdom. If an author does this, he will certainly find the human species to be more variegated than any other, but, with pertinacity, the varieties may be classified so that no one's behaviour evades scientific analysis. Thus the schemes and stratagems of a Valérie Marneffe are classifiable and predictable to the novelist–zoologist, however astonishing they may be to her lovers. And her will, though strong, is not remotely free.

So it is with women in general. Balzac was obliged to acknowledge several varieties of women but in his *Physiology of Marriage* tried to establish that there is an eternal feminine nature which society is apt to warp but cannot eradicate. Woman, he argued, has a destiny involving both physiological and psychological pains, but above all devoting her to man's use. Therefore we are supposed to regard the Valéries of this world who use men as perversions formed by society, rather as someone might artificially create a new species of plant. However, they are formed: their wills are an illusion — or else operate within narrow limits.

Balzac's attitudes and methods were in part pseudo-scientific in the sense that, wishing to account for human conduct as well as representing it, he thrust aside behaviour that did not fit his theories. His observations of manners, though wonderfully sharp, were often (not invariably) at the mercy of his classifications, rather than the other way round. Balzac's nearest English equivalent in his own day, Thackeray, was different again. To a degree the world of *Vanity Fair* is Balzacian and yet in no other major English novel, except for the novels of Defoe, do we find such freedom from social or sexual determinism. Admittedly it is easy, all too easy, to relate the natures of Becky Sharp and Amelia Sedley to their parentage and backgrounds, but Thackeray's attitude to these (and other) characters shows that he saw them as self-determined creatures.

As the two girls are presented it is clear that the personality of each constitutes a strategy for life. Within a range of possibilities and limitations each one has adopted, more or less deliberately, a particular pattern of behaviour with the object of gaining satisfaction from her environment. And for both Becky and Amelia we can see the origins of the strategies but not their inevitability, for in theory the girls could have developed quite different natures. So, Becky's father was a drunken, irresponsible artist who married a French opera-singer. The mother died young, whereupon the father beseeched Miss Pinkerton (at whose academy for young ladies he gave drawing lessons) to take in the seventeen-year-old Becky as an articled teacher of French. Soon afterwards the father died of drink. When we first meet Becky, she, the charity-girl and offspring of a bohemian couple, is leaving school with her friend and opposite, Amelia. Becky and her dissolute father had been great pals in the old days, hanging around Soho together and typically making fun of the pretentious Miss Pinkerton whom Becky had met on a visit to the school in Chiswick. We can say that Becky derives her intelligence and unprincipled ways from her father and we can assuredly add that her resolve to secure a (preferably well-to-do) husband stems from her poverty. Nevertheless, Becky's chief traits are not the automatic results of either inheritance or imitation of her parents.

It seems that as a child Becky was bright, easy-going, fun-loving. Then came the catastrophe of her parents' deaths and she was plunged into the snobbish sphere of Chiswick Mall. Her reaction was lonely anger which rapidly gave rise to the habit of deception. Apparently this was her act of self-choice, one possibility amongst several. From these early days at the school onwards, Becky is mainly a dissembler and an adventuress. Thus she changes into a character quite different from her father. She is above all calculating, which he evidently was not. He lived for pleasure and immediate gratifications of the flesh, while Becky seems if anything sexually cold and is for ever using her acquaintances for long- or medium-term ends. He presumably was not much of a poseur but Becky's first action on meeting a potentially useful person is to strike whatever pose will serve her interests. So far as Becky is concerned social life is competition and sincere people (such as Captain Dobbin, the patient lover of Amelia) are both rare and stupid. Obviously this chief strand of Becky's nature is the result of a desire to wrest from society what will not readily be given to her, yet she enjoys the sport for its own sake. She lives by her wits even when she has no need to do so and starts fresh adventures, such as the liaison with Lord Steyne, when she has secured her earlier objectives.

The remarkable thing about Becky is that she knows as well as Thackeray himself how worthless are the prizes she pursues. Thus the summit of her career is her presentation to the half-witted King – 'George the Good, the Magnificent, the Great', as Thackeray calls him. For a while afterwards Becky is so full of herself as to snub even some aristocratic ladies of dubious reputations, but this is simply the pride of victory, for she presumably knows (Thackeray is not clear on this point) that to her the King's value is no greater than the intrinsic value of any trophy. Similarly Becky is perfectly aware of the viciousness of Lord Steyne, her grandest admirer.

There is a sense in which Becky *plays at* being a woman. Whenever it seems advantageous to do so, she makes pitiable gestures, weeps, casts down her eyes, assumes helplessness and so forth. For all that she is not less of a real woman. On the contrary she exposes time and again the extent to which (in Thackeray's view at any rate) womanly manners can be a masquerade. I do not suggest, and Thackeray certainly does not at any point contend, that they are entirely a masquerade, but in *Vanity Fair* there is a flow of implications that outward behaviour is regularly in the service of self-centred designs. Captain Dobbin, a genuine altruist, is the only exception of any note and he is finally seen as rather an ass for worshipping such a girl as Amelia Sedley.

Amelia of course is the subject of an apparent *volte-face* on Thackeray's part in the final chapter. Throughout the novel she has been treated with respect and affection (coupled occasionally with a little amusement) and then at the conclusion of the tender scene of Amelia's reunion with her faithful Dobbin come the famously damning words.

> The vessel is in port. He [Dobbin] has got the prize he has been trying for all his life. The bird has come in at last. There it is with its head on his shoulder, billing and cooing close up to his heart, with soft out-stretched fluttering wings. This is what he

has asked for every day and hour for eighteen years. This is what he pined after. Here it is – the summit, the end – the last page of the third volume. Goodbye, Colonel – God bless you, honest William! – Farewell, dear Amelia – Grow green again, tender little parasite, round the rugged old oak to which you cling.[14]

In part Thackeray is here making fun of an entire literary – and to some extent social – convention: that the height of felicity is reached when a worthy fellow gains an amiable, helpless girl. But there is no doubt about the condemnation of Amelia's helplessness. Are we therefore to assume that Amelia's personality involves, like Becky's, a degree of choice? Her father, a stockbroker, worshipped her and wished to spare her every pain: at the time of his financial ruin, for instance, one of his great anxieties was for the ill effect the family trouble would have on 'Emmy'. Once Amelia depended upon the manly strength of her father: at the end of her story she has obtained yet another stalwart man. At no point does Thackeray suggest that Amelia's sweetness is a pose, but time and again he develops scenes in which she averts her gaze from uncomfortable facts. She has been protected and throughout her story has the habit of instantaneously blotting out of mind whatever it does not suit her to contemplate, for example, aspects of Becky's behaviour or of George Osborne's. People generally do not disclose their selfish designs in her presence and they sometimes say to her in effect: 'You are too decent to appreciate what I am going to tell you, but the rotten truth of this world is . . .' And Amelia does not contest this estimate of her or seek to know more about the truth in question.

In such ways as these Thackeray's attitude towards his variously unpleasant, rascally or mediocre personages is the reverse of Balzac's. The latter 'blames society' as they say, or more widely, a complex of forces outside the control of the individual – race physiology, historical patterns, iron laws of one sort or another. He is ambiguous in his condemnation of individuals for actions which he regards as involuntary in some ultimate sense. But Thackeray is unwavering in his (good-humoured) criticism of thoroughly specific characters. He offers no social or psychological theories but regularly implies that his people could decide to behave differently. His women, no less than his men, may contend with their environment as they please and their chosen way constitutes, or at the least consolidates, their characters.

However, for some time we have been considering only male observations and suppositions. It is one thing to be as acute as Balzac or Thackeray and quite another to look upon women with the eyes of a genius who is also a woman. And when the woman genius writes principally about herself do we not get a very different story? According to Virginia Woolf in *A Room of One's Own* what we get, though different, is by no means the whole truth because the woman's vision is confused by bitterness and by subservience to male modes and categories.[15]

Virginia Woolf's argument (to which we shall inevitably return in later chapters) is partly concerned with integrity in the sense of unimpaired wholeness. Charlotte Brontë, for example, faithfully represented elements of her own vision but was constrained to link these elements with various falsehoods. The falsehoods, according to Virginia Woolf, are the consequence of ignorance, imposed masculine values and anger about the imputation of inferiority to women. Therefore Charlotte Brontë's novels include fine parts yet lack 'integrity'.

It will be profitable to try to see *Jane Eyre* in this way, qualifying Virginia Woolf's judgements, and building upon them. Jane herself, the first notable self-projection in English literature by a woman of strong talents, is above all an individual. It is hard to imagine anyone, male or female, inventing her from external observation alone. Labels do not fit her very well and she is a product neither of the Balzacian sort of 'scientific' classification nor of loving observation after the manner of Stendhal. Jane Eyre is a distinct person largely because of her style which is more subtly individualized than the styles given by their creators to such earlier women characters as Moll Flanders and Clarissa Harlowe. Paradoxically, however, Jane's is a copy-book style: she is in this sense (though in this sense alone) a mature version of a model schoolgirl. Of course what we encounter is Charlotte Brontë's own manner: there is little distinction between the personality of Jane and that of her creator, and therefore there is little difference of personal styles. Charlotte Brontë wrote her novels with great care, as Mrs. Gaskell tells us in the *Life*.

One set of words was the truthful mirror of her thoughts: no others, however apparently identical in meaning, would do . . . It [the right word] might be provincial, it might be derived from the Latin; so that it accurately represented her idea, she did not mind whence it came; but this care makes her style present the finish of a piece of mosaic.[16]

We can deduce from the novels that Charlotte Brontë had this diligent manner of composition, but the important point is that 'Jane Eyre' is likewise a perfectionist giving us the mirror of her mind. Jane is at once intimate and restrained, passionate and dignified in such a way that her feelings are absorbed by the reader even when they are not nakedly expressed.

> While disease had thus become an inhabitant of Lowood, and death its frequent visitor; while there was gloom and fear within its walls, while its rooms and passages steamed with hospital smells, the drug and the pastille striving to overcome the effluvia of mortality, that bright May shone unclouded over the bold hills and beautiful woodland out of doors. Its garden, too, glowed with flowers: hollyhocks had sprung up tall as trees, lilies had opened, tulips and roses were in bloom; the borders of the little beds were gay with pink thrift and crimson double-daisies; the sweet-briars gave out, morning and evening, their scent of spice and apples; and these fragrant treasures were all useless for most of the inmates of Lowood, except to furnish now and then a handful of herbs and blossoms to put in a coffin.[17]

To some extent this entirely typical passage resembles a prize-winning school composition. It is also emphatically a girl's or woman's composition: from the range of English fiction the only male parallel that comes to mind is the early 'feminine' Lawrence, the Lawrence of *The White Peacock* (which happens to include a funeral scene in fine weather, a contrast betwen death and burgeoning nature). Nevertheless the formal beauty of the passage, not excluding the pleasantly stilted phrase, 'the effluvia of mortality', and markedly including the melancholy close, is pure Jane Eyre. If, following Virginia Woolf, someone were to say that Charlotte Brontë has failed to break through the correctness imposed upon her by a masculine culture we must reply that the very correctness is self-expressive. Jane is a 'good girl' despite or because of her capacity for rebellion, her accurate observations of people, her sceptical intelligence and her obvious though undisplayed sensuality.

Has Jane Eyre, which is to say Charlotte Brontë, forced her rambling woman's thoughts into a strait-jacket of schoolmasterly syntax? How can we know the answer to this? In *A Room of One's Own* Virginia Woolf points out that the English sentence has been formed by men, but then asserts that for a woman writer to express herself properly she must re-fashion the sentence.[18] Here is a complex question which is discussed in a later chapter,[19] but for the moment it is enough to state one's conviction that Charlotte Brontë can have felt no greater discrepancy between thoughts and words than many male writers (who also have their difficulties). Surely anyone reading Charlotte Brontë's novels has, correctly, the impression that he is in real contact with the mind of the author and that the felicitous propriety of her prose was a true expression of the personality she had become – however she started out. In any event, in the relationship between Jane and Rochester, and especially in the portrait of Rochester, Charlotte Brontë's fantasies were clearly enough expressed without the dubious benefit of an experimental style.

In everyday life Charlotte Brontë had similar, though cruder, fantasies. According to Margaret Lane in her book *The Brontë Story*, Charlotte dreamed of 'a world where heroes were amoral and unscrupulous, "viciously beautiful", handsome dukes who possessed noble wives and passionate mistresses, who begot bastards, ruined their friends, and were at all times wonderfully eccentric and sardonic and sarcastic'.[20]

However unrealistic he may be, Rochester is a toned-down version of such fantasies. He is rather ugly instead of 'viciously beautiful', his wickedness lies in the past and was not considerable, and whenever he is sardonic he is generally thoughtful over Jane. This then was Charlotte Brontë's dream moderated towards probability and indeed towards circumstances that she imagined might satisfy her in real life. At the end, after the fire and Rochester's partial recovery, he is not a Samson shorn of his strength nor is he emasculated. Jane becomes 'absolutely bone of his bone, and flesh of his flesh', and she bears a son who resembles the virile father. But he is finally a pious man. Thus the marriage of Jane and Rochester is a union of equals, Christian and at the same time, one is led to assume, richly carnal.

For all their differences of talent, temperament and vision Charlotte and Emily Brontë seem to have had the same dream of relationship between the sexes. It was, I suggest, a worthy dream founded upon a realistic assessment of male and female possibilities. Thus the recurrence in Charlotte's novels of a master–servant or master–pupil relationship does not mean that she (of all people) desired to be led, tutored, or even emotionally protected, by a man. Similarly, the maiming of Rochester is neither a symbolic castration nor, as one critic has put it, 'the symbol of Jane's triumph in the battle of the sexes'.[21] On the contrary what Charlotte Brontë plainly wanted was total rapport of mind and spirit with a man who would dominate her in the sexual act, and in that act alone. This is evident in Lucy Snowe's relationship with Paul Emmanuel in *Villette* and in Shirley Keeldar's entire personality in *Shirley*. It goes without saying that she would ideally have denied the man his social and legal advantages over her, since these spoil the very rapport of which she dreamed. When Jane Eyre says that after her marriage to Rochester she became 'absolutely bone of his bone and flesh of his flesh', Charlotte Brontë can be seen wishing away, not indeed the biological distinctions to which she refers, but every non-biological distinction. Likewise, when in the ninth chapter of *Wuthering Heights* Catherine Earnshaw makes her celebrated declaration of identity with Heathcliff, we are faced with the same notion of total merging between man and woman. 'Whatever our souls are made of', Cathy says to Nelly Dean, 'his and mine are the same.' A little later she expands on this assertion.

> If all else perished, and *he* remained, I should still continue to be; and if all else remained, and he were annihilated, the universe would turn to a mighty stranger : I should not seem part of it . . . Nelly, I *am* Heathcliff ! He's always in my mind : not as a pleasure, any more than I am always a pleasure to myself, but as my own being.[22]

Critics tend to respond to these remarks with enthusiasm but little curiosity, seeing them only as one of the high points in a strange, in fact an unparalleled, novel. But what do the remarks mean ? Cathy is excited though not hysterical, and she knows what she is talking about. Furthermore, though Cathy and Heathcliff are only components in the pattern of the novel, they clearly meant more than any of the other characters to Emily Brontë – as they do to readers. To us each is a distinct individual and Cathy, for all her wildness, is a complete woman, while Heathcliff is as masculine a man as anyone could hope or fear to meet. And yet the correspondence of their souls is due to the sex-distinction, for Cathy could never be so at one with another woman, nor Heathcliff with another man. Their thoughts and feelings flow together *because* they are of opposite sexes. The merging is not overtly sexual, like the merging of Jane Eyre and Rochester, but it rests upon sexuality. She and he, says Cathy, are like the 'eternal rocks beneath'; beneath the efflorescence of nature, so that what Emily Brontë is presenting – or perhaps discerning in her 'mystical' way – is an underground confluence between the sexes from which a host of variegated forms grow upwards into everyday life. If Cathy and Heathcliff are, as everyone says, elemental, the implication is that differences of character between the sexes, far from lying at the roots are in reality blooms – and often cultivated blooms at that. This, at any rate, seems to have been Emily Brontë's vision. Bodily differences were to her, as to Charlotte, nature's source of psychological unity.

This attitude shared by two of the Brontë sisters is of course implicit and is not expressed by either of them as a theory. However, in one extraordinary novel of the mid-nineteenth century the author openly speculates along similar lines, and that novel was a product not of Europe but of New England. Initially Hawthorne's *The Scarlet Letter* received both good and bad reviews and it was some of the latter that accused him of falling victim to a 'French virus', so to speak.[23] It was suggested that Hawthorne understood little of Christianity, had failed to condemn adultery in the proper spirit and had brought his heroine to something approaching a state of grace without causing her to repent. Hester Prynne's punishment should have been adequate but it did not make her realize how grievously she had sinned.

What the reviewers, favourable and unfavourable, missed, and what even later critics have not emphasized, was the prophetic nature of *The Scarlet Letter*. Though it is an historical novel it is also a piece of 'legislation' for the future. Hawthorne's prime purpose was not to illustrate seventeenth-century puritanism but to combat puritanism in the society of his own day and he therefore looked forward to a time when fear and guilt should be replaced by truth and love. It was necessary, he thought, to root out the 'Black Man', the figure of evil believed by the people of Hawthorne's novel to lurk in the forest behind their township.

But it is clear that this Black Man (one of the clearest instances in fiction, not so much of the Freudian 'id' as of the Jungian

'Shadow') is, in Hawthorne's view, a product of male supremacy. He is there in the woods because the patriarchal community so abominate and chastise the sins of the flesh. Hester Prynne, through her sufferings and in particular because she is made an outlaw, becomes a prophetess of a new order – an order, not of licence but something remarkably like the motions of some latter-day humanistic psychologists. And this new order, it seems, depends upon the equality of women with men.

In the novel Hawthorne is tentative about the origins of secondary sex-characteristics but enthusiastic about the need to modify them. In the thirteenth chapter he writes as follows:

> A tendency to speculation, though it may keep woman quiet, as it does man, yet makes her sad. She discerns, it may be, such a hopeless task before her. As a first step, the whole system of society is to be torn down and built up anew. Then the very nature of the opposite sex, or its long hereditary habit, which has become like nature, is to be essentially modified before woman can be allowed to assume what seems a fair and suitable position.[24]

A tendency to speculation did not necessarily make women sad, or even angry, in the nineteenth century (George Eliot for instance was not sadder than male intellectuals of her time) but the remark is fair enough as a generalization, for Hawthorne's generation and ours. Nevertheless Hawthorne's words show a fine awareness of woman's position. They suggest that women generally lack interest in speculative thought, or indeed the capacity for it, simply because they also lack power. Such thought, even or especially in its most disinterested forms, is a prelude to change and is pursued by people who feel themselves to be actual or potential lords of creation. Then, Hawthorne realized the immensity of the task confronting women, a task which he nevertheless seemed to feel must be undertaken. It was not a matter of tinkering with a few laws but of tearing down the 'whole system of society'. Even that would not be enough because women (or men, for it is not clear which is the 'opposite sex' here) must change their nature. Nor is it certain whether woman's nature is unalterable or the result of 'long hereditary habit' and therefore possibly capable of change.

The chief point about Hester Prynne is that her estrangement from the community leaves her free to think more radically than other characters in the novel. She is a lonely, creative thinker, and a heroine in every sense of the word. She begins to see the truth because she is not involved in the day-to-day business of the town. And what she glimpses is that 'at some brighter period, when the world should have grown ripe for it, in Heaven's own time, a new truth would be revealed, in order to establish the whole relation between man and woman on a surer ground of mutual happiness.'[25]

The Scarlet Letter was first thought of as a story about witch-craft and dark forces of evil: Hawthorne was even compared with Poe. In a later phase of literary criticism the novel naturally became a subject for sub-Freudian analysis. To-day it would be foolish to claim that Hawthorne's whole purpose was the liberation of women, but that element of his purpose is thrown into sharper relief. More broadly, Hawthorne aimed at enlightenment and he seems rightly to have assumed that the real enemies of enlighten-ment are not ignorance and superstition but fear and power. In one respect *The Scarlet Letter* was extraordinarily ahead of its time, a fact that has been obscured by its historical character, by the quaint dignity of the style and by veneration in the twentieth century for those features of the psyche which it was Hawthorne's purpose to help us to outgrow. He dealt with dark matters in order to thrust them behind; not indeed to repress them but to demon-strate what he believed to be their origins in moral cowardice. Some nineteenth-century realists, whom we shall be dealing with next, were in this regard less 'advanced' than Hawthorne.

4 The Later Nineteenth Century

'Realism' is and was from its inception a vexed and varied designation which we should to-day, perhaps, use in a purely convenient way (avoiding the questions) or, at the opposite extreme, take as the starting-point for a fascinating, important and necessarily inconclusive discussion. What is not possible is to employ the term literally and so assume, for instance, that Flaubert, George Eliot, Tolstoy and Henry James – the authors under consideration here – presented portraits of women that are somehow more valid, more empirically right, than the portraits produced by their gifted forebears. Tolstoy, commonly seen as the exemplary realist, thought that all art was a 'beautiful lie', and that it worked in his day, as it had worked in the ages given to fable and legend, by providing moral guidance. What alone mattered was the quality of that guidance. George Eliot's self-justification for writing fiction was that fiction could supremely strengthen the reader's capacity for fellow-feelings. Truth to life was relatively important – as a means of educating the moral imagination. Henry James thought that the writing of fiction should itself be a moral enterprise and *therefore* an aesthetic one. He believed that beauty and truth coincided, but the truth he sought was not in the least a matter of documentary fact. As for Flaubert, with whom we begin, he, the 'father of realism', hated contemporary realism on the grounds that only dolts could be reconciled to the real world.

Madame Bovary was designed, partly at least, to demonstrate the superiority of art over life and only incidentally to show the folly of confusing the two. For Flaubert had no ethical intent and never supposed that reading about Emma would make people less inclined to behave like her. Nor for that matter did he believe that his showing-up of the bourgeoisie would help to reform them. However, the pertinent questions about *Madame Bovary* concern

Flaubert's motive for creating his heroine and her status, in his eyes, in comparison with the rest of the characters.

Emma delights in the inherited notions of romantic culture – novels, the opera, romanticized history. We are told that at sixteen she was a worshipper of such ill-fated women as Mary Queen of Scots, Joan of Arc and Heloise. She is at odds with her Norman community of Yonville-L'Abbaye, neglects the realities of debts and her lovers' instincts for self-preservation, and so ends in suicide. But her creator was at odds both with the community and, on the face of it, with dreams such as Emma's. In his novel Flaubert attacked the bourgeoisie while also mocking the fantasies by which his heroine tried to evade the sterility of bourgeois life. Yet he famously told people, 'Madame Bovary, c'est moi.' In what way, then, was Emma a projection of Flaubert?

As a child Flaubert was himself a dreamer and already a writer.[1] At his boarding school in Rouen he wrote historical adventure stories filled with noble personages. His mental world was normal for an imaginative boy, since he enjoyed tales of revenge and murder, furiously reading Dumas, Hugo, Scott, Byron. But he was more than commonly captivated by such literature: this was not a phase he would outgrow in the usual sense of coming to accept the dullness of adult life. Within a short time there crept into his stories a strain of disillusionment which was certainly affected but nevertheless developed into his genuine adult attitude. During his teens he became recognizably more 'Flaubertian', ensuring that the characters he invented should suffer as a result of their ingenuousness or optimism. Death awaits them, sardonic and yet surprised that they have not taken him seriously. It does not seem that Flaubert then desired death (though he sometimes did in later life) but rather that he was baffled and scornful because people refused to face the truth. He loved truth: why did others hate it? At eighteen he wrote:

> If ever I take an active part in the world, it will be as a thinker and demoralizer. I shall only tell the truth, but it will be horrible, cruel, and naked.[2]

He was not sure that he would 'take an active part in the world', because doing so entailed all the usual lies and self-deceptions. It is possible, of course, to regard such an attitude as mere rationalization arising from a passive nature : Flaubert was overwhelmingly receptive and disliked action. To do anything in society was to impair his minute and multiple awareness. But his contemplative capacities and his lack of involvement did help him to see, most shrewdly, the shabbiness of much social life. In addition he was convinced that pious hopes, programmes of reform (of self or society) and seeming decencies were illusory. At the same time, as a ludicrous or painful paradox, his upbringing had given him a yearning for achievement; a yearning, in other words, for what he himself regarded as worthless.

Flaubert's art, and especially *Madame Bovary,* perhaps constitutes a way out of this dilemma. He took an active part in the world by exhibiting the futility of taking an active part in the world. He achieved something by ridiculing common forms of achievement. But unlike earlier writers who may be said to have done roughly the same, he of course did not hold out the consolations of religion. In *Madame Bovary* there is no God, but to compound Flaubert's rejection of common alternatives, even the atheist character of the novel, the chemist Homais, is a humbug who ends up with the Legion of Honour.

In the writing of *Madame Bovary* Flaubert became a strange, indeed a unique, sort of realist, *because* he found reality so distasteful. Other writers who offer us what appears to be only moral or physical squalor are covertly sentimental or hopeful. Flaubert's novel is utterly cynical, partly for the plain reason that it depicts only wretchedness of one sort or another and partly in consequence of its rigorous organization and sparely beautiful style. In other words the aesthetic qualities both describe and offset the subject-matter, in effect saying to the reader, 'See how appalling life is, but see also how the mind may create beauty without departing one iota from the evident truth'. For this reason we are exhilarated rather than depressed by Flaubert's cynicism. The style at least is inspiriting so that no competent reader of Emma's depressing story is actually depressed. This does not mean that Flaubert tricked himself, or that we his readers do so, since he was quite sure that art is only art and that it is the only genuine alternative for an honest observer.

At the same time, after some attempt has been made to appreciate Flaubert's stance, it is reasonable to question it. Surely it is true that everything in *Madame Bovary* conspires to produce what Sartre has called 'a realism more spiteful than detached'.[3] Sartre means to suggest not only that Flaubert's picture is a half-truth, but also that his response to life is 'womanish', helpless, a sort of jeering resignation. It apparently relies upon the belief that the world, including human nature, is a given, unamenable to creative thought.

But from another point of view Flaubert's very jeering is creative: it is not at all as helpless as it looks, or as Flaubert seems sincerely to have supposed it to be. It is also implicit, for Flaubert is scarcely anywhere so careless as to mar the objectivity of his tone. But there are tiny moments when he seems to let slip his identification with Emma, or at least some qualified support for her, as for instance in the eighth chapter of Part 4 when he speaks of 'that innate cowardice that characterizes the stronger sex'.[4] In fact as we know from Flaubert's letters of the period (1851 to 1856) he was partial to his heroine, though he chose her in the first place for her central trait of self-glamorization. In our estimate and, I believe, in Flaubert's Emma is superior to her milieu because she is spiritually misguided where everyone else is crass. There is no word of praise for Emma in the novel, yet it is impossible not to prefer her to other characters. Where can this preference, this slight partisanship, have originated, if not in the mind of the creator? Emma is surely a greatly reduced and vulgarized Flaubert whose essence lies in the refusal to accept the nullity of Yonville. She knows, as others do not, that life is intolerable at its present level, and this is Flaubert's own knowledge expressed through the figure of a misguided woman. Another way of grasping the matter is to see Flaubert as a maturer, vastly more sophisticated Emma who instead of entertaining dreams composed an exquisite pattern of words, who controlled fictional events as she imagines she can control people and who made the writing of his novel an alternative to social commitment such as she rashly undertakes.

Emma is mentally isolated from first to last, though she is often unaware of this. To begin with she is a bored dreamer at home in her father's farmhouse, then after her marriage to Charles Bovary she is alone, either because Charles is attending to his patients or because when the couple are alone together there is no point of contact between her fancies and his dismal preoccupations. Emma's first affair, with Rodolphe Boulanger, is a gallantry on his part, a self-induced passion on hers. We observe Emma working up her emotions to the proper, sanctified level of intensity. The emotions are real for all that and in fact Flaubert remarks that in everyone feelings grow to the extent that they are cultivated and uttered.

Emma's self-dramatization is regularly juxtaposed with scenes that are prosaic, painful or dully vicious. At the Yonville agricultural show (Part II, Chapter 8) Rodolphe's advances to her are first conducted beside an arena full of pigs and cattle and later punctuate the grandiloquent flow of the deputy Prefect's speech from the platform. Emma's love for Rodolphe is at its height at the time when her husband, in hopes of medical fame, is operating disastrously on the club foot of Hippolyte, an ostler. It is typical of Flaubert that he thus brings together the stench of gangrene and an idyll in a moonlit garden. After Rodolphe deserts her Emma is for a while neurasthenic and then moves into a brief religious phase initiated by a 'heavenly vision' of a puerile sort. This period of 'Catholic melancholy' gradually wears away and on renewing the acquaintance of the law-student, Léon Dupuis, in Rouen Emma once again becomes 'the "woman in love" of all the novels, the heroine of all drama, the shadowy "she" of all the poetry books'.[5] But her relationship with young Léon is marked – 'cursed' one would call it in a more fanciful context – by the appearance of a blind beggar of extreme, mutilated ugliness, and it is this beggar's pretty, silly love-song which is the last thing Emma hears before her final convulsion from arsenic poisoning.

Emma is estranged from other people in Yonville and Rouen. When she feels at one with them, at times with Rodolphe but more completely with Léon, the harmony is either an illusion or takes place in a never-never land. In *Madame Bovary* society can foster neither vital connections between individuals nor any but the crudest aspirations. However different Emma may be from her creator she shares his loneliness, his love of beauty and his need to organize the world. Furthermore author and heroine coincide at the centre of that imaginary spectrum which runs from extreme masculinity to extreme femininity. His attitude to society was submissive and fatalistic, in other words 'feminine' in the traditional sense; but he nevertheless retaliated against society by an art that is 'masculine' in its precise organization. The images which compose Emma's daydreams are exceedingly feminine (satins, lagoons, flowers, dying swans, 'pure virgins rising to heaven'), but she thrusts towards her fantasy-goals in a way that is, or was, more common for men. This is presumably what Baudelaire meant when he remarked that Emma possessed 'at once the folly and the will of a man'.[6]

It was propitious for Flaubert to 'pretend' to be a woman. From the standpoint of a somewhat masculinized woman he could better express his judgement of small-town bourgeoisie than by speaking in his own voice or by inventing a hero like himself. Such a hero must have been rather feminine and therefore, by the standards of the time, unimpressive. And the faults of the society, in particular its drabness and pettiness, would have been less marked in contrast to the vision of a somewhat effeminate – which is to say, an eccentric – man. Emma Bovary is scarcely eccentric despite the fact that she never meets a true companion. Some of her traits had been attributed to women for many a day, along with the assumption among readers of popular fiction that society safely provides scope for such adventures as Emma dreams of.

It seems that whenever an author masquerades as a member of the opposite sex some broadly similar motive is at work. It is always a matter both of self-expression and of social criticism. In ancient literature, as we have noted, one of the readiest ways for a dramatist to question contemporary notions of justice was to place himself in the position of a woman. Mainly for this reason Euripedes, for instance, elevated the traditionally bestial figure of Medea by seeing Corinth partly through her eyes. Similarly in later literature we have observed how Defoe in *Moll Flanders* and *Roxana* expressed his views about individual freedom and social necessity by imagining himself (a not much altered self) in the positions of his two heroines.

It is not rare for an author to divide himself into a man and a woman who are locked in a deadly contest. Thus Richardson, before he was finally prevailed upon to depict a good man, found it congenial to feminize his ego-ideal in the figure of Clarissa and put her in opposition to his subterranean dream embodied as Lovelace. This sort of manoeuvre is interesting because it consists not merely of exteriorizing a 'male' and a 'female' facet of one's make-up but also of causing the favoured facet (which may be of the opposite sex) to emerge triumphant. And of course this is never simply self-analysis conducted in a void but criticism of society as well. The author makes a recommendation to his readers based upon concrete social conditions. Plainly one of the neatest ways to this is through the portrait of a marriage or a love-affair. Evidently this was George Eliot's method in *Middlemarch*.

It is generally recognized that those of George Eliot's characters who come nearest to being self-portraits are Maggie Tulliver in *The Mill on the Floss* and Dorothea Brooke in *Middlemarch*. Of course these characters differ a great deal and Maggie is closer to her creator in nature and circumstances, but each is a projection of the author. What in certain phases of development they have in common is a preference for ideas and images over actuality. This preference among others George Eliot inveighed against to the end of her career, not solely because she despised it in others but also because she felt she had reason to be ashamed of it in herself.

In *The Mill on the Floss* at the time of her family's troubles the thirteen-year-old Maggie Tulliver turns to a regular reading of the Bible, Thomas à Kempis and a work called 'The Christian Year'. In other words, she reads and dreams about virtue but fails to increase her practice of it. At this point George Eliot characteristically comments as follows :

> This is the path we all like when we set out on our abandonment of egoism – the path of martyrdom and endurance, where the palm-branches grow, rather than the steep highway of tolerance, just allowance and self-blame, where there are no leafy honours to be gathered and worn.[7]

The reference here is universal (Maggie follows a course which 'we all' follow at such times) though George Eliot was generalizing from her own childhood. When her father, Robert Evans, fell ill and her mother, Christiana, shortly afterwards died, the young Mary Ann Evans took on a considerable burden of household duties to which her nature was quite unsuited. She had a yearning for knowledge such as few women or men have ever possessed and she was, so to speak, 'wickedly', that is time-wastingly, imaginative.[8] Besides, like any embryonic artist she must have desired self-development, but she was set amidst people (some of them like the Dodsons of *The Mill on the Floss*) to whom such a desire must have been incomprehensible and bad. Some leading aspects of Maggie Tulliver's nature in relation to her circumstances are a reasonably faithful (though smoothed) reflection of Mary Ann Evans's in childhood. Maggie is bright in all aspects of her being : she is clever, emotionally vigorous, imaginative and physically robust. In every important way Maggie is ahead of her family and indeed she is the clear star of her small town of St Ogg's. But her kinsfolk and neighbours think she is, if anything, inferior, because she is ill-adapted to their ways. Then, in comparison with her brother, Tom, she cannot give much practical help just when such help is needed.

George Eliot remained to the end of her days a probing critic of every manifestation of individualism, including the notion of the artist as 'outsider'. To her a Flaubertian solution would have seemed preposterous and immoral. The exceptional person should serve the community; certainly he should not sneer at it for its failure to match his requirements. However, unlike so many people who – to-day more than in George Eliot's time – talk fervently, almost evangelistically, about social responsibilities – she was aware of the tendency of a community to estrange some of its most promising members. Of course she did not so describe the matter, but it will be salutary for us to consider George Eliot's much-discussed analyses of 'egoism' for once in this light. The point is that such analyses sometimes include portraits of persons in whom self-centredness is a product of nobler impulses than the community can appreciate. This is true of several of George Eliot's characters : of Adam Bede, Maggie Tulliver, Romola, Felix Holt, and Dorothea Brooke and Lydgate in *Middlemarch*. It is normal for critics to accept George Eliot's own appraisals of these characters, to the effect that they must halt their movements towards estrangement, mortify their pride, abandon their daydreams, come to understand the sinfulness of casting oneself as the hero around whom lesser mortals sing in chorus.

But George Eliot's moral analysis rested upon the attempt to resolve a personal dilemma. She wanted to be at one even with simple folk, yet she had a massive intellect. Her soul throbbed to grand music but she wished, as a child at least, to be *en rapport* with souls of clay. She dreaded isolation and yearned for community. Moreover, she suffered regularly from a sense of personal unworthiness which made her both hope for and fear some indubitably honourable worldly attainment. She hoped for it as proof of her value as a human being, but she feared it since she felt it would be unfitting, undeserved. These important aspects of George Eliot's personality are implied rather than stated in one modern biography, that by Gordon Haight, while another recent biographer, Ruby V. Redinger, does conduct a thorough analysis along such lines.

Another important contradiction with which George Eliot had

to wrestle was sexual in nature. Professor Redinger describes this complication in the following words :

> But in George Eliot's time, one had to be all man or all woman – or at least pretend to be in public. As hers was an extraordinarily powerful nature, it is little wonder that for many years during which she was caught between the need for and fear of masculine aggressiveness and feminine passivity, her sense of identity was blunted and her sense of unworthiness augmented. Where in the great family of man – woman did she belong ?[9]

Professor Redinger is confident that George Eliot eventually overcame this problem, and perhaps she did, but it is pertinent here to look at an example of the use she made of it. In *Middlemarch* George Eliot took hold of two aspects of her so-called 'bisexual' nature and dramatized one of them as Dorothea Brooke, the other as Edward Casaubon whom Dorothea marries. At the same time Dorothea and Casaubon display in markedly different ways the yearning for achievement, 'greatness', perfection, which George Eliot understood and condemned in herself.

Dorothea and Casaubon are so antithetical; she is so high-souled and he so mean, that at first this fact is hard to accept and possibly it would never be accepted if George Eliot had not pretty certainly told someone that Casaubon was based upon herself. According to the well-known anecdote mentioned by John Cross in *George Eliot's Life* (1887), when a friend asked her from whom Casaubon was drawn 'With a humorous solemnity, which was quite in earnest, she pointed to her own heart'.[10] There seems to be nothing ambiguous here, especially when we recollect George Eliot's regular and at times pedantic determination to avoid being misunderstood. She of all people would have known that the friend in question could misinterpret at the drop of a hat. George Eliot cannot have meant, 'I invented Casaubon' but 'Casaubon, c'est moi.' In any event, George Eliot admitted in a letter to Harriet Beecher Stowe : 'I fear that the Casaubon tints are not quite foreign to my own mental complexion'.[11] Nor is this identification hard to understand, since George Eliot suffered from Casaubon's desire to excel and his horror of failure or rejection.

Casaubon's anxiety to impress is in direct proportion to his sense of inadequacy. However, he is an extreme case because without knowing it he feels himself to be, almost literally, a nonentity.

Therefore he yearns for unqualified superiority, for a sort of absoluteness of being that cannot be touched by criticism. Specifically he wants to be a great scholar, but he apprehends that role as static and impregnable. In effect this means that Casaubon wishes to exist without proper relationships, since relationships are challenging and unpredictable: one cannot rehearse and control them. George Eliot, like the existentialists of our century, seems to have believed that our valid existence, our 'authenticity', far from being necessarily corrupted by others, cannot blossom without them. But Casaubon is afraid that his spirit will wither away through contact with other people, unless of course they act purely as advisers and acolytes. George Eliot writes of him as follows:

His experience was of that pitiable kind which shrinks from pity, and fears most of all that it should be known: it was that proud narrow sensitiveness which has not mass enough to spare for transformation into sympathy, and quivers thread-like in small currents of self-preoccupation or at best of an egoistic scrupulosity.[12]

George Eliot herself did again and again what Casaubon never dares: she made her experience, or in other words herself, known through books. Casaubon, on the other hand, ensures that his great work, the 'Key to all Mythologies', is never completed, never published, because he is terrified that errors of fact or weaknesses or argument will be detected by fellow-scholars. Thus he makes a virtue, scrupulosity, out of what is really a vice in him – and in any event his book, unlike the works of George Eliot or of any novelist great or small, is calculated to conceal the author's inner life. Nevertheless, George Eliot suffered from Casaubon's fears: she knew them intimately. Although she had long wished to write fiction, G. H. Lewes had to push her into writing her first stories, those that make up *Scenes of Clerical Life*. After that for many years Lewes tried to keep from her even the smallest and most ill-conceived pieces of adverse comment, because he knew that criticism would blight her powers.[13] George Eliot, like Casaubon, regularly felt that her remarks or gestures were, unless she was extraordinarily careful, vulnerable to criticism. For all or for most of her life (it is not clear which) she lacked a secure sense of identity: sometimes when she spoke she disconcertingly heard her own voice; she suffered almost as a matter of course from the physical pains of nervous tension. For all her popularity she was fearful about the reception of her books. In these and other ways she thoroughly understood the condition, craven but pitiful, of Casaubon.

This surely is the reason why Casaubon is so penetrating a study. But in sharp contrast George Eliot was also possessed of great ardour, unshared in the smallest degree by Casaubon but poured into Dorothea. Those rapturous passages which too often occur in George Eliot's novels – and which modern critics point to as weaknesses – represent maturer, talented versions of Dorothea Brooke's tendency to cause the environment to lose its awkward edges, to melt, as it were, into her eager will.

Dorothea is of course quite unlike George Eliot in important ways, having pure, dignified beauty and belonging to a high bourgeois family, but in one key respect author and character are the same. At the beginning of her story we are told that Dorothea knows 'many passages of Pascal's *Pensées* and of Jeremy Taylor by heart; and to her the destinies of mankind, seen by the light of Christianity, made the solicitudes of feminine fashion appear an occupation for Bedlam',[14] Dorothea is impractical: she has a 'theoretic' mind and is unable to reconcile local concerns with her exalted dreams. By the end of her story, after her grotesque marriage to Casaubon has ended with Casaubon's death and after she has become the inspiring and useful wife of Will Ladislaw, Dorothea is a different person. Rather, Dorothea has evolved (though the evolution is completed in a single night) by causing her zeal to fasten realistically upon objects and persons near at hand. She has grown content, even profoundly happy, with prosaic life and no longer dreams of greatness – for herself or for others. Thus Dorothea is a heroine and no heroine, because in George Eliot's view (perhaps mistaken) the days of the 'great' man or woman were already over by the second half of the nineteenth century. In particular terms, Dorothea has the soul of a Saint Theresa though a humble destiny, because the modern world calls not for sainthood but for obscure and unassuming decencies.

This in outline is Dorothea's impressive and affecting story – a progress from pride to humility, from illusions to reality – but does it not in the end perpetuate the sort of error it seeks to rectify? Dorothea's conversion is itself a piece of wish-fulfilment on the part of her author. In reality the aspirations of a Dorothea are likely (at best) to mature, perhaps to the point of tragic consciousness, though not altogether to lose their grandeur. But it was precisely grandeur that George Eliot wished to do away with, because it is wicked and because the grand person is liable to feel alienated from the community – as George Eliot herself remained uncomfortably alienated. Much of her skill went into disguising the fact that the conclusion of Dorothea's tale is a dream of improbable integration.

In other ways, however, Dorothea's career reflects the emotional essence, though not the detail, of episodes in George Eliot's life. In her twenties George Eliot laboriously and sickeningly translated David Strauss's *The Life of Jesus,* a myth-demolishing but arid work, and this activity may well be represented by Dorothea's marriage to Casaubon. The latter is not a portrait of Strauss himself (whom George Eliot long after the period of translation met on several occasions) but in all probability an embodiment of the feeling Strauss's work gave her – a feeling of oppression and dessication. If we add to this the intense self-doubt of George Eliot herself, the doubt and its concomitant fear of rejection, we almost certainly have the root elements in the genesis of Casaubon. But George Eliot as Dorothea Brooke comes eventually to marry a vivacious and chivalrous man whose affection leads her to the fulfilment of her destiny. Will Ladislaw, Casaubon's nephew and in personality Casaubon's opposite, is surely a romanticization of some of the qualities George Eliot found in George Henry Lewes. In fact Lewes was ugly not carelessly handsome like Ladislaw, and Lewes's domestic life was greatly and sadly complicated, but his characteristics – his liveliness of manner, intellect and sensibility, his bohemianism, his protectiveness – are present in glamorized form in Ladislaw.

Presumably the sort of process we have been considering in George Eliot's writing may take place only when an author's nature is not emphatically 'masculine' or 'feminine'. The fictional characters who are the result of just such a process are not themselves extremes of the sexes. Thus, the admirable Dorothea is so far from being exclusively feminine that many a man would fight shy of her (as Lydgate does to his cost in the novel), while Casaubon is something of an 'old maid'. Conversely George Eliot's manly men, Adam Bede, for instance, or Tom Tulliver in *The Mill on the Floss,* are results of acute external observations. It seems to be rare for an author to present the very mental texture, as opposed to the overt behaviour, of a character of the opposite sex with whom in his daily life he has little in common. It is for this reason that some of Tolstoy's portraits of women, notably Natasha Rostov in *War and Peace* and Anna Karenina, are more remarkable than is often recognized. For there is little to compare between the self-projections of a Richardson or a Flaubert and Tolstoy's evident capacity to occupy, as it were, the mind of a woman poles apart from his own richly variegated but scarcely feminine mind.

Tolstoy's characterizations of women are reckoned to be marvellously accurate, yet he wished to confine women to their traditional roles. Even today women readers and critics find little fault in the portraits but Tolstoy's views about the psychology and social functions of women were unqualifiedly Biblical. This is not necessarily a paradox but it is very interesting. Let us first consider Tolstoy's theoretical opinions.

In 1870 his close friend Strakhov, the critic and eulogist of *War and Peace,* published a study of the position of women, declaring them to be fashioned by God for men's solace and for procreation. Strakhov regarded the feminist movement as a monstrosity which sought to pervert not simply the laws of society but the God-given, irreversible nature of womanhood. With all this Tolstoy agreed, adding only that unmarried or unmarriageable women might well serve society in other ways – as nurses, for example, or in some unfortunate instances as prostitutes.[15]

The abundant biographical material confirms that such, with minor qualifications, was Tolstoy's regular attitude. His eldest daughter, Tatyana, mentions in her memoir that the family used to accuse him of what they called 'womanophobia'.[16] This sounds light-hearted enough (Tolstoy was not a crude domestic tyrant) but, it seems, his view was indeed like Pozdnyshev's in *The Kreutzer Sonata,* that emancipation makes women 'mentally diseased, hysterical, unhappy, and lacking capacity for spiritual development'. The 'phobia', in other words, was a reaction not to women in their 'proper' state but to their condition in consequence of false teachings. Tolstoy's was the common assumption (held with uncommon vehemence) that the capacities of the sexes are antithetical or complementary – though man was in every important way the leader. His opinions on the subject were banal. 'With women', he told his sister-in-law, 'reasoning leads nowhere. It is useless. Their intellect doesn't work properly. And I'll say more. However reasonably a woman may judge, she will nevertheless always act by her emotions.'[17]

Tolstoy's knowledge of women was, he said, acquired by

studying them after his marriage. 'Even before my marriage,' he once confided to his daughter, 'it had dawned on me that I knew nothing about them whatever, and it was only through my wife that I got to know them.'[18] What all this suggests, I believe, is that in the fiction we encounter a most astute combination of empiricism and prejudice.

The empiricism is plainly there, on page after page of *Anna Karenina* in particular, so that even modern women are bowled over : they do not rise up with the usual denunciations. And yet the story of Anna herself, in carefully designed contrast to Levin's and Kitty's creative struggles, is a study in degradation caused by a distortion of womanly nature. Anna's tale is a 'gloomy tragedy',[19] as Henri Troyat has called it, but the tragedy is not produced simply by social forces.

Indeed it is gloomy, unrelieved either by phases of joy or by the stylistic felicities of a Flaubert or a Zola. (In comparison *Madame Bovary* is sourly amusing and *Nana* is exuberant.) In a severely functional style, with what appears to be complete understanding though not an ounce of sympathy, Tolstoy recounts a pretty well unbroken decline. The seed of this decline is sown at the moment when Anna first sees Vronsky at the Petersburg railway station, and the consummation is reached when she crouches on the tracks at another station, perplexed by her own actions. Tolstoy makes his tale blacker than Euripedes' tale of Phaedra, who is Anna's remote ancestress. The love-making of Anna and Vronsky is never ecstatic : there is nothing here reminiscent of the coming-together of Dido and Aeneas, or of Criseyde and Troilus. From the beginning it is mainly a matter of doubts, forebodings and misconceptions : these alone intensify and ripen.

To say this is not to overlook the short periods of *relative* happiness for Anna and Vronsky, such as part of their time in Venice, but just to point out the absence (unusual by the standards of great love-tragedies) of exultancy. It is doubtful whether this feature is in itself a measure of Tolstoy's truthfulness : on the contrary it signifies his refusal to allow even some qualified merit in erotic love. For him there were none of the compensatory or ennobling possibilities of tragic passion that are present in the literature of the Christian Middle Ages and are not entirely absent from classical drama. Such passion, to Tolstoy, was simply wrong, a disease which if it is virulent enough must run its full course. It should be emphasized that Tolstoy's attitude is unusual among the great writers of tragedy: only in a superficial sense is it traditional. For the Greeks the tragic heroine often had a touch of the sublime in her make-up. This is true not only of Sophocles' Antigone, but even of Aeschylus' Clytemnestra and Euripedes' Medea. The Phaedra of Euripides decides to kill herself not in madness, nor yet solely to bring misery on Hippolytus and his father Theseus, but in part 'to bequeath', as she puts it, 'an honourable life to my children'. The medieval tragic woman is a product of the contemporary urge to elevate women as well as of the priestly desire to denigrate them. Moreover, she experiences great happiness before her downfall.

But Anna at the start is merely not unhappy, not consciously and profoundly discontented over her situation as wife to Karenin and mother of her young son, Seryozha. She is also, of course, beautiful and extraordinarily charming. After the ball (in Chapters 22 and 23) at which she more or less unwittingly captivates Vronsky and ousts Kitty Shcherbatsky from his affections, she begins at once her degeneration. It is as if a bacillus has entered her bloodstream, and the bacillus is a consuming and exclusive lust. Obviously it takes a while to gather strength, or even to fill her mind and be clearly recognized, but once there it cannot, evidently, be dislodged. The process, in this most realistic of novels, is not only without justification; it lacks explanation as well.

For Tolstoy chronicles the happenings in *Anna Karenina,* including the psychological events, but does not in the usual sense analyse them. Absent are the sort of generalizing comments with which Balzac sprinkles his pages and the theoretical explanations we find in George Eliot. George Eliot would tell us what Anna is thinking and would in addition diagnose Anna's moral condition. Covertly, Tolstoy's manner, his celebrated 'objectivity' or 'moral neutrality', is actually more *ex cathedra* than the manner of a George Eliot, because there is less opportunity for readers to interrogate him. In effect he says to the reader as if he were a chronicler: 'Don't ask me why these things happened. They did so happen; it is the way of the world, and you had better pay heed.'

As we have it, then, Anna falls pathologically in love, like the heroine of an ancient drama. But in Tolstoy there is neither a vengeful goddess nor a modern explanation in the terms of theoretical psychology. Fairly early in the novel Anna tells Vronsky that she dislikes the word 'love' because, she says, 'It means too

much to me, much more than you can understand'.[20] After the
first sexual act when Vronsky is innocently talking about his happiness, Anna is disturbed that he should think in such a way. She
herself feels shame and horror with an admixture of joy, but
cannot now or at any stage of their relationship contemplate real
happiness. Anna feels degraded physically and causes Vronsky to
feel, as he gazes upon her wretched but still beautiful face, that
he has committed a murder. Why is he made to feel like this?
Because she is no standard hedonist, a light-of-love, but a chaste
woman into whom, by little more than his mere presence to her
sight, he has injected a slow-working poison. The poison works not
simply because she cannot take such adventures lightly but because
there is some factor in her that co-operates with it.

No one in the book understands Anna. Not Karenin of course
though he gives a crude parody of an understanding when he
asserts to his wife, 'All you want is the gratification of your animal
passion'.[21] In a sense that is all she wants, though the passion must
be gratified with one man only and it is bound up, as Anna in a
corner of her mind knows, with decay and death. To Princess Betsy
Anna is just 'inclined to take things too tragically'[22] as if Anna
could shake herself into a sensible frame of mind. The worldly,
agreeable officer, Serpukhovsky, is both right and wrong (in
Tolstoy's eyes) when he tells Vronsky that 'women are all more
materialistic than men. We make something tremendous out of
love, but they are always *terre à terre*'.[23] He is probably meant
to be right in his general view, but wrong with the full force of
dramatic irony not to see that some women do fly away from their
earthy habitat and are therefore doomed. Kitty, after she has
married Levin, is prone to regard Anna as merely an evil woman.
Dolly Oblonsky remains grateful to Anna for patching up the
Oblonsky's marriage, but is shocked to find that Anna has calmly
decided on birth-control methods with Vronsky. Above all,
Vronsky himself is regularly bewildered and grows appalled at the
turn his life has taken – a tragic fate for a non-tragic man.

It is not uncommon in fact for readers to feel that Anna is a
woman of great promise enamoured of an unworthy man. But
this response cannot be in accordance with Tolstoy's intentions.
There is nothing much wrong with Vronsky and the love Anna
brings him is manic in its intensity. It is not that some man
somewhere would be worthy of her but that what she wants
is against nature, which is as much as to say, in Tolstoy's belief,

against God. To Tolstoy an exclusive concentration upon physical love (a man and a woman each living solely for the emotions and sensations aroused by the other's body) is, contrary to some naive notions, the height of unnaturalness, a perversion of the soul. Tolstoy's point is that shutting one's eyes to the needs of people one meets, to society at large, to the diverse features and demands of daily life is opposed not only to God's ordinances but to human nature as well. Such a way, if we persist in it, is bound to lead to madness or death. On the other hand what is right and Godly is also in the purest sense natural. When in the eleventh chapter of Part 8 a peasant lets Levin into the secret of right living this is roughly what the peasant's words mean. Referring to a particular good man the peasant says that he 'lives for his soul, he does. Remembers God'.[24] Taking into account the drift of the novel and noting especially Levin's subsequent contemplation of these elementary words, they imply that one should not act against one's ingrained (Kantianly innate) moral sense.

The soul in this sense must be impaired not simply by specific acts of wickedness and by vice in the usual sense but also, and more effectively, by obsessions and *idées fixes*. Thus the love of Anna for Vronsky, like every *grande passion* is in Tolstoy's view, a means not of heightening the soul but of debasing it. When Tolstoy chose as the epigraph for his novel the words from 'Romans', ' "Vengeance is mine; I will repay," saith the Lord,' he surely meant that man is governed by inexorable laws of which the law concerning erotic love is, in the novel, the most striking example.

Where, then, is Tolstoy's 'womanophobia' and where is his legislation for womankind? Neither can be located within *Anna Karenina* which is a triumph of formal and stylistic neutrality. Even such formal links as the railway deaths (the accident to a guard in Chapter 18 and Anna's suicide) are unexceptionable, since the first death suggests to Anna's despairing mind the manner of her own. Nevertheless the novel, for all its minute detail, has the effect of a parable, and not merely in the lesson Levin learns. The reader is nowhere urged to generalize from Anna's tale but he is meant to carry away the impression that something older and stronger than Russian mores in the 1870s brings about Anna's fate. The absence of explanation for Anna's conduct (such as might in theory have been provided by glimpses of her earlier development) reinforces Tolstoy's tacit teaching that a decent and generous woman is the very last person who should give herself up to sexual love. Such a woman is not, as she is in Fielding for example, the secular guardian of virtue, but among her strengths and severe limitations there is no scope for commerce with Aphrodite.

For an artist Tolstoy's view was extreme : he so firmly separated truth from beauty. Unless an artist was extraordinarily vigilant he was far more liable to mislead than to enlighten, since apart from anything else, he could be fatally tempted by the beauty of his medium. In Tolstoy's work there is barely an echo of the great medieval (supremely, the Dantesque) fusion of moral and aesthetic values. Henry James, on the other hand, believed that these two sets of values, far from being opposed, were bound up together. He asserted that he did not write in order to teach (doing so was a *vice anglaise*), yet critics have normally, inescapably treated James's works as exquisite ethical studies. Ideally, I suppose, the reader of James would enhance his powers of perception and *thus* (rather than by example, percept or theory) refine his discriminations in daily life. But James did not hope or expect that anything of the sort would happen.

James's outlook was both secular and tragic. It was secular in the sense that, unlike Tolstoy, Flaubert and (despite her rejection of Christianity) George Eliot, he seems wholly to have accepted life, or the 'World' with all its corruption. As a corollary he had no general or codifiable scheme of values against which his characters are measured. One character is, or grows, better than another, but does so as a result of keener awareness in specific, unrepeatable situations. From James, therefore, there are no lessons to be drawn except the lesson of fine awareness – and of a sort of courage. James was a 'tragic poet', I think it is right to say, in Nietzsche's sense of the term, which has nothing to do with pessimism. James's superior characters acknowledge Nietzsche's formula for superiority : *'amor fati'*. Each comes to love his (or commonly *her*) fate. They affirm life and some of them are in one way or another sacrificed. I have in mind a passage from Nietzsche's *The Birth of Tragedy*, which is in turn a repetition of words in *Twilight of the Idols*.

Affirmation of life even in its strangest and sternest problems : the will to live rejoicing in its own inexhaustibility through the sacrific of its highest types – *that* is what I call Dionysian, that is what I recognized as the bridge to the psychology of the tragic poet.[25]

An interesting feature of James's fiction is the recurrence of bravely flawed women: indeed, except in the characterization of Milly Theale in *The Wings of the Dove,* whose goodness is bound up with her knowledge of her approaching death, he displayed no zest for purity. In James it is as if some taint or error is indispensable for his, and consequently for our, admiration. But of course there is no juvenile fascination with guilt and no softening of its effects.

Some of his female characters whom we respect, such as the young Maisie Farange in *What Maisie Knew* and the mature Mme de Vionnet in *The Ambassadors,* are culpably enmeshed in some sort of corruption. Maisie at the end of her novel is no innocent but a calculating girl and Marie de Vionnet is throughout *The Ambassadors* rather sadly vulnerable (though the fact is for long concealed). But of more immediate interest are those pairs of ladies so composed by James that one member of each pair triumphs over the other, yet does so in the midst of her own suffering. In these pairings James's evident purpose was not to contrast good and evil but to dramatize different responses to tragic destinies. The woman who most wins our esteem – or was intended by James to do so – is the woman with the more complete grasp of her inescapable position. She grows resolute and, in the special Jamesian sense, intelligent.

It is wrong for instance when considering *The Portrait of A Lady,* to think simply in terms of the 'good' Isabel Archer as against the 'bad' Madame Merle. To be sure, Isabel is not blameworthy in any ordinary sense and her nemesis (a life allied to a loathsome husband and a sad, sequestered stepdaughter) is classically 'unfair'. It is a proper nemesis because it is the result of an offence not against decency but against the nature of things. In this fundamental way James is a tragic writer: he arranges consequences which have little to do with the preferences of popular Christianity or of humanitarianism.

Isabel Archer is mistaken, not in assuming that she can chart her own course but in believing that she can determine the quality of her destination. She wishes to do something free and noble with her life, something more original and elevated than, for example, entering into a conventionally good marriage with a man such as Lord Warburton or Caspar Goodwood. No doubt there is, as critics have commonly suggested, some sexual wariness in Isabel's rejection of these two virile suitors, but the wariness is bound up with a general distaste for being the mere recipient of her fate. She feels that she must not simply accept things but rather go after them for herself. (Diana, the divine archer, was a huntress as well as the guardian of chastity.) A marriage to either Goodwood or Warburton would be expected and unheroic. Such a choice would be less a choice than an acquiescence and would, in any event, be spiritually commonplace. Consequently Isabel comes to take the 'grand' and perverse step of fettering herself to an unregarded man, Gilbert Osmond, against whom she has been properly warned. But Osmond is essentially low (for all his finesse), malevolent, a despoiler, and he withers up the lives of Isabel herself, Madame Merle and his daughter, Pansy.

Isabel finally returns to Italy and to her husband partly of course to befriend Pansy shut away in her convent, but also, it seems fair to deduce, because she feels she must accept the fruits of her own choice. With only a modicum of subtle encouragement (from Madame Merle) Isabel once walked into a trap: to walk away now would be to deny her own self-responsibility and therefore, paradoxically, her freedom. Osmond never inveigled her into marrying him, never even deceived her about his nature but was in fact Mephistophelianly candid. Thus Isabel, as one of the 'highest types', in Nietzsche's phrase, is willingly sacrificed rather than descend to the level of those, the great majority, who wriggle away. She passes from a condition of youthful, innocent pride at the beginning of her story to a condition of sublime, disillusioned self-respect at its conclusion. I am not sure if this is a Christian progress but it is certainly age-old, Attic, reminiscent of Sophocles' *Antigone*.

James regularly and with complete credibility gives to people the fate they have earned. This is not a matter of his being unsentimental (which is common enough) but of his preferring the stance of willing endurance. A contented Isabel Archer would not, one feels, impress him. Her motives are good enough, if presumptuous, but they lead naturally and in one sense satisfactorily to a sort of imprisonment. Isabel could stay out of the prison only at the cost of confirming herself as exactly the commonplace sort of person she has chosen not to be. In this sense going back to Osmond at the end is actually the intelligent thing for Isabel to do, and *therefore* the moral thing. Appreciating this is not easy because it is usual to distinguish between intelligence and morality while James, in the final analysis, never does so.

This is why in *The Portrait of A Lady* Madame Merle is inferior to Isabel Archer. She is not precisely wicked (as Isabel recognizes) and of course she is extraordinarily clever, but her stratagems produce the wrong results, as stratagems normally do in James's fiction. She, who was for some seven years Osmond's mistress and is the mother of Pansy (though Pansy is and remains unaware of the relationship), now schemes to marry Isabel to Osmond chiefly so that Pansy might profit from the alliance in terms of both money and affection. In the event Madame Merle loses everything: the friendship of Isabel, the prospect of Pansy's coming to like her and the dubious benefit of her connection with Osmond. But she is pitiable, not tragic, just because she has failed to rise to that plane of co-operation with her fate which is the dwelling of all James's superior characters. They, unlike Madame Merle, observe, understand and discriminatingly act, but they do not manipulate.

This is the distinction between other pairs of Jamesian women. It is not a distinction which necessarily produces in us hostility to the manipulator, but it leads logically to her defeat. There are readers of *The Wings of the Dove* who prefer Kate Croy to Milly Theale and readers of the *The Golden Bowl* who exalt Charlotte Stant above Maggie Verver. These partialities are perfectly understandable because Kate and Charlotte are both 'underprivileged' and have a kind of fighting magnificence. But James himself (who nevertheless spoke very well of these 'inferior' ladies in his prefaces) remained true to his tragic consciousness.

There is little doubt that in *The Wings of the Dove* Kate Croy does outstrip Milly Theale in terms of sheer interest, though Milly is a bright figure as well as a figure of beneficence and muted pathos. Each is a heroine in her way; certainly it is not a matter of heroine and pseudo-heroine. Milly is good and doomed, while Kate, having struggled for riches as well as love, gets both only in alloyed form. As in *The Portrait of a Lady* (and as so often in James) the plot hinges on a trick which is crass neither in conception nor in execution. Kate Croy, who is unable to marry her lover, Merton Densher, through lack of money, schemes to cause the dying Milly Theale to leave a fortune to Densher. Nothing is dissembled except Densher's reciprocal love for Kate and anyway – so Kate's casuistical argument goes – it will be an act of fulfilment for Milly to do such a generous deed. In the event Milly's death is hastened when she learns the truth (from an unsuccessful suitor,

Lord Mark) and the money nevertheless inherited by Densher will assuredly poison his marriage. 'We shall never be again as we were!' says Kate to her downcast lover in the final sentence of the novel.

The Jamesian point (which has parallels in many of his other novels and stories) is that Kate, for all her brilliance, her daring vitality of body and mind, has sought to push things in the direction she wishes them to go and must suffer for it. Here, as elsewhere in James, there is exploitation by one without money or privileges, and this is James's special, modern version of classical hubris. Certain people of high intrinsic worth feel compelled to reach out for what they want, for what perhaps they deserve, but the act of reaching out is also a deceitful act and entails a nemesis. There is nothing to be done about it : life had for James that sharp, exciting and in some way satisfying bitterness.

In James's final novel, *The Golden Bowl,* one of the two chief women characters, Maggie Verver, triumphs over the other, Charlotte Stant, by an act of self-sacrifice. Maggie marries the Italian prince, Amerigo, thus bringing her father's American riches to the restoration of the declining fortune of an ancient Italian family. Adam Verver, Maggie's immensely rich father, marries Charlotte Stant, Maggie's brilliant but penniless friend from schooldays. But Charlotte has been, and after the marriage continues to be, Prince Amerigo's mistress. A further and critical complication is that Adam and Maggie Verver are intensely attached to each other. It is Maggie who fortifies both marriages by ensuring, with a kind of delicate toughness, that her father and his wife quit the London scene for America. In this way, by bringing about a barely tolerable severance from Adam Verver, Maggie halts the corruption which is eating away at the lives of all four characters. At the same time Maggie's stature rises and she wins the wholehearted love of her husband as she ceases to be emotionally protected by her father. The point is that once again the two chief women are both impressive persons. Charlotte Stant is so brilliant as to gain the allegiance of many readers (and moreover she, like Kate Croy, is poor to begin with), but the palm is awarded to Maggie, the woman who makes the hard choice, having learned that in order to win it is necessary also to lose.

In these last few pages we have been concerned with only a tiny selection of characters from the vast range of James's productions. Nevertheless, it is clear enough (and it would be clearer still if we chose to track the matter through ea⁻ˡy, middle and late novels of James) that he was especially interested in the tragical-heroic possibilities of the woman's position in his milieu. He did not, of course, identify himself with his remarkable female figures : they are studies of character (that is, of dispositions and choices) in those sections of society where the circumstances and consequences of a choice are least mitigated or confused by external factors such as public work or insignificant daily activities. Thus the tragedy – as so many of James's dramas may properly be called – is pure, complete and exclusive. Given this leisured domestic sphere, the woman, either as heiress or as poor adventurer, was a ready vehicle for the sort of discriminations of value that James wished to make. But clearly there is more to it than that. James was interested in what people suffer rather than in what they assertively do : the doings in his novels, though they are dramatically striking, serve as revelations of awareness. The superior person acquires and acts upon a perfect understanding of the situation. In this respect also the woman's social position, her dependence or 'relative being' (even when she is rich) causes her so often to be a suitable bearer of James's insights. Then, James (like Richardson, though more exquisitely) was fascinated by traps and snares. Many of his chief characters seem to wander for a while in a roomy mansion, then a door slams behind them. That for James was the essential condition of life and he loved to show how people exercise not so much their freedom as their sense of freedom. In James's period women of the class he depicted could so completely carry his theme.

But in that period an alternative point of view already flourished. 'Alienation' in Marx's sense had not entered the vocabulary but many writers were sure that the nature of women was warped, not fulfilled, by their circumstances. Some writers contemporary with James in part copied and in part sought to produce new women freed from cultural constraints. It is to these writers we should now turn.

5 New Women

In 1854 or 1855 Turgenev conceived an idea which by the end of the decade had blossomed into the novel, *On the Eve*. This preliminary notion was the character of Elena Nikolayevna, the heroine who, as he later wrote, 'was then still a new type'. It seems that Turgenev had noticed in Russia an interesting and as yet rare phenomenon: the emergence of women in search of a destiny that should transcend, though not necessarily replace, the domestic round.

Such a woman was dissatisfied with ordinary society and was reluctant to become or to remain a mere wife, but she did not hanker after a position in the market-place. The dissatisfaction was neither capricious nor, at that period, remotely fashionable. It was connected with a belief that man-made values and explanations were faltering. Where was the sense in things and why did people tolerate so many pointless lies? The woman was forced into becoming some sort of philosopher, crusader or pioneer and looked for a man who would share her quest or, preferably, act as a guide. Sometimes it seemed necessary, though unpromising, to bully a complacent man into an awareness of his own and almost everyone else's futility. This is a preliminary sketch of the type to whom the term, 'new woman' (variously used in the nineteenth century) is here confined.

Portraits of such women in modern literature sometimes amount to stories of frustration but commonly they do not. Certainly Turgenev's Elena, who has a good claim to be the first of her fictional breed, does what she wants, though this is not to say that she is in an ordinary sense happy. She is the odd, attractive daughter of a retired lieutenant of the guards who cannot make her out or cope with her: she is, he says, 'a sort of enraptured republican girl'.[1] Elena is intelligent, alert, questioning rather than opinionated, but nevertheless censorious about moral faults. She befriends a beggar-girl, weeps over hurt animals, cannot bear the callousness she detects around her. In outline her story is that she gives no encouragement to two rather dilettante suitors, a sculptor and a philosopher, but instead marries a Bulgarian insurgent and leaves Russia with him to take part somehow in his country's struggle against the Turks. Elena's husband, Insarov (a taciturn, politically committed man of action), dies in Venice as the couple are *en route* for Bulgaria, and Elena carries on alone in the hope of joining a nursing organization and so helping Insarov's native land in the coming war.

It is clear that so early as the 1850s Elena must indeed have represented a new type. She is a prophetic study of a sort of woman (far from the only sort) who is now attracted to liberation movements but is still rarely copied in serious literature. Someone might suggest that historical circumstances straightforwardly force into being the Elenas of this world: a country is corrupt or tyrannized, so women fight back alongside the men. However, it is notable that Turgenev presents us with a girl who is positively looking for a cause. There is nothing historically vital to be done in Russia and so Elena goes elsewhere. She wants love but cannot dissociate love from a larger social purpose. This is not, obviously, a definable and specific goal, still less a personal ambition, but is felt in the beginning purely as an emptiness wanting to be filled.

In nineteenth- and twentieth-century imaginative writing there are few thorough parallels to Elena, since most fictional new women confine their adventures to personal relationships conducted in comparatively humdrum surroundings. They are drawing-room pioneers, but they possess Elena's sense that meaning encompasses the drawing-room. Above all, they feel a need to make their distinctive patterns of life if necessary amongst people whose patterns are familiarly sterile.

The first major writer for whom such characters were of more than sporadic or subordinate interest was Ibsen: from his plays especially (though not of course exclusively) images of unfettered women spread across Europe and to America. Our understanding to-day, after a century of Ibsen commentary and scholarship (in terms not only of literary criticism but of psycho-analysis, political theory and studies in mythology as well), is that such images were simplified and exalted versions of Ibsen's heroines whose roles are often complex. But in the main these women are what nineteenth-century audiences already took them to be – agents of demystification and of a particular kind of self-fulfilment. To say this is not

/er of the forces with which the women contend,
at Ibsen gave to women rather than to men the
erence, rational meaning.

o take the earliest play to have an appreciable
eme – Solveig, the simple maiden, waits some
hero to return from his wanderings during which
alize his identity. After a clumsy and sometimes
Peer Gynt passes his life in various occupations
oroad, always supposing that in order to 'be him-
to pursue his desire of the moment. He practices
calls 'Gyntianism' but what the Troll King tells
, meaning adaptation to whatever function seems
nally profitable. In the end he is saved from the
Button Moulder's casting-ladle by Solveig who smilingly answers
his riddle : his self, she tells him, lies in her faith, hope and love.
Peer Gynt's personality has hitherto had no core, so Solveig clearly
means that she will be able to create his true personality *ab initio,*
even though he is now getting on in years. It is not that he possesses a seed of selfhood which her love may cause to ripen or
flower, but that he has so far been quite null, an imitation man.
But for this miracle to take place Peer Gynt must give himself un-
reservedly to her. This will not entail submission to Solveig, because
her whole purpose is to bring Peer Gynt to life as a unique individual.

This idea in varying forms is present in many of Ibsen's plays :
what he preached (though the preaching took the form of a quest,
not a dogma) was the realization of selfhood through love. It
seems, however, that for love to produce its effects both parties
must be truthful. The woman may not serve the man by taking
him, as it were, on roundabout and shadowed paths but by cutting
a straight, clear path through the forest. At times it is almost as if
Ibsen thought in terms of 'love-and-truth', a composite quality,
rather than of two qualities that should support each other.

So, *A Doll's House,* which remains after exactly a hundred years
the play of women's liberation, is nevertheless (as Ibsen himself
insisted) not a recommendation that unsatisfied wives should for-
sake their families. It is a study of one particular though widely
representative family, the Helmers, in which both husband and wife
have always supposed their union to be best cemented by role-
playing and pretence. Indeed it was Torvald Helmer who at the
outset of their marriage fostered this manner of life, but Nora,

his wife, has for long played up to him. What is significant, of course, is that it is Nora who in the exhilarating final scene rises to heights of calm maturity, leaving her home for no destination, with no parent, friend, lover or institution to turn to. Up to that point she and Helmer have mutually sustained their make-believe life together : in other words they have settled for a form of security which depends upon a stingily managed 'output' of love and truth. It should be added that Ibsen was no hedonist and did not imagine, as audiences seem often to imagine, that Nora must be happier in the future : she is a heroine because she might end up destitute or mad. In some of Ibsen's later plays the qualities he advocated lead to death, regarded as a proper consummation.

But in Ibsen it is almost always a woman who first sees the light, or has never been in the dark. Throughout most of the plot of *Ghosts* the two leading women are both in their different ways un- satisfactory, in the sense of failing to guide the hero, Oswald, to an acceptance of his fate. Since Oswald is suffering from hereditary syphillis, his only route is towards degeneration and death, but his mother, Mrs Alving, is a 'loving mother'; that is she tries to console her son and to keep distressing facts from him – partly, however, because she herself is scarcely innocent. Regina Engstrand, on the other hand, whom Oswald thinks of marrying, turns out to be the 'pagan' sort of woman whom Ibsen has often been presumed to admire. In fact Regina is callous as well as candid, so that when she learns about Oswald's sickness she rejects him on the spot and within seconds decides to take up with Pastor Manders for whom she feels no affection. Finally Mrs Alving becomes honest with Oswald and with herself, and both of them await the inevitable horror, not in fear or sadness but with a kind of joy. Mrs Alving, we might say, learns to practise love-and-truth.

The earliest of Ibsen's complete and completely characteristic heroines (Solveig is too slight a figure to count) is Lona Hessel in *Pillars of Society* (1877). She is the woman – not young but well into middle age – who talks of letting 'some fresh air' into society, specifically the society of a Norwegian coastal town where her relative by marriage, Karsten Bernick, is a rich shipbuilder. Lona is one of Ibsen's agents of transformation (normally women) in that through her influence Bernick makes a public recantation of his and other citizens' devotion to financial profit. Ibsen's explicit point is that the true pillars of any society are not important members but, as Lona stirringly puts it, 'the spirit of truth and the spirit of freedom'. It is worth noting that in the final exchanges of the play Bernick is still under what turns out to be a false impression: that 'true loyal women' are the pillars of society. Since this is an evasive, 'chauvinistic' sentiment, Lona has to put him right by insisting that the matter has nothing to do with one sex rather than the other.

No doubt this is what Ibsen believed, but anyone must carry away from the plays the impression that women (a select few) are better qualified than men to let in fresh air – whether this process leads to renewed vigour or to a species of triumphant disaster. On one level this potentiality of women is presumably a result of their position on the sidelines: they are not, or were not then, caught up in the pursuit of power, not required to be 'honourable' in business or the professions, not dynamic contributors to ethical codes. On another level it seems to me connected with Ibsen's Promethean nature. He associated sex not with warmth and security but with danger and victory, the bare mountain rather than the hearth. In Ibsen's plays there is on the one hand the thrusting, Faustian nature of the man (though he is usually a small-town bourgeois) while on the other hand there is a woman who can break down whatever deceitful and unloving relationships he might have built up. He is not supposed to relinquish ambition but to find the right path forwards. If he is a world-beater all well and good, the point being that he must choose his own rules as well as his own game. And choosing the rules does not mean cheating (that is, lying) for on the contrary, it is the existing rules that are always in some degree false. Sometimes – so Ibsen's implication runs – one's right path leads right away from the ordinary world of confused and middling souls: in practice this means death with a woman at one's side.

It is the *raison d'être* of Ibsen's 'superior' women to know all this, whereas the man, who has fallen in with the present, rotten order of things, does not. Perhaps he knew it once and has forgotten. At all events an Ibsen heroine might save the man or in effect kill him. It makes no difference: she is still in the right. She might also kill herself – as Rebecca West does in *Rosmersholm*.

Rebecca West once seemed set fair to help John Rosmer, an ex-clergyman, in his lately-discovered vocation of delivering a secular message of benevolence and co-operation to mankind, but in the end their way is blocked and so the couple die together. Rebecca, having brought about the suicide of Beata, Rosmer's wife (since Beata was physically and intellectually sterile) now finds her spirit ennobled and 'infected', as she calls it, by vaguely Christian ideas of guilt and charity. At the same time Rosmer loses his evangelistic ardour and has nothing left to say. Consequently he announces his decision to do away with himself and this is presumably a deliberate test of Rebecca. She rises to the challenge by deciding to join Rosmer, so together they jump into the mill-race beside the house, as Beata did a year or so earlier. Rebecca is a thorough-going though 'immoral' heroine. The ennobling and infecting elements of Christianity go together in Ibsen's evident opinion, and it is these by which Rebecca and Rosmer are defeated. But their defeat is also a victory, an anti-Christian martyrdom.

Rebecca West is an enlightened woman who feels herself being drawn back into the dark and commits suicide before it is too late. It is not, surely, that Ibsen wished to modify the values of enlightenment but that he, unlike glib progressivists, was aware of its spiritual hazards and of its need for self-sacrifice. In his plays generally women try, often with some success, to free themselves from age-old mysteries. For instance, Ellida Wangel, the heroine of *The Lady from the Sea,* has always been lured and frightened by the unknown and shapeless, by everything the sea represents in this play. She finally elects to stay with her husband rather than run off with a fascinating seafaring stranger, just because Wangel gives her the choice. Her fears and bewitchment vanish when the great choice of her life is put into her hands. There is perhaps an implication that women are drawn to mystery and muddle because of their lack of self-responsibility. More widely, it may be that the entire sphere of magic and irrationality is attached to the 'feminine principle' as a means of conferring a form of potency on those who are socially powerless. If this was Ibsen's belief, it is similar to the attitude we earlier noted in Hawthorne (Chapter 3).

In harmony with such a pattern of thought Ibsen's women at their most destructive are yet not *femmes fatales.* A siren character obviously aims to destroy the masculine spirit, just as the original sirens would have killed Odysseus out of pure hatred for any kind of striving and voyaging. But, it seems, when an Ibsen heroine causes a man's death, or her own, it is because the alternative is what we are nowadays apt to call an 'inauthentic' life. Solness in *The Master Builder* has for years confined himself to putting up dull houses for the residents of his town and has repressed his knowledge that he once aspired to make magnificent, soaring edifices. But a twelve-year-old girl, Hilda Wangel, once saw him in a moment of triumph and now as a lovely young woman (the very figure of the younger generation which Solness fears) she seeks him out and encourages him not merely to erect a tall spire but to climb, despite his vertigo, to the top of it. Solness falls to his death and Hilda in ecstasy exclaims, 'My – my Master Builder!'

The 'Freudian' connotations are plain (and of course Freud himself wrote most interestingly on Ibsen) but it is clear also that Hilda is supposed to have recalled a man to his right, heroic destiny. Hilda does not set out to kill Solness but to make him into the kind of Viking-figure she has always, childishly, dreamed about. Hilda can be understood as nothing more than an irresponsible young woman (*necessarily* irresponsible because she is a woman) and this is how in *The Second Sex* Simone de Beauvoir sees her.[2] She illustrates the enforced immaturity of women and their need for vicarious satisfactions, in this instance the satisfaction of someone else's heroic death. But for Ibsen she was also presumably a rescuer of a defeated soul. It is not possible to detect much sympathy for Solness in the play (even though he may in part represent the author) but rather a feeling that Hilda, though brash and adolescent, is right. That is why the play ends with Hilda's jubilant words: Solness, the older generation, has handed on to the next generation the affirmative spirit which is, tragically, demanded.

Ibsen's last plays were less realistic than their predecessors, but this cannot be said to have altered the basic theme with which we are concerned. Indeed Irene and Rubek in *When We Dead Awaken* (1899) are the most perfect exemplars of it. Rubek is a great sculptor in decline. Years before, Irene modelled for him and the statue was called 'The Day of Resurrection'. But Irene put all her vitality into the modelling and ever since she has been a living corpse. Meanwhile Rubek has married, made money, and lived without vigour. Irene, accompanied by a nun (in other words the Church, the spirit of 'goodness'), arrives at the resort where the Rubeks are staying and there, and later at a mountain sanatorium, she brings Rubek to a realization of the tragic values he has relinquished. In the last act Rubek leaves his wife, Irene leaves her nun, and the pair climb to a mountain-top where they are buried by an avalanche. This is an elementary account of a spare, parabolic play; nevertheless it brings out, correctly I believe, Ibsen's feeling that the right woman saves a man's soul and her own at whatever cost.[3]

Ibsen's attitude towards women was distinctive and was not so much copied as simplified or softened by other writers who supposed themselves to be in sympathy with it. (Sometimes, though rarely in the period of his greatest influence, 1880 to 1900, other *avant-garde* writers quite detested Ibsen's women so that, for instance, Stringberg's *The Wife of Herr Bengt* and his *Miss Julie* are deliberately and virulently anti-Ibsen plays.) In the main, however, there was a general movement along roughly the same lines in the last decades of the century. No doubt this was in part a reflection of what is now a much-documented movement in society, but it was more than that. The writers we are concerned with were ahead of their times, looking forward, cultivating a crop of ideas rather than distributing a crop already grown. And each of course used the general movement for his own peculiar purposes, yet each one singly and all of them collectively had an effect upon the next generation – not, it goes without saying, an effect any one of these writers would have welcomed as precisely matching his hopes.

Our inescapable impression now, a hundred years later, is that men writers felt themselves to be in a cul-de-sac of values and looked to women for a way out. When I say 'looked to women' I do not mean that they literally and conscientiously did anything of the sort, but rather that they used *images* of women as a means of moving onwards. Ibsen's women (Nora as well as Rebecca West, Mrs Alving as well as the quasi-mythical Irene) are not 'real'; still less, so we have often been told, are the women of Shaw – whose *The Quintessence of Ibsenism* is surely a distortion of Ibsen for his own purposes. The new woman of real life, by the end of the century much in evidence, and the new woman of literature were fairly different creatures, partly for the age-old reason that the invented characters were designed to further their authors' particular aims. Nevertheless authors emphasized at least one social truth : that women in Western society were merely accomplices in the value-system which was now visibly breaking up. It had never been *their* system, but one that they acceded to or exploited. From the writer's point of view it was not, obviously, that he could invent a woman character of messianic proportions, but that he could produce a female critic, or perhaps a gallery of critics. Such women were well placed to diagnose the condition of society, sourly or with joyful confidence according to the disposition of their creator. As a rule it was not their function to formulate new goals, but – at their most radiant – to release new energies.

So far as Shaw was concerned women were intrinsically less given to intellectual falsehood than men. They told social lies naturally, but they could spot a lying idea a mile away. In fact they knew that ideas should be distrusted, ignored or used for personal advantage. Shaw's women characters commonly have a capacity to tell when an idea is an accurate summary of social facts and therefore, in that sense, true. Further, they realize that words themselves, the materials of ideas, are generally tools and weapons rather than honest coins. Consequently there is a marked tendency for women in Shaw's plays to know where their interest lies, while many of his men are ineffectual creatures who either fail or else blunder into comically qualified success. Of course the plays also include unillusioned, manipulative men (Napoleon in *The Man of Destiny*, General Burgoyne in *The Devil's Disciple*, Sir Andrew Undershaft in *Major Barbara*, the Earl of Warwick in *Saint Joan*, King Magnus in *The Apple Cart*) but such men aid the Life Force, when they do so at all, chiefly by moderating the errors of others. The women, on the other hand, even the decidedly mediocre, are active agents of the Life Force. Two of Shaw's best characters, Caesar and Joan of Arc, illustrate these distinctions by rising above them.

In a sense Caesar is the Shavian manipulator raised to a higher power, but this power includes a visionary quality. In addition, Caesar is a well-drawn character, since the formula to which he is built is properly confused by minor contradictions. He is a superman, but wry, fallible, and even at times a little absurd. Thus the opening remarks of *Caesar and Cleopatra* are meant to be both accurate and pompous. Caesar's address to a Sphinx contains a correct reading of its riddle. 'I am he,' Caesar grandly proclaims, 'of whose genius you are the symbol: part brute, part woman, and part god – nothing of man in me at all.' These words, which indicate the solemn meaning of the entire play, are followed by a deflation of Caesar when Cleopatra (a giggling, non-moral adolescent) surprises him in this silly act of talking to a statue, calls him a 'funny old gentleman', and later tells him that it is the wrong Sphinx.

It is clear from the Preface to the play, and would be absolutely clear without it, that Shaw wished to controvert the values of Shakespeare's *Antony and Cleopatra* by arguing that romantic love belongs to the childhood of the human race and has no justification or purpose other than reproduction, ideally the reproduction of higher types of men and women. Caesar himself is at least a forerunner of such types, one who exploits nature even as he exploits (not without mishaps) the follies of ordinary people. He is able to do this because he is 'part brute, part woman, and part god'. In other words he belongs to nature like a brute and he cooperates with nature like a woman, but he transcends these functions by his quasi-divine comprehension and acceptance of them. What he does not do is project his own vanities and petty designs upon the world, like a commonplace man.

Caesar is getting on in years, but Joan of Arc is a teenager with the result that her misjudgements are far graver than his, but she too is 'godlike' immediately before her martyrdom and then after death in the Epilogue to *Saint Joan*. She, like Caesar, is not a creature of her sex. She is instead a conscientious servant of history in the sense of one who knows where the forces of the age are tending and that her vocation (the calling which her voices disclose to her) is to aid these forces. But ultimately she knows also that the making of independent nations out of the components of the Holy Roman Empire is merely a link in the chain of history, the next thing to do. More aptly perhaps, history resembles a tower to which each generation adds a portion: higher up (Joan hopes or believes) there will be a suitable position for disinterested souls.

The success of *Saint Joan* over the years may be partly due to the fact that it is at once romantic and anti-romantic. It is romantic in the sense of Promethean and it is anti-romantic in the sense of knocking down beliefs about womanhood, sexual love, chivalry, puritanism, the vileness of the Inquisition and the inherited wisdom of the Church. Joan herself embodies this important characteristic of the play : she is an attractive heroine with next to no interest in sex; she arouses chivalrousness yet makes fun of it; she excites emotions while espousing reason and common sense; she heralds the coming of romantic individualism but yearns for a community of like-minded saints. Mainly, though, she is a woman who is not womanish but has the attributes of a complete (though unworldly) human being. Adapting the peculiar sense in which Caesar claims to have 'nothing of man' in him, we may say that she has nothing of woman in her.

Although Joan and Caesar are thoroughly different characters, each represents the same ideal. Ellie Dunn in *Heartbreak House* shows signs of developing into a member of the same small category and so perhaps does Barbara Undershaft in the final scene of *Major Barbara*. Vivie Warren *of Mrs Warren's Profession* has some of the appropriate qualities – resolute practical sense and a capacity to surpass her sex – but, since she is an early figure and Shaw had not yet realized his ideal, she offers only a hint of the conclusive attribute of down-to-earth spirituality. Lady Cicely Wayneflete in *Captain Brassbound's Conversion* is likewise an impressive but incomplete version of this higher type of individual.

These are prominent examples of the true Shavian woman. They are also 'new women', though Shaw's strategy, and possibly his genuine belief, was to suggest that they are not new at all. Other women in the plays are 'Shavian' in a different sense altogether. Such characters as Candida, Ann Whitefield and Eliza Doolittle are intended to be admirable for their vitality and sureness of instinct, but not for additional, finer traits. Indeed it is their vitality and instinctual confidence which make them seem new, though they are meant to express traditional and common patterns of thought, to express what the humblest of their sex have always known.

Interestingly, Joan of Arc and her lesser sisters who combine to form the small class of Shaw's exalted women are not, with the exception of Lady Cicely, consistently sure of themselves, and the paragon of them all is placed in the Middle Ages. In fact Shaw, like other, greater innovators (consider Marx or Nietzsche) believed that he was not so much dealing with novelties as disclosing the historical condition of mankind. To Shaw this condition consisted of a handful of superior persons and multitudes of the spiritually unawakened. His ideal for both sexes was a version of that age-old ideal which Aldous Huxley was later to isolate and term 'non-attachment'.[4] Nevertheless, few writers before Shaw, and scarcely any after him, have allowed women this particular virtue. Of course his faith, without which he would surely have been a hopeless pessimist, was that the proportion of non-attached persons would increase over the centuries, if we willed them into existence. Such people he saw as having a minimum of secondary sex-characteristics. So it is that in the fifth part of *Back to Methuselah*, 'As Far as Thought Can Reach', the He-Ancient and the She-Ancient are barely distinguishable; and Lilith, who is beyond sex in every sense, looks forward in her final soliloquy to a time when not only men and women but also matter and spirit shall be identical. Shaw's admired characters are intended to be precursors of that time, minimally conditioned by physiology or cultural patterns.

Most of Shaw's women characters are strong-minded, but so are many of his men. In this respect he was unusual in the period of his greatest influence (roughly from the late nineties to the early twenties) since this was notoriously the phase of the sensitive or subjugated hero. The common theme in such varied stories as those of Edwin Reardon, Hanno Buddenbrook, Ernest Pontifex, Edwin Clayhanger, Paul Morel, Philip Carey, Stephen Dedalus and Joseph K. is the oppression of sensibility by coarseness. For a good part of his story at least, each hero is the victim of crudely vigorous personalities and crude (though not necessarily poor) circumstances. We are encouraged to feel that promising males of this generation were exceptionally liable to be mistreated by fathers, employers, unfeeling associates and vulgar women.

But when we think at random of fictional heroines of the period the picture is different. The woman is typically a bright star to begin with, grasping her world not as a burden but as a challenge, though she may undergo great trials and end (as Hardy's Sue Bridehead ends) with her lustre dimmed. Generally, though, the heroine comes through triumphant, so that her adventures have not so much awakened her to life as confirmed her early sense of life's possibilities. Naturally this optimistic attitude towards women varied from the facile to the heavily qualified, according to each author's disposition. In Chekov's *The Three Sisters* Masha, Irina and Olga are survivors who exchange their joyous illusions for hopeful awareness. In Wells's *Ann Veronica* the heroine simply blooms as all her trobles melt away. In Arnold Bennett's *Clayhanger* and the related novels Hilda Lessways is steeled and aged by her troubles but not defeated.

But what, first of all, of the gloomy treatment of new womanhood? Robert Gittings in the first of his biographical works on Hardy, *Young Thomas Hardy,* draws an interesting and it would seem authoritative distinction between the 'New Woman', so called, of the 1890s and 'The Girl of the Period' of the 1860s.[5] He points out that the former was apt to be a socialist, a supporter of the suffragette movement and member of some sort of women's society. She was emphatically a political person. However, thirty years earlier a number of relatively isolated women of strong intellectual tendencies were influenced by Auguste Comte and John

Stuart Mill. They were at once sceptical and ardent, and each saw herself as an individual who happened to be a woman. Men were not necessarily enemies or even rivals, but companions, colleagues, lovers or husbands, on an intellectually equal footing. Robert Gittings is sure that Hardy's Sue Bridehead in *Jude the Obscure* is such a 'Girl of the Period' transposed into the nineties. But she is a new woman in our sense of the term.

Indeed Sue is probably the best portrait of the type in the range of late nineteenth-century fiction. I use the word 'type' advisedly, since Hardy himself used it. In a letter of 1895 to Edmund Gosse he wrote that 'Sue is a type of woman who has always had an attraction for me, but the difficulty of drawing the type has kept me from attempting it till now'.[6] The implication here is that Hardy had observed more than one woman of roughly Sue's cast of mind. He may well have known intimately a particular girl, for the first thing to be said of Sue is that she is, in all her awkwardness and diversity, more like a living human being than all but a handful in literature. From one point of view she is certainly a type, a member of a Victorian category (with descendants living to-day): from another point of view she is utterly herself.

Sue cannot have been dreamed up to further an 'argument' of her author. Rather, she must have originated in an actual woman whose personality haunted Hardy. Once it was thought that Hardy's cousin, Tryphena Sparks, may have been the girl in question, but scholars now rule out this possibility.[7] At all events Sue Bridehead is plainly a creature of flesh and blood forced into Hardy's pessimistic scheme. But the forcing process is convincingly managed, partly because it seems to have the retrospective inevitably of real life.

We are told that Sue Bridehead started out magnificently: at one time, before her story begins, 'her intellect scintillated like a star',[8] causing her to view with cheerful indifference the Creator whose blind, primordial will never contemplated the evolution of such sensitive human creatures as have now inherited the earth. When we first meet Sue she is a slight, nervous, elegant figure, a composite personality in whom 'male' and 'female' traits are nicely blended. At one point she remarks to Jude Fawley that she has 'mixed with them [men] – one or two of them particularly – almost as one of their own sex'.[9] A little later Jude tells her in dismay that her mind its 'quite Voltairean' and he is pained by her 'epicene tenderness'.[10] Subsequently Sue's husband Phillotson, is also plunged into gloom by her capacity for sexless, 'Shelleyan' affection, such as she feels for her cousin, Jude.[11] What happens of course is that Sue marries the school-master, Phillotson, who is physically distasteful to her, runs off with Jude to whom she bears children, and then, after the children have been killed (by the eldest of their number who also hangs himself) returns to Phillotson intent on being a loyal, sacrificial wife.

Sue begins as a bright pagan, an enthusiast for classical antiquity, and ends as a Christian with the awful conviction that guilt, remorse and pain rule human life. In one particular this progress is reminiscent of Ibsen's Rebecca West since both she and Sue are finally women who have 'veered round to darkness' – a phrase which Hardy gives to the despairing Jude Fawley.[12]

But Rebecca West kills herself in defiance of Christianity, or rather to escape from it, while Sue throws herself into the role of penitent. Hardy's attitude was more ambivalent than Ibsen's, I think. He admired his heroine, even as he must have admired her real-life original, but was then (in the nineties) determined that she should be brought down. Her hopes *must* be dashed, her intellect destroyed because Hardy had become convinced that her precise combination of intellect and sensitivity could not, in the present or the foreseeable future, survive. So it comes about that this most promising of literary new women is turned into a melancholy wreck.

In this way Hardy seized hold of some feminine characteristics he had observed, probably during his youthful period in London, and worked them after years of patient thought and self-development into his own mature and bitter vision. On the other hand the early H. G. Wells was enormously, and according to his own later convictions mistakenly, optimistic.[13] As a result his pre-eminent liberated heroine, Ann Veronica Stanley, is a study in what must now be seen as too easy triumph over the petty, the ignoble and the vicious.

Wells remarks in his *Experiment in Autobiography* (1934) that Ann Veronica 'came as near to being a living creature as any one in my earlier love stories. This was so because in some particulars she was drawn from life'.[14] Curiously enough, this is exactly the impression the novel fails to give unless by 'some particulars' Wells means the external facts of his heroine's life. Anne Veronica's world seems faithfully observed – the Surrey suburb, the train journeys to Waterloo, laboratory work at the Central Imperial

College, the suffragettes' conversations, the brisk and jolly slang, even at a pinch the prison cell – but what seems engagingly unreal is Ann Veronica's personality. This novel, more than some of Arnold Bennett's, supports Virginia Woolf's thesis in her essay, 'Mr Bennett and Mrs Brown', to the effect that a lifelike personality cannot be created out of external bits and pieces.

Ann Veronica is really an Edwardianly sterling girl who is caused, as it were, to break with her father, to mix with suffragettes of various degrees of crankiness and distaste for sex, to be pawed by a would-be seducer, to get locked up in prison, to enjoy a love-idyll with a married man. And these episodes have chiefly the effect of maturing her beauty, making it richer and less 'suburban'. Finally Ann Veronica is able to marry Capes, her lover, and is reconciled with her father. In those parts of the novel dealing with the heroine's studies the science of biology is used, not so much to distinguish fundamental from superficial sex-differences as to advocate a zestfully experimental way of life. But the whole is a romance in which the pangs of evolutionary growth are represented rather than its necessary tragedies.

Nevertheless this novel was far from innocuous in its day and of course it landed Wells in a good deal of trouble with readers, librarians and even fellow-writers. This happened because many readers of Wells, to whom Shaw was amusingly perverse and Ibsen an unlikely influence upon one's womenfolk, realized that this girl, Ann Veronica, was very seductive. In a way those detractors of Wells were right: the novel is enchanting propaganda for new womanhood, generous but misleading. It is also – though hostile critics in 1909 failed to notice the fact – as paternalistic as many a popular romance.

Ann Veronica is an attractive but ersatz new woman, 'got up' to fit a thesis. Arnold Bennett's Hilda Lessways as she appears in *Clayhanger, Hilda Lessways* and *These Twain* is the reverse: she seems to emerge from the society of her time without schematic contrivance or doctrinal fuss. She represents something about her generation precisely by being out of the common run, a true individual who nevertheless could exist only in reaction to the conditions of the eighties and nineties.

Nor can it be said that Hilda Lessways owes much of her verisimilitude to Bennett's minute reproduction of her surroundings, since she, unlike other well-drawn characters in the three novels, is curiously alien. Perhaps Bennett included traits of his wife,

Marguerite in the portrait. Marguerite Soulié was born in southwest France, left her village as soon as she could, worked successively as a dressmaker, lady's companion, governess, and at thirty-three fell in with Bennett.[15] What may have happened (we can only conjecture) is that Bennett tried to capture, to explore indeed, some of his wife's fascinating characteristics while placing his fictional creation in altogether different circumstances. Whatever the case, Hilda is convincing partly because the author himself and his hero, Edwin Clayhanger, fail to fathom her.

She is of a different order of creation from other notable figures in the *Clayhanger* novels: from old Darius Clayhanger, for instance, from George Cannon who bigamously married her and from Edwin himself. The difference is that these characters are known through and through: they are so completely grasped and documented that they remain, for all their impressiveness, *literary* characters. But the organic structure of Hilda's personality reaches back into darkness. At the same time, it is not that Bennett wished to make her into a 'woman of mystery', except to a dramatically fitting degree in *Clayhanger*.

Hilda is not strenuously political and she has only fitful concern over women's rights. She is merely, though extraordinarily, an honest person to whom perceptions, feelings, ideas and professed sentiments should always be in harmony. Around her she finds conspiracies to accept, to believe, to cling together beneath arbitrary banners. Edwin first arouses her interest because at a dinner-table (in the eighth chapter of *Clayhanger*) he exclaims, apropos of the Bradlaugh case, that 'You can't make yourself believe anything' and that 'There's no virtue in believing.' Edwin has no idea of the immensity of what he is saying: he doesn't know that at all times, in 'liberal' as well as in 'reactionary' periods, group-loyalties and group-myths take precedence. Most people make themselves believe something or other as a matter of course. Hilda feels that Edwin may be an interesting man and in her efforts to find out for sure she arouses in him a sense of his own singularity.

Hilda is not only unremittingly serious: she is also for the most part unhappy. She is a stranger to laughter, often scowling, pensive or bitter, and – to compound her unlikeliness as a heroine – her features (black hair and olive skin) are by common standards rather ugly. But her unhappiness is restless, far removed from melancholy, and her 'ugliness' is sensual. It is clear in *These Twain*, the story of a combative marriage, that Edwin and Hilda are bound together sexually but are often at odds in other spheres. Sex permeates their lives: it is not occasional, routine or diverting. Each grasps what Bennett at the close of *Clayhanger* calls the 'exquisite burden of life', a burden which (though Bennett is never explicit) seems to include vigorous sexuality and which neither of them is disposed to lighten by dishonesty.

As I have implied Bennett does not refer to Hilda as a 'new woman' or seek to categorize her in any way. Yet that is what she is. Her essence lies in her freedom – a freedom less of action than of thought and personality. She is an independent person who expects to fight rather than to wheedle or to bully in the manner of a wilful woman of the past. She is aggressive, of course, but not in pursuit of narrow, personal objectives. There is probably no social role she could comfortably undertake, including of course the role of prosperous wife which she assumes in *These Twain*.

Perhaps it should be made clear at this point that our own use of the phrase, 'new women', should not summon up an image but rather a sense of breaking free from images. If new womanhood was not an attempt to defy categories what of any real value could it have been? In the mid-century when Turgenev noticed his Elena-figures (a scattered few) there was no sense of a new group, militant and therefore to a degree like-minded, rising up. By the end of the century, at the time of Hilda Lessways, women were of course banding together and producing for themselves another set of imperatives. One melancholy tendency in such situations is always the same: the originating figures, whether discovered in life or constructed largely from authors' imaginings, soon give way to tedious and simplified copies. More precisely the copies fill the pages of books while actual individuals try to force their own true diversity into standard moulds. As it happens, it is unlikely that more than a trifling number of women ever tried to resemble either E. M. Forster's Margaret Schlegel or D. H. Lawrence's Ursula Brangwen. These were not in any sense popular figures, but each in her way represented a departure from the usual (male or female) expectations of women. The important point is that each is a proper character to be noticed here, yet they are downright opposites.

Forster makes plain his high regard for Margaret Schlegel who has always 'a profound vivacity, a continual and sincere response to all that she encountered in her path through life'.[16] It is she alone of his women characters in this and other novels who never makes a blameworthy mistake, never performs a selfish action and never gives way before male or female foolishness. One interesting fact is that she is the mistress of what she describes as a 'female house', a house that even in her father's day was dominated by women's conversations, plans and general dispositions. And this London house, Wickham Place, is regularly bubbling with intellectual or artistic activities of a serious (though not solemn) nature. The Schlegel sisters, Margaret and Helen, are not dilettante. Neither pursues an art-form or a branch of learning single-mindedly, but they are plainly intended to be the best sort of amateurs, interested in a fair range of cultural activities and, most importantly, never failing to relate those activities to the demands of everyday life. The only dilettante in the house is the bored, disparaged but undeniably clever brother, Tibby.

Wickham Place is a female house partly because it is dominated by two women but also because it does not accommodate what was then, in 1910, a man's professional or business ethos. More accurately, personal relationships are not sacrificed to the sphere of work or, for that matter, to intellectual ideas. This does not mean that the conversation is trivially personal or that talk about ideas is abandoned so soon as someone feels uncomfortable, but that the frame of mind of anyone present is naturally and candidly brought into the reckoning. Everything rests upon relentless candour and everything – politics, music, ideas – flows effortlessly into a proper consideration of personal needs. Conversation is apt to move readily from, say, train-times to forthright notions about the world at large. Margaret will launch into such remarks as these :

> I was going to say that the Continent, for good or ill, is interested in ideas. The Literature and Art have what one might call the kink of the unseen about them, and this persists even through decadence and affectation. There is more liberty of action in England, but for liberty of thought go to bureaucratic Prussia.[17]

The style here, it must be admitted, is Forster's own : the passage reads like one of his essays or the authorial comments he never scrupled to insert into his novels. The observation is interesting enough, probably true and certainly well expressed. So that is how Margaret can talk, and yet her principal feature is not engaging talk but practicality. She holds her family together, unites the family with the philistine but moneyed Wilcoxes and is, much more widely, held out as being a *practical* guardian of Western (or at all events European) values. This means that she has political as well as intellectual acumen. It is she who speaks sensibly about money and at the meeting of the discussion group (in Chapter 15) maintains against the rest that poor people should be given not subsidies but cash. At the same time she has no illusions about the physical conditions or the psychology of the Edwardian poor.

Forster's intention in this novel was of course to show that the supposedly practical men of Britain are monstrously impractical and to demonstrate that people such as the Schlegel girls should inherit the nation. Accordingly Margaret is married to the successful businessman, Henry Wilcox, brings him to his knees after the killing by his son, Charles, of the aspiring Leonard Bast and is finally mistress of Howards End. In effect she brainwashes Wilcox and takes over the house which has all along represented the continuity of British society. In the end, as the corn is cut, Margaret is fully in possession. A practical woman who is also an intellectual has conquered. Forster admired such a combination of lively mind and worldly ability : he deplored the usual modern division between those who think and those who get things done.

But how complete is Margaret Schlegel? She doesn't want children, as she tells her sister in the closing scene; she is content with an older man whose energies were always bound up with coarseness of mind and are finally quite diminished. In other words the values Margaret embodies rest upon a curiously circumscribed and weakened sexuality. Her marriage, though it solves the specific problems posed by the novel, is a feeble marriage by the standards of much of the best literature down the ages : it is merely a convenient and not unhappy arrangement. Forster always managed in his fiction to treat sexuality as one element in human affairs (sometimes of course an explosive element), but he never saw it as the driving force. In the great struggle between Apollo and Dionysus Apollo too readily wins, because Dionysus is just a mischievous spirit rather than a mighty god. Certainly Margaret Schlegel is a particular (and in my view, plausible) person, but the novel as a whole pretends to tackle wide-ranging social questions. It does so by limiting the very, Dionysian forces which, it may well be, in secondary and often disguised ways produce the questions.

It must be admitted that Forster did not foresee at the time he wrote *Howards End* (1910) either the furious breaking of Apollo's bounds or the way in which women writers would shortly be disclaiming a good deal of what Margaret Schlegel stood for. Before then, however, D. H. Lawrence had set out to 'bring down' such a woman as Margaret by demonstrating what he saw as the need for almost any woman to obtain a man of greater spiritual power than her own.

Lawrence believed that by a law of nature nearly all women require masculine guidance. In his 'Study of Thomas Hardy' he allowed that a few 'specialized' women are exempt from this law and that Sue Bridehead (for whom he had a surprisingly high regard) was one of this select number.[18] But other women, however personally remarkable, must for their psychological well-being find mates whose spirit they can venerate. This is why in *The Rainbow* and *Women in Love* he produced such brilliant creatures as the Brangwen sisters, but ensured that one of them, Gudrun, should reach the verge of madness and the other, Ursula, should yield herself to a man modelled upon himself.

Ursula and Gudrun are emphatically new women, though they are never classified by the author in this way. And for once, in *The Rainbow,* we see through Lawrence's genius how the actual social manifestation came about. For what the first half of *The Rainbow* shows, and shows convincingly, is a decline in the self-confidence of men brought about by rising industrialization. Lawrence's narrative, though it concerns three generations of a particular family living in the English north Midlands after about 1860, is plainly representative of something happening in other industrialized nations. Ursula Brangwen is the eldest daughter of a weakened, defeated man and a dominant but shallow mother. She grows up with no great opinion of her mother and a strong though exasperated love for her father. Consequently she feels that she must find her own route through life. Since *The Rainbow* has become one of the best known novels in English there is no need to go into detail, but the essential feature of Ursula's youth is a kind of brave and blundering determination to maintain her own being. By the end of the novel she has received a decent education, had two love-affairs, one with a woman and the other with a man, obtained a miscarriage and finally experienced a vision that the future – for society as a whole – will be more fruitful than the immediate past.

At the outset of *Women in Love* Ursula and Gudrun (who

played little part in the earlier novel) are embarked upon their adult lives and cannot decide whether marriage is necessary or desirable. By Lawrentianly natural processes (there is no husband-hunting of course) Ursula comes to marry Rupert Birkin, a not uncritical version of Lawrence himself, while Gudrun determines to reject the potential dominance of her lover, Gerald Crich, and ends her story by going off to Dresden where she will plainly degenerate. The difference is this: Ursula, for all her enforced independence, never loses sight of the possibility that male leadership is *biologically* necessary, while Gudrun 'pervertedly' rejects this possibility.

The main question is how far, if at all, Lawrence misrepresents feminine nature in order to promote his doctrine. The consensus among critics, women as well as men, has been that Lawrence was an extraordinarily good observer of women, or, to be more precise, that he had profound intuitive understanding of them. And of course the feminine influences of his childhood, especially the rapport with his mother and the long friendship with Jessie Chambers, were decisive. But these factors do not mean that Lawrence was incapable of misrepresentation in the service of his own powerful needs. On the other hand some objections to Lawrence's 'legislation' by women readers, including readers who affirm his accuracy over many particulars, do not amount to convincing testimony either.

Surely what we find in Lawrence is an almost unmatched presentation of the 'woman's point of view' coupled with a determination to show that in the final analysis it is the woman's nature to submit. She is supposed to submit only to a man who demonstrates his mastery, and even then her acts of submission must be anything but regular domestic grovelling. We are given to understand that the woman should yield herself not to the man in his daily pettiness, but to the 'god in him'. If there is no divine element in the man, no independent or exploratory quality, then the woman knows in her heart that she should not yield, and if she does so she abuses herself. So there is a division in Lawrence's fiction between such women as Ursula Brangwen, Alvina Houghton, Kate Leslie and Constance Chatterley who possess this wisdom and those such as Miriam Leivers, Gudrun Brangwen and Hermione Roddice who do not.

Lawrence's attitude in this regard was anything but unique to him, yet it should not be confused with some commonplace masculine assumptions. Lawrence was quite clear that there is no question of an automatic masculine superiority. He seemed to know how it feels to be a woman who must tolerate male fatuities or give herself up sexually to a man she cannot respect. But the important question is how the attitude affects such women as the Brangwen sisters. The answer is that they who so readily see through the pretences and weaknesses of ordinary men can rise to completeness only through the medium of extraordinary men, 'sons of God' in Lawrence's Biblical phrase. Then they will join the ranks of womanhood down the ages; they will come home to themselves.

However, in *Women in Love* Lawrence depicts a period in which, in his view, few men have this godlike quality. The rest, whatever their conventional worthiness, honesty, bravery, prostrate themselves before the false idols of the age – money, science, social class, misconceived notions of democracy and spiritual equality. Each of the Brangwen sisters is a new woman and has no use for these idols: the difference between them is that Ursula wants to find a 'son of God' while Gudrun sets her will against manhood, which is to say against God. For while God is not in every man, a woman may encounter Him only through a man.

This is a simplified but so far accurate account of an aspect of Lawrence's doctrine. If the doctrine is 'chauvinistic', it is so only in the last analysis, since Lawrence was utterly sympathetic towards Ursula, his most complete heroine. And it must be emphasized that Ursula is wayward, contemptuous of both masculine and feminine norms, in love with abstract learning, adventurous intellectually as well as emotionally. Everyone knows that Lawrence thought in terms of a male–female polarity, ideally a balanced tension between the sexes, but he did not believe that the everyday consciousness and character of a commendable woman must be qualitatively different from a man's.

In fact it was some women writers – the subjects of the next chapter – who insisted on pervasive distinctions of personality between men and women. Virginia Woolf in particular set out to argue and fictionally to demonstrate that there truly is, and always must be, 'feminine psychology', a psychology which men writers down the ages (poets, dramatists, novelists, divines, philosophers and psychologists) had always misrepresented. The response of Virginia Woolf and some other women in the twenties was a reaction not so much against shallow, popular views but against those individuals, notably Shaw, Wells and Bennett, who supposed themselves to be championing the cause of women.

6 Virginia Woolf and her Contemporaries

Virginia Woolf's *A Room of One's Own* remains after fifty years and a torrent of feminist publications a most stimulating discussion of the relation of women to literature. This book, an expanded version of two papers read at Cambridge in 1928, is concerned with the difficulties of women writers. They have been hindered not simply by domestic exigencies but also by the problems of presenting, or even acknowledging, a female vision. Fictional women created by authors of both sexes are misrepresentations. Down to the eighteenth century almost all authors were men and 'a man is terribly hampered and partial in his knowledge of women'.[1] Since that time authoresses have been obliged to wrestle with a man-made and therefore alien culture.

Literary portraiture of women has merely extended the main cultural function of their sex, namely to promote the confidence of men. For 'women have served all these centuries as looking-glasses possessing the magic and delicious power of reflecting the figure of man at twice its natural size'.[2] This memorable comment refers not only to petty vanities but also to the feats of civilization, to the arts and sciences, the voyages of exploration, the laws, the revolutions and the military conquests. In other words, men have looked into the eyes of women and seen magnified images of themselves. But then by a magical process the images have become reality.

This process, the very psychology of masculine achievement, takes little account of the real woman. She is scarcely seen, for the man does not objectively scrutinize her face. She must stay an unknown creature who fosters the man's ego-ideal. Virginia Woolf says of woman in social and cultural history that 'Imaginatively she is of the highest importance; practically she is completely insignificant'.[3] Here for example is Antigone, noble and defiant, while there in Sophocles' Athens were only drudges, idlers and concubines.

However, it seems that even in ancient Athens women may have been far from 'completely insignificant'. Modern scholars are no longer sure on this point: H. D. F. Kitto, for instance, in his book, *The Greeks,* argues that impressions of women given us by the Greek poets cannot be wildly inaccurate. The great tragic heroines, he asserts, were surely not entire inventions.[4] This is a common-sensical view, for is it possible that Sophocles could have imagined his Antigone or Aeschylus his Clytemnestra in the absence of any social basis for these images? This of course is a qualification of Virginia Woolf's point, not an invalidation. There remains the fact which we noted in the first chapter that male writers of ancient Greece exploited women in order to promote certain attitudes or ideas.

Much the same process is evident throughout the ages. But Virginia Woolf and some other writers of her generation believed that the centuries of masculine 'distortion' of women had thrust the feminine psyche into obscurity. It was not revealed in poetry, plays and novels, but lurked in the shadows, bewildered, resentful and more or less incorrigible. Even the greatly talented women writers had failed to bring this psyche into the light of day. Being obliged to use a masculine structure, such as the conventional novel, and an orderly, logical syntax created by men, they too had manufactured false models of femininity. Adding insult to injury the older generation of writers in Virginia Woolf's day had, she felt, sought to free women by conferring masculine possibilities upon them. If anything, Shaw, Wells and Bennett had made matters worse. Perhaps they were chivalrous; certainly they were presumptuous and ignorant. For the minds of women were still hidden away; undiscovered treasures in caves, untapped sources of health and, conceivably, of moral improvement. Certainly there was something deeply immoral about this *mental* subjection.

This is the aspect of Virginia Woolf's argument in *A Room of One's Own* (and elsewhere among her writings[5]) which concerns us here. To see how far it can be accepted let us first consider her observations on the English sentence. Virginia Woolf points out that when the English women novelists came on the scene they had to hand only the masculine sentence of eighteenth-century prose writers such as Johnson and Gibbon.

It was a sentence that was unsuited for a woman's use. Charlotte Brontë, with all her splendid gift for prose, stumbled and fell with that clumsy weapon in her hands. George Eliot committed atrocities with it that beggar description. Jane Austen looked at it and laughed at it and devised a perfectly natural, shapely sentence proper for her own use and never departed from it.[6]

But, we must ask, if Jane Austen was able to devise a sentence for her own use, why could the others not do so? It is well known that the prose Jane Austen most fondly 'looked at' was the masculine prose of Dr Johnson. His structures entered her mind and were these adapted to the requirements of her vision. If indeed she also 'laughed at' Johnson's style, she did not laugh it quite away. Then, if Charlotte Brontë had her mishaps, this was not because she was using an altogether uncongenial style. On the contrary she did wonders with language and, moreover, it was plainly a feature of her character to *admire* the very kind of prose she tried, often with great success, to write. I do not think we can say that her admiration was misplaced; that she was a schoolgirl aping her masters. To the extent that Charlotte Brontë wished her compositions to be elegant and 'correct', this desire was an integral part of her being. George Eliot in fact began as a model school-child, trying always to lose crudities of speech and writing. Later, as a novelist, her manner (which steadily improved from *Scenes of Clerical Life* to *Daniel Deronda*) was designed to convey exactly her usually grave, often complex and sometimes exalted thoughts. Her infelicities cannot simply be the result of copying a man's heavy-handed or formally dignified ways. In any event, the mind of George Eliot was most comprehensively expressed in the writing : there was no alternative Mary Ann Evans hovering outside the study.

Virginia Woolf assumes too readily the existence of another Charlotte Brontë and another George Eliot, each independent of the culture she inherited; independent somehow of the world in which she lived. It was Virginia Woolf's unvarying belief (expressed in the fiction and the essays) that every individual has a 'self', a core of being which has come naked and vulnerable into the world. She never entertained the possibility that this 'self' is purely a dynamic interplay between the will of the individual and his circumstances. I fancy that Charlotte Brontë's self, her woman-self, is what we encounter in the novels; it was not something else tucked away and inexpressible. Even her unappeased yearnings are communicated, in the style as well as in the plots and characters. Whatever did not go into the novels in some form (muted and disguised perhaps) was presumably trivial to her. To imagine Charlotte Brontë confronting different linguistic possibilities is to imagine not a truer Charlotte Brontë but a different person.

Virginia Woolf further believed that the forms of literature had generally been masculine forms. 'There is no reason to think', she wrote, 'that the form of the epic or of the poetic play suits a woman any more than the sentence suits her.'[7] Even the novel, the 'most pliable of forms', may not be fitted to reflect a woman's mind. But to think along these lines is once again to suppose that a woman's mind has little essentially to do with her position in society; that it is not in considerable measure a product of her subordination to men. Virginia Woolf's view was that women in general (not all of them) have ineradicably certain qualities of consciousness which complement, in salutary and creative fashion, the masculine qualities. She assumed that if all gratuitous curbs and misrepresentations were removed this feminine consciousness would stay substantially the same. Certainly the bitterness and the defensiveness would go, but there would remain the free-flowing, non-logical, unregulated, emotional and unashamedly subjective concern with the material world. We cannot confidently share this view, because the mental qualities with which Virginia Woolf invested her womanly women in the fiction are patently connected with subordination. They may be the cause of that subordination, in which case there is little beyond common justice to be done. Such personalities as Virginia Woolf's own Clarissa Dalloway or Mrs Ramsay will never rule; will never determine either laws or cultural patterns. Alternatively it might be that the traits of a Mrs Ramsay are a response to lack of public responsibility, to restraint of political influence, to an absence of the need to solve theoretical problems; above all to small-scale and intimate spheres of concern.

One of Virginia Woolf's chief objectives as a writer of fiction was to display the feminine mind, to announce to her readers that what they had encountered even in such impressive writers as Tolstoy and Proust was a falsification of women. So far the highly talented women writers had worked in the shadows cast by men: now it was time to move out into the sunlight. Accordingly, in 1921 Virginia Woolf made a new departure with the publication of the volume of short stories, *Monday or Tuesday*. The early novels had been conventional in form; that is, they had been fashioned after 'masculine' models. Though *A Voyage Out* had charted the self-discovery and the death of a young woman, it had nevertheless followed the pattern of the male *bildungsroman*. Even *Night and Day* with its echoes of both Jane Austen and George Eliot had exhibited but little of a woman's vision. So Virginia Woolf began, tentatively but bravely, to see if her own true way of responding to people and situations could be captured in some new kind of stories. *Her* way of course, but she was sure that it was also to a degree everywoman's way. After that in a remarkably short time she progressed from cautious exploration in *Jacob's Room* to a large measure of success with *Mrs Dalloway* to complete triumph with *To the Lighthouse*. Each subsequent novel was a fresh formal experiment, since Virginia Woolf could not tolerate repetition and, besides, there were new things to say. *Orlando, The Waves, The Years* and *Between the Acts* are formally distinct from one another and each is a considerable departure from the orthodox novel. Having discovered her self and a sufficiently variable medium (in terms both of structure and prose style) for expressing that self, Virginia Woolf had, it seemed, opened up a new path for other women writers.

But scarcely any have gone down that path. Her contemporaries did not work along similar lines, and later generations of women novelists have for the most part either reverted to traditional ways or conducted experiments for quite different purposes. Nor, despite the linguistic innovations of the past forty years, in particular the loosening of the old grammarians' forms, have we seen a marked 'feminization' of sentence-structures. There have been many admirers of Virginia Woolf's idiosyncratic and lasting work but no disciples.

The reason, I suggest, is bound up with the nature of fiction, with why it gets written and read. Virginia Woolf wanted to display the truth – for instance about the workings of women's minds in quotidian circumstances – but the truth in this limited sense is not what writers and readers, however discriminating, actually want. At least they do not want much of it, because they believe that the mind is properly employed in *forging* meaning.

There are times, admittedly, when Virginia Woolf writes like an existentialist, anticipating up to a point the Sartre of *La Nausée;* that is, she seems to feel that 'out there', beyond the order created by the mind, is mere chaos. For example, the 'Time Passes' section of *To the Lighthouse* is a paradoxical and impressive attempt to suggest in words a wordless universe. There is no Word in the gospel sense and there are no meaning-conferring words in the ordinary human sense. However, unlike Sartre, Virginia Woolf wished the shapes of each of her works to comply with its own peculiar emotional, aesthetic and imaginative demands. There should be an absolute minimum of interference either from tradition or from the reasoning intellect. Feelings and impressions must be the raw material dictating, or at all events heavily influencing, the finished structure. Thus, by avoiding the Procrustean bed of orthodox narrative and the requirements of 'masculine' reasoning, something akin to everyday felt experience would be grasped. Such experience might very well not be the final Reality (since Virginia Woolf acknowledged mystical possibilities) but it was the worldly reality that fiction had always, falsely, pretended to communicate.

So far Virginia Woolf's assumptions seem vulnerable only to that familiar naturalistic – or alternatively Marxist – belief that social reality, even or especially when it is not discerned by the day-to-day processes of consciousness, should also inform a work of literature. Such processes are in part a response to that reality, though the individual is commonly unaware of the fact. Therefore, so the argument runs, the subjectivist vision of a Virginia Woolf is incomplete, if not downright false. This is a reasonable and, since about 1930, a widely-held view, but it does not completely explain why Virginia Woolf's kind of pioneering has not been followed by other women. The main reason, I suspect, is that both men and women, however much they value the works of Virginia Woolf herself, generally esteem the dynamic properties of mind more highly than she did. Without thinking about the matter, they accept the need to manipulate and control experience by the usual architectural or myth-making or ratiocinative devices. They acknowledge implicitly that fiction is not a product of the receptive powers alone, or of receptivity controlled by the aesthetic impulse, but may also be a drive towards domination in which 'masculine' reason, facts, theories also play their parts. There is a point in *To the Lighthouse* when the unqualifiedly feminine Mrs Ramsay contemplates her inability to share a man's type of knowledge – of square roots, of Voltaire's notions, of the character of Napoleon. Then the movement of her mind is described in the following way:

. . . she let it uphold her and sustain her, this admirable fabric of the masculine intelligence, which ran up and down, crossed this way and that, like iron girders spanning the swaying fabric, upholding the world, so that she could trust herself to it utterly, even shut her eyes, or flicker them for a moment, as a child staring up from its pillow winks at the myriad layers of the leaves of a tree.[8]

Thus Mrs Ramsay sees the world as a sort of infinitely large sheet or tent swaying in the wind : it would crumple or float away but for the girders of masculine intelligence which keep it tolerably firm. These girders are not the stuff of the world; perhaps indeed they are unreal, purely mentalistic, though they are indispensable. Now, bearing in mind that Mrs Ramsay is an extreme type; that, for example, numerous schoolgirls are happy with square roots, Virginia Woolf is here acknowledging the necessity for everyone of the girders. Her own novels have a minimum of such scaffolding, or more accurately, the scaffolding is supple, not firm like iron. It is evident though that many women writers themselves wish to erect firm girders. To weaken these supports is undesired apparently as well as undesirable. In this way we all, men and women, falsify the real world as a matter of need, but also, surely as a legitimate and joyous exercise of the will. This activity, the activity of a Homer or a Tolstoy, a George Eliot or many a latter-day woman novelist, is not 'escapism' but a principal function of the human (not simply the masculine) mind. Women perhaps come into their own to the extent that they share the task of putting up a framework.

Nevertheless, that Virginia Woolf rejected precast framework is a cause not of weakness in her novels but of their peculiar merits. After *Night and Day* she achieved for each novel a fair coincidence of medium and message. Thus *Mrs Dalloway* is about degrees and kinds of relatedness of human beings to one another, varying from lonely madness to self-compromising sociability. Clarissa Dalloway maintains fruitful links between herself and others (or more generally brings people together) by repressing or manipulating her real being. At the other extreme Septimus Warren-Smith wandering about the London streets with his Italian wife is so cut off from the world around him that at times he feels, paradoxically, consumed by that world. Accordingly one feature of the form of the novel (there are other, more obvious features) is designed to show two mental spheres, that of Clarissa and that of Septimus, moving along their separate tracks and finally merging. These spheres fit together, so to speak, when towards the end of the novel Clarissa learns of the suicide of Septimus and realizes that she and this young ex-soldier (whom of course in her Mayfair milieu she has never met) have a certain kinship. The very form of the book, insofar as we can separate form from content, supports this notion of ultimate unification.

To the Lighthouse has received so much exegesis that it is necessary here only to recall two principal features. First, the three parts of this novel constitute through their imagery a sequence of light (or meaning), darkness (or meaninglessness), followed by light once again – this time as the representation of a more comprehensive meaning. The darkness, it seems, is a necessary accompaniment of the light. Then in terms of 'plot', young James Ramsay shifts from his childhood self-identification with his mother to teenage rapport with his father. Meanwhile Lily Briscoe, the artist friend of the family, comes to realize that for her artist's vision both the radically feminine Mrs Ramsay (now dead) and the radically masculine Mr Ramsay are indispensable dual components.[9] Once again the architecture of the novel unites with its images, characters and events to make a whole uniquely expressing Virginia Woolf's understanding at that period of her development, in 1927.

Virginia Woolf's criticism of the conventional novel is to the effect that the medium confounds the message. In her most characteristic work the two are barely separable. In *The Waves* the agreeably varied succession of what for convenience we may call 'interior monologues' (though the phrase is inaccurate) joined with the movements of sun and sea, culminates in the reflections of one character, the rounded, empathetic Bernard, to form a singular but apposite pattern. This pattern itself (one could almost *draw* it) implies Virginia Woolf's leading idea at this point in her career – that of oneness achieved through individuality. Bernard's final 'soliloquy' expresses the same idea. Being extraordinarily self-confident, he is extraordinarily and healthily malleable : therefore he experiences in old age a few visionary moments during which he sees a landscape as it truly is, while he is eclipsed yet secure. Likewise *Between the Acts* – to offer one final illustration – establishes by its design as well as by its people and happenings a connection between one commonplace day in the thirties and extensive periods of the social history of Britain. Indeed pre-history is nicely (and rather comically) envisioned, so that the novel gives us a moment in time, a single sunny day, which expands towards timelessness.

Such formal experiments as these of Virginia Woolf are by their nature unrepeatable, yet they might have been expected to suggest to other writers, women especially, a new way of working. This has happened to an unimportant extent. Women writing in the interval between the wars often managed to be 'true to themselves' without departing much from the orthodox novel. Alternatively, the departure from orthodoxy has taken a different turn. Dorothy Richardson's succession of volumes which make up the composite novel, *Pilgrimage,* tends to be classed with the works of Virginia Woolf, but this is a very rough classification. What Dorothy Richardson lacked (or cheerfully eschewed) was Virginia Woolf's sense of shape, since *Pilgrimage* is purely a sequence. Dorothy Richardson was enticed by her recognition (a personal recognition rather than a simple acknowledgement) that the prime difference between art and life is that art is shapely while our experience merely unfolds. So *Pilgrimage* is an immense unfolding of impressions, seemingly undirected. At the same time the impressions are fashioned into normal, connected prose and the work is unified. The unity lies chiefly in the fact that everything is perceived, felt, contemplated by one person, Miriam Henderson. It is her pilgrim's progress from the nineties to the early years of the First World War.

The pilgrimage is not in the traditional sense a moral quest and the progress is not appreciably an ascent of any kind. Furthermore, it might be more accurate to say that the adventure was the author's own, not just because author and heroine are, evidently, rather alike, but also because the act of writing was more than usually adventurous. Dorothy Richardson tells us in the Foreword she wrote in 1938, when twelve of the thirteen volumes of *Pilgrimage* had been completed, how she stumbled upon her method. She set out 'to produce a feminine equivalent of the current masculine realism', threw away a good deal of manuscript and then found herself producing what she calls 'contemplated reality'.[10] She had long wanted to discern the truth about her own thoughts and beliefs, but it was not until she discarded the usual methods of realism that this truth began to appear. The first chapter of what eventually became *Pointed Roofs* (the opening volume of *Pilgrimage*) was written with the joy of discovery.

In 1913, the opening pages of the attempted chronicle became the first chapter of 'Pilgrimage', written to the accompaniment of a sense of being upon a fresh pathway, an adventure so searching and, sometimes, so joyous as to produce a longing for participation, not quite the same as a longing for publication, whose possibility, indeed, as the book grew, receded to vanishing point.[11]

Dorothy Richardson, unaided, recognized what had been glimpsed by some people before her and is now a commonplace: that realism is not, psychologically speaking, realistic. Balzac, she says, was a realist without knowing it, and while this is misleading (for it was merely the term that had not been coined in Balzac's lifetime), she also remarks that for Balzac realism had something to do with the relation between the human spirit and 'a relatively concrete and coherent social system'. Arnold Bennett, she writes, is a conscious realist, portraying his individuals in a decaying society. As for her younger contemporaries (chiefly men), they too are deliberate realists, but for them the word connotes 'explicit satire and protest'. The realism of Balzac, Bennett and, presumably, such a writer as Galsworthy had, for Dorothy Richardson, little to do with felt experience. It was full of ideas, willed constructs, attitudes maintained in the teeth of the author's own feelings and observations.

Then, during the war, news came to Dorothy Richardson of Proust, apparently engaged on a similar task to her own (though in fact *A la Recherche du Temps Perdu* is vastly more organized and, in the end, more 'masculinely' philosophical than *Pilgrimage*). Later she realized that important features of her work had been anticipated by Henry James and even so early as the late eighteenth century, by Goethe. However, Dorothy Richardson's project was, and remains to this day, without reasonable parallel. Her method and her conviction are stated by the heroine, Miriam, on the penultimate page of the last volume, *March Moonlight*.

While I write, everything vanishes but what I contemplate. The whole of what is called 'the past' is with me, seen anew, vividly. No, Schiller, the past does not stand 'being still'. It moves, growing with one's growth. Contemplation is adventure into discovery; reality. What is called 'creation', imaginative trans-formation, fantasy, invention, is based upon reality. Poetic description a half-truth? Can anything produced by man be called 'creation'? The incense-burners do not seem to know that in acclaiming what they call 'a work of genius' they are recognizing what is potentially within themselves.[12]

So Dorothy Richardson qualified the claims of art and the prestige of genius. No one properly creates anything: at best people simply observe. In effect, her way was to take the term, 'realism', pretty well literally and to push the doctrine as far as it would go in the direction of subjectivism. As we read *Pilgrimage* we are encouraged to feel that phases of Miriam Henderson's consciousness are omitted purely because they are unimportant to her. If the break between one phase and the next seems arbitrary, it is so after the manner of anyone late in an evening recalling the events of the day. What is recalled is for some, often unfathomable reason significant, while the rest has fallen into oblivion. Therefore Miriam's consciousness is not exhibited as an unbroken flow and this may in part be what Dorothy Richardson had in mind when she referred dismissively to those who can 'persuade themselves of the possibility of comparing consciousness to a stream'.[13]

The clue to the entire procedure lies in Dorothy Richardson's trust in contemplation, her belief that the truth for each of us resides in 'contemplated reality'. The idea is that to make sense of life it is necessary to break the codes by which we mostly live. We should ponder only those fragments of experience that rise up, demanding attention, and they should be pondered without preconceptions. There is no need – in fact it is positively harmful – to subject such fragments to logical analysis or moral scrutiny, since they will yield up their own 'logic' and their own moral consequence. These acts of pondering, of contemplation, may employ grammatical prose (in one's head or on paper), but so far as possible language must not be allowed to distort experience. The original raw experience is the truth, and no idea has value unless it matches the experience. In philosophical terms Dorothy Richardson resembled a Husserlian phenomenologist, forever 'bracketing-off' her experience in order to grasp it accurately.

One illuminating result of Dorothy Richardson's procedure is that the heroine, Miriam, is not a readily definable character. At the same time she is unmistakably a person. A critic who tried to describe Miriam would find himself either using vague terms or specifying what she is not. For example he might lamely say that she is observant or he might notice that she is not much given to fantasizing. Therefore this novel suggests that characters in fiction are generally false: it lets the cat out of the bag. Further, it reinforces the belief that character in everyday life is to a degree a product of habit, will and cultural influence; that people tend to 'screen out' those perceptions and feelings which they cannot accommodate in the moulds they have made for themselves.

This is not inescapably a matter of gender. Miriam's personality lacks firm contours not because she is a woman (as though there were nothing further to be said) but in consequence of her creator's determination to be accurate and contemplative at all costs. Here is something approaching real mimesis as opposed to the selective mimesis practised by other writers, however talented. This figure of Miriam encourages one to believe not exactly that Pope was right when he remarked, 'Most women have no characters at all,' but that women have been less prone than men to will themselves unvarying characters. The distinction here is gradual not sharp, and plainly admits many exceptions. Furthermore, there remains the possibility that the groundwork of the distinction is as much political as biological.

However, the psychological realism sedulously practised by Dorothy Richardson is thought to reflect the workings of feminine minds only. We have noted that she saw herself as producing a 'feminine equivalent of the current masculine realism'[14] and Virginia Woolf wrote that Miss Richardson had developed 'a sentence which we might call the psychological sentence of the feminine gender'.[15] The trouble with such remarks is that they foster a confusion between *what* people think about and *how* they do their thinking. As it happens Miriam Henderson's thoughts are neither more nor less logical, objective, ideational than many a man's: they are simply tied to her womanly situations. Miriam has next to nothing in common with Joyce's Molly Bloom – to take the chief modern example of supposedly uncorrected femininity. Molly is just semi-literate, and if this means she has evaded the influence of grammarians, logicians and their like, it doesn't follow that she had *thereby* preserved her essential womanliness. An 'evolved' woman such as Miriam has not travelled away from her authentic nature. And this nature, it seems to me, is merely human, for even Miriam's (that is to say, Miss Richardson's) preference for contemplation over action, her reluctance or inability to compel her world into some kind of scheme, might well be taken to represent a phase in cultural development rather than an ever-lasting fact of womanhood.

It is generally true that at this time (I am thinking roughly of the period from 1910 to 1930) notable women writers sought to define feelings and moods. They were not Jamesian so much as Chekovian, since they steered clear of those hard rocks of choice which often mark the high points of the drama as well as the moral import of James's works. It was Chekov more than any other writer who showed the twentieth century how to let moral significance emerge from a complex of feelings, with little reference to principles or rational explanations. This quality of Chekov was seized upon by writers of short stories more than novelists, by women more than men and by no one more eagerly than Katherine Mansfield.

Katherine Mansfield's strong, sad, bitter feelings are precisely though obliquely expressed in her stories. Not only were the feelings real but the characters and events were often enough mere re-arrangements of actuality. The stories, it seems, rely upon exact observation of people, places, gestures, fragments of conversation. In other words, there is a good deal of objectivity, but what matters is the composite emotion of each story. For Katherine Mansfield the mental state was all in all : she was not in the least a philosopher, an historian, a journalist, a politician, but simply an experiencing subject and an artist who had no use for general conclusions. Even James, for all his disparagement of ideas in fiction, implies a con-sistent personal 'philosophy' and so perhaps (though this is dis-putable) does Chekov, while Katherine Mansfield conveys only pointless and generally painful experience. She is the complete suffering woman, since even her satire (which of course pervades many of the stories) suggests no expectation of a corrective.

Nevertheless, there is no doubt in a story where the fault lies and consequently there is an imaginable corrective, namely that individuals should, in the terminology of a later period, be 'com-mitted' to one another. Not, it goes without saying, to God, to country, to a cause, but with entire honesty to friends and lovers. At all events, Katherine Mansfield's stories commonly deal with abandonment or isolation : someone is set apart through an aware-ness, or perhaps, as for instance in 'Je ne parle pas français', by acts of desertion.

In writing 'Je ne parle pas français' Katherine Mansfield saw through the eyes of one of her lovers, Francis Carco, for it is he in the person of a Parisian writer called Raoul Duquette who tells the story. Duquette reveals himself in every sentence: a small, dark, cynical, gleefully selfish man to whom, for some reason he cannot fathom, women offer themselves. One of his friends is an English student of French literature modelled upon John Middleton Murry, at that time another lover of Katherine Mansfield and later of course her husband. This friend, named Dick Harmon, is handsome, courteous and at times secretive in the way of one who possesses amusing knowledge which he does not wish to share with others. Harmon, it should be added, carries in his wallet a photograph of his good-looking and beloved mother. After a spell back in England Harmon returns to Paris with an attractive young Englishwoman nicknamed 'Mouse'. The couple repair with Duquette to some rooms Duquette has rented for them, where after a spell of fatigued and stilted conversation Harmon makes an excuse to go out for a while. But he never returns: instead he leaves in an adjoining room a note for Mouse, explaining that he cannot continue their liaison because it would kill his mother if he did so. Mouse is left with Duquette who, after promising to visit her the next day, fails in his irresponsible way to turn up.

Now, Mouse is Katherine Mansfield herself and the story expresses her fears, caught between the self-seeking Carco and the weak Murry. She is purely observed, puzzled over, neglected, while Carco–Duquette unabashedly displays his thoughts and Murry–Harmon is nicely caught in an action which, in Katherine Mansfield's evident view, sums him up. It is true that Duquette does not mention the sort of lascivious images that would in life cross his mind; nor does he manage more than mild hints of the homosexual feelings Dick Harmon presumably arouses in him, but the story may be all the better for such reticence. However, the important fact is that Katherine Mansfield saw herself as a victim, one to whom people generally, but men especially, would sooner or later be disloyal.

Whatever the ultimate reasons for this attitude a leading feature of it was a sense of her own incorruptibility in relation to the self-serving devices of others. The stories make plain a regular feeling that love and friendship seldom ripen as they should because of selfishness, and that in consequence the world at large is set upon a hopeless course. In an important letter to Murry written while she was working on 'Je ne parle pas français' she described this general apprehension as her 'old original' inducement to write fiction.

The other 'kick off' is my old original one, and (had I not known love) it would have been my all. Not hate or destruction (both are beneath contempt as real motives) but an *extremely* deep sense of hopelessness, of everything doomed to disaster, almost wilfully, stupidly, like the almond tree and *'pas de nougat pour le noel'*. There! as I took out a cigarette paper I got it exactly – *a cry against corruption* – that is *absolutely* the nail on the head. Not a protest – a *cry*, and I mean corruption in the widest sense of the word, of course.[16]

The widest sense of the word seems to have included, for Katherine Mansfield, almost any kind of exploitation, any equivocation, any bad faith. Many of her stories deal with emotional dishonesty and for that reason might be termed 'cries against corruption'. In 'Psychology', for instance, a man and a woman fail to let their friendship develop, because of some kind of calculation or reserve chiefly on the man's part. The man arrives for tea at the woman's studio where the couple talk agreeably about literature, and then at six o'clock, when the conversation is circling about in familiar fashion, he announces that he must leave for another engagement. For a while over the sandwiches and cakes the situation seems pleasantly normal, since 'they were both old enough to enjoy their adventure without any emotional complication'. Only a little later does the woman realize that this occasion matches previous occasions too perfectly. They are repeating themselves, not in the detail but in the tenor of their meeting. After the man has gone an 'elderly virgin' comes unexpectedly to bring the woman violets and the contrast is striking, for the man has whiled away an hour or so but the bearer of violets is a true – that is, a self-committing – friend. The story is not about shyness, but about the wary check people place on their feelings, and this is perhaps a species of corruption.

Then, in 'The Garden Party' a young girl, Laura, dimly but sympathetically grasps that the death of a proletarian neighbour should cause the people at the big house, her house (based, incidentally, upon Katherine Mansfield's childhood home in a suburb of Wellington, New Zealand) to abandon their day of cream cakes and meringues, of a band playing on the lawn and guests strolling beside the flowers. The garden-party proceeds nevertheless, and in the dusk at the behest of her snobbish mother Laura takes a basket of left-over food to the neighbour's poky house where she is obliged to view the corpse. The sight impresses her deeply and places in proper perspective the junketing at Laura's own house. The attack in this story is partly upon class divisions, of course, but there is also a *cry* against the readiness of individuals to blot out of mind whatever inconveniences their plans or pleasures.

In story after nicely-observed story we are caused to share the writer's sense of a blight on human relations, for each episode has the universality of a particular action perfectly caught. Thus the office boss of 'The Fly', after being reminded of his son's death in the war, maintains his composure by drowning a fly in ink. His grief, his cruelty and the connection between them are specific but at the same time general in their implications. Similarly 'The Canary', Katherine Mansfield's last story, is the soliloquy of a woman whose pet bird has died, but it is also a comment (this time explicit) upon sadness or a sense of loss lying in wait behind all human emotions.

Katherine Mansfield never quite succeeded in marshalling her ideas about the distinction between art and life, though the subject was important to her. We can tell from her journals that she was fascinated by Shakespeare's accuracy, so that one of her own aims was to represent speech, thoughts, actions, motives with something approaching a Shakespearean nicety. At the same time she thought of the artist's vision as necessarily apart from day-to-day reality with the result that, for her, the artist's task was 'to create his own world in this world'.[17] In other words she worked always to infiltrate her vision into things as they objectively are, and indeed this is what artists of a representational sort generally achieve in some degree. However, she would not allow that an artist's success in this endeavour might alter the way in which others see the real world. To express the matter differently, the truly objective sphere barely exists for most of us, for we see to an appreciable extent through the eyes of generations of artists. We are apt to grasp not their objective perceptions but the dynamic use they made of those perceptions. Katherine Mansfield herself, for instance, was extraordinarily accurate, though what readers apprehend, what must sometimes modify their own picture of life, is her sorrow. And this of course was her true, subjective aim: to cause others to share her desolation.

She was convinced that 'the attempt of Hegel to change subjective processes into objective world processes will not work out',[18] yet this Hegelian transference, as she appears to have understood it, has been fairly consistently brought about by creative thinkers of one sort or another. She evidently took Hegel to mean that the development of the human species is a process of thoughts becoming external facts. An artist *acts* through his work, which is to say that he wills, whether he acknowledges it or not, certain alterations in the real world. In some degree, minute or expansive, his work contributes to social and psychological change. Sometimes, of course, an artist is so pessimistic as to refute this fact entirely, but his very pessimism, when it is cogently enough expressed, helps to make some change in the existing order. No artist secures for future generations exactly what he in his day lacked and his work may well have perverse and bitter consequences. Nevertheless it bears fruits. What Katherine Mansfield rather pessimistically did was to expose, with exquisite art, the sort of devices by which people evade one another. She believed that there could be no end to such evasion and we cannot say that she was wrong. Nevertheless, her stories are precursors of that modern movement which takes the showing-up of bad faith to be a principal aim, and this movement has itself altered (not merely reflected, but altered) consciousness itself. Further, as a result of Katherine Mansfield's stories readers have learned a good deal about woman's dependency, her position on the sidelines of history, and such knowledge has helped the movement of women into the centre of the arena.

Now, of course there have appeared down the ages isolated women who behaved simply as political or cultural leaders, showing little awareness of themselves as members of a generally dependent group. In Katherine Mansfield's time and well beyond it such a woman was Gertrude Stein whose consciousness of herself as a representative of the beleagured sex was happily deficient. Everyone knows that Gertrude Stein's contribution to the modern movement was considerable, both through the example of her own writing and through her advice to other American authors, notably Sherwood Anderson and Hemingway. She helped such authors to rid their works of pretence, under which heading must prominently be included verbal mannerisms borrowed from former periods of English literature and no longer fitting. Indeed for her a very high proportion of even the best literature of the past was now, in the early twentieth century, hopelessly unsuitable as a model of good writing. The writer could serve either God or mammon, the first meaning the spirit of his own age, and the second meaning the moribund spirits of former ages.[19]

Accordingly, after the comparative conventionality of the early books (*Things As They Are,* originally entitled *Q.E.D.,* and *Three Lives,* published in 1910), her works are thoroughly radical, proceeding from sentence to barely punctuated sentence and either disregarding or curiously using cultural influences from the past. It is perhaps wrong to speak of Gertrude Stein's 'aim', as if it remained constant throughout a long, prolific career, but she seems chiefly to have pursued the unimpeded expression of mind alone; that is, the minds of individual characters viewed as sets of interior events loosely related to the exterior events which the characters perceive.

Biographers and critics do not explain why she made this remarkable attempt, except by suggesting that her experiments as a student at Radcliffe College (then, in the 1890s, called Havard Annexe) might have helped to promote some of her ideas. At Radcliffe she learned Philosophy from Santayana and Royce, and Psychology from William James. After that she studied Medicine at Johns Hopkins but was bored and some two years later went off to Paris with her brother, Leo. In Paris, settled at 28 rue de Fleurus, Montparnasse, she made the acquaintance of artists and started collecting their as yet cheap and sometimes unregarded paintings. Far from being two opposed sides of her nature, her scientific bent and her enthusiasm for the latest art coincided, since she had an empirical interest in the mind and the paintings fed that interest. For the artists were, to Gertrude Stein's great delight, not only breaking free from the past (or serving God) but also seeking to represent what they saw rather than what their education or common sense told them was actually before their eyes. In other words, a Matisse or a Cezanne painting records a moment in the mind of the artist as distinct from the objectivity of the objects which appear in it. In this way the canvas asserts the vital importance and the distinctiveness of the artist's thoughts and feelings. Moreover, since these mental activities fall into recognizable patterns the paintings embody the artist's character.

Even in those two early books, *Things As They Are* and *Three Lives,* but more especially in her later works Gertrude Stein attempted with words what the artists were successfully doing in their medium. More precisely, it seems that she looked for a literary equivalent, and this exploration, which passed through changing and sometimes questionable phases, lasted for the rest of her life. The theory, I think, can be stated simply in outline, though a full exposition would require a separate and elaborate study. First, Gertrude Stein concentrated upon the mind of an individual in a story rather than upon his visible style or actions. However, each mind in what she liked to call its 'bottom nature' displays a pattern or rhythm which constitutes the character of the person, and this character is not unique but is classifiable along with the characters of many other persons past and present. Character, then, consists in the first instance of a repetitious mode of thought and feeling, and the writer defining his own or another's character ought repetitiously to render words which match that mode. The proper or the most valuable object of literature is to capture mental phases, a single though possibly complex phase in a poem, a progression of phases in prose fiction. It would often be necessary to find words for a non-mental thing (for instance a rose), at which point the writer should be at pains not to confuse his feelings with the inherent qualities of the thing. His feelings must of course be expressed, but not as though they belonged to whatever it was in the world that had aroused them.[20]

A writer should, furthermore, try to secure immediacy of attention, so that the reader's eyes as they follow the work are at least momentarily arrested by each block of words. The reader must be encouraged to concentrate upon the words rather than allowed to use the words merely as humble signs. In this way the reader, like the writer, would be wholly engaged upon the work of art itself. He would of course notice its resemblance to aspects of everyday life, but only in a subordinate way for his chief object is delightfully to engage his own mind with the mind of the author, to stay for a while in a mental and verbal sphere. As for events or actions commonly used to form the story, these must be minimal since they are unimportant in themselves. Such happenings could safely be left to inartistic myth-makers (of whom, at least in the form of crime authors, Gertrude Stein was very fond), since the true writer is overwhelmingly concerned with psychology and of course with language. Physical actions are unimportant to him, because he wishes to capture mental structures, especially as they constitute characters.

Moreover, since such character-structure are apt to remain the same throughout the changing circumstances of life, writers might profitably emphasize the fact by using the present tense. In any event American writers are different from English writers who as members of a conquering island-race naturally see life in terms of development or story, of one action leading to another. English writers know the end of the story and have indeed a strong sense of beginning, middle and end. But for Americans writing now there is chiefly a sense of the pregnant present moment. For Americans are currently making themselves while the English are well past their peak. This, roughly, should be the twentieth-century American way to separate the art of literature, an art of psychological units called 'words', from anecdote or narrative which points away from the mind and towards the world.

This brief account of Gertrude Stein's methods and purposes is no doubt open to question and is obviously incomplete. I have extracted pieces of argument from her lectures (delivered in the thirties in the USA[21]) and merged these with what I believe to be the implications of her literary practice. At all events her influence was considerable between the wars. She immediately influenced, among others, Sherwood Anderson and Hemingway who in turn, taking from her what they required, passed on to countless other authors a fresh denotative style. And this style in all its individual variations declared a new grasp of the human personality. For as the nineteenth century progressed British authors had increasingly emphasized a distinction between the personality of an individual and his world. He as a consciousness and a coherent group of idiosyncracies confronted his fictional world. Further, objects in that world were commonly superfluous or were given irrelevant qualities. In various ways they exceeded the needs of the story. By such means British writing and European works in general fostered the sense of a gulf between the consciousness of a character and whatever at any moment he is conscious of.

But Gertrude Stein and other American writers saw the personality itself as a mode of being-in-the-world. It was an existential pattern, not a cause of actions but a more or less complex rhythm of the actions themselves. This fact meant that in American writing there was an absence of reflection (itself an inward form of action) and of character-description; a lack of stress upon the sheer 'style' of the personage. The fictional character was what he did and was little else. At the same time scenes and objects in the world around that character were depicted clearly and immediately, just as they struck the eye of the observer. These were, without prior or unnecessary knowledge, what they seemed to be in a narrative instant.

Thus consciousness itself was confined to a series of objects and events, so that the reader properly gained an impression that a character and his world were in harmony with each other. For consciousness does not resemble a searchlight shining upon things but is simply the momentarily illuminated qualities of the things themselves. It is a general term for a multiplicity of happenings rather than a specific and theoretically separable faculty.

Such insights eventually worked their way to Europe so that by the late thirties Jean-Paul Sartre, for example, was reckoning John Dos Passos far above the reflective Marcel Proust and utilizing this new awareness in the growth of his philosophical notions.[22] But the entire movement towards re-integrating man with his world had started in Europe, especially in the works of French artists. Gertrude Stein saw some of the possibilities for literature, as Virginia Woolf saw them when, in 1910, she attended the first post-impressionist exhibition in London. So far as Virginia Woolf was concerned that exhibition announced an actual change in human character, a change which literature must set about recording.[23] However, it is important for us to note a distinction between the views of these two women rather than their common recognition of the significance for writers of French paintings. Virginia Woolf had an artist's sense of shape and design, while Gertrude Stein was unprofessionally a scientific psychologist, interested in words as instruments of mind and character. Virginia Woolf was scientifically and philosophically weak and the range of her acute regard was small. In her youth she had been overwhelmingly impressed by the contrast between her rational father, Sir Leslie Stephen, and her lovingly non-rational mother, Lady Julia Stephen. For her so much fell into place if these Victorian parents were viewed as specific representatives of everlasting types, or indeed of universal principles. She was angrily impatient over the patriarchal falsehoods she detected in writers of the older generation, in Shaw and Wells especially. Such writers overlooked precisely those spheres of human nature that she was well qualified to irradiate. And was not Freud himself (whose works were first published in English by Virginia Woolf's Hogarth Press) assuring her that after puberty girls naturally – not culturally – grew in a different direction from boys?

On the other hand Gertrude Stein concentrated upon what she observed in the people she met. She was a true empiricist, taking it for granted that culture represents wishes, hopes and fears rather than unassailable facts. And what she saw were individuals distinguished from one another fundamentally, but susceptible to arrangement in classes of personality-types. Either she observed no evidence of a generalized maleness or femaleness absolutely dictating culture patterns or was not impressed by what little evidence she saw. It seems likely that she would have agreed with the following remarks of the anthropologist, Margaret Mead:

> We may go up the scale from simple physical differences through complementary definitions that overstress the role of sex difference and extend it inappropriately to other aspects of life, to stereotypes of such complex activities as those involved in the formal use of the intellect, in the arts, in government, and in religion.[24]

It is now necessary to turn our attention to the literature of the last thirty years or so, asking, of women's writings in particular, how far such 'inappropriate' stereotypes have been discarded. For women's liberationists broadly speaking fall into two camps, the first assuming with Virginia Woolf that the great thing is to emphasize and exalt the 'woman's vision', the second believing, on the contrary, that the way ahead must surpass that ancient and almost magical category.

7 Creative Evolution

When women started to write for publication in the eighteenth century they were obliged to see themselves as somewhat freakish, certainly audacious. They enlisted in an age-old male profession and felt it necessary to justify their temerity. They wrote to improve conduct and manners, to spread abroad those refinements which it was part of the function of their sex to foster in the family. The woman's expressed vision at that time was in some degree a corrective to the man's, and it may well be a mistake to imagine a secret vision lurking behind the published words. These were not modern women without a modern woman's opportunities, since otherwise their lives would have been intolerable. We should not readily postulate a disturbing gulf between their inner thoughts and their utterances.

Whenever cracks are widening into such a gulf a few people strive to build across it with words or other artistic means. For example, at the end of the eighteenth century Mary Wollstonecraft's *Vindication of the Rights of Women* was not, in one sense, a hugely belated argument but a timely and prophetic recognition in the wake of the French Revolution. It helped to intensify a gathering sense of injustice and to change both the image and the reality of womanhood. For most of the nineteenth century many (but not quite all) women writers set to work with a strong sense of their femininity pressing upon them, while male authors, whatever the scope of their problems, naturally took their manhood – its obligations, its privileges and its very nature – for granted. Manhood was not a question until some writers towards the end of the century, Ibsen outstandingly, sought to raise women to a lordly, pioneering level. In the following generation, roughly from 1910 to 1930, Lawrence and Virginia Woolf in particular conducted a reaction, each claiming in a different way that new womanhood was a falsity, or more precisely that certain psychological differences between men and women lay beyond the sway of culture. Manhood also had now to be defined, or at least reaffirmed, especially since the rise of industry and technology seemed to be throwing men into confusion or robbing them of their initiative. Lawrence therefore argued that men, whatever their shortcomings, were meant by nature to be the explorers. This was not, however, purely a literary reaction in the narrow sense, for it was aided by, among others, the anthropologist, James Fraser (or by interpretations of his *The Golden Bough*) and by the early psycho-analysts. These individuals were confident that inescapable distinctions of a more than biological kind separated men from women.

But then the matter settled for a while so that women beginning to write in the 1930s and 40s regarded themselves simply as authors confronting the social scene. An interesting general feature of those notable women who entered the world of letters in this period is their lack at that time of expressed feminist concern. I am thinking chiefly, though not exclusively, of Simone de Beauvoir, Nathalie Sarraute, Mary McCarthy and Carson McCullers. In the first of these authors the concern lay dormant throughout the urgencies of the war and issued with immense vigour in *The Second Sex* (1949). This is a generous and fair-minded book, shot through with Sartre's type of existentialism and borrowings from Marx. As part of her conclusion Simone de Beauvoir looks to the future in the following way :

> On the contrary, when we abolish the slavery of half of humanity, together with the whole-system of hypocrisy that it implies, then the 'division' of humanity will reveal its genuine significance and the human couple will find its true form.[1]

It is taken for granted here that the present forms of the division of humanity are not inevitable, that human beings are all warped by circumstances and the warping of women is a special category of the general deformation. What we find in culture, ancient and modern, is never the 'true' woman, for she (like the 'true' man) will not be realized until all impediments are cleared away.

In this manner *The Second Sex* takes the opposite view from many feminist works, notably from Virginia Woolf's *A Room of One's Own*. To Virginia Woolf the feminine mind was eternal and fundamentally constant, but hitherto unexpressed. A modern woman had the chance to clear away the debris of the ages, allowing that mind to find its own structures and words. Believing this, Virginia Woolf could also believe that the Elizabethan age might well have harboured a woman of Shakespeare's degree of talent but not his chances. She seems to have regarded talent as a quality or force independent of circumstances for its existence, though obviously not for its fruitful exercise. She thought that her own mind in its essential patterns resembled the minds of countless women of the past and doubtless of the future. To Simone de Beauvoir, on the contrary, the feminine mind may eventually be not much different from the masculine, and both are as yet entangled with many alienating circumstances. The great thing is for men and women to advance together overcoming obstacles. But one giant obstacle is just that notion of the eternal feminine taken over by Virginia Woolf from centuries of enslavement.

As it happens the eternal feminine is not even seriously implied in the best women's writing since the 1940s (though notions of roughly that sort are still asserted in fiction plainly designed for women readers). Indeed personalities in a wide variety of fiction are less liable than of old to be presented as fixed entities moving through changing scenes, but rather as ill-defined organisms pulsating to the world around them. Obviously the character has certain habits of thought, goals, recurring images, a remembered past and so on : she is herself and no one else, but that self is an interplay with present circumstances, not an essential and theoretically independent set of facts. At one extreme a man or woman in a spy thriller may be a little more than a tiny group of physical traits and a mind fuctionally engaged with a succession of hazards or pleasures. At the other extreme in seriously-intended fiction it is often no doubt the mind that matters, but here the 'mind' means a number of internal activities connected, phase by phase, according to mood and exigency and having naturally a certain style but no essential explanation. Let us approach an illustration of this by considering first not a story but a paragraph from Carson McCullers's autobiographical article, 'How I Began to Write'.

By that winter the family rooms, the whole town, seemed to pinch and cramp my adolescent heart. I longed for wanderings. I longed especially for New York. The firelight on the walnut doors would sadden me, and the tedious sound of the old swan clock. I dreamed of the distant city of skyscrapers and snow, and New York was the happy mis en scène of that first novel I wrote when I was fifteen years old. The details of the book were clear : ticket collectors on the subway, New York front yards – but by that time it did not matter, for already I had begun another journey. That was the year of Dostoevski, Chekov and Tolstoy – and there were intimations of an unsuspected region equidistant from New York. Old Russia and our Georgia rooms, the marvelous solitary region of simple stories and the inward mind.[2]

This is a record of part of the year 1932 in which Carson McCullers decided to become a writer, rather than a musician as she had previously supposed. It is also, no doubt, an indication of her fifteen-year-old character, since she and the yearnings she records were for all important purposes fused. And this is how she presents some of the characters in her fiction. We should note also that in Carson McCullers's account there is no sense of the legislative capacity of literature but only of its beauty. Dostoevsky and Tolstoy, possibly Chekov as well, did seek to affect real life, though so far as Carson McCullers was adolescently concerned they made engrossing works of art, each complete in itself yet belonging to her 'marvelous solitary region'. She was drawn to that region but not at this or any stage of her career did she wish to promote a doctrine.

Nevertheless, she grew convinced that if ever writers in the American South passed beyond their 'naivete' (as she called it) and became a sort of philosophers, their work would be better. 'If and when', she wrote, 'this group of writers is able to assume a philosophical responsibility, the whole tone and structure of their work will be enriched, and Southern writing will enter a more complete and vigorous stage in its evolution.'[3]

It seems, then, that Carson McCullers regarded her own writings as belonging to an early, innocent stage when all a Southern writer could honestly do was make up stories based upon the life around her, without seeking overmuch to guide the reader's moral feelings. Her stories and novels follow this prescription so extraordinarily well that we might wonder if she made it up to suit solely her own temperament. But this is not so, for when we turn again to other writers of the South whom she mentions – Ellen Glasgow, Erskine Caldwell and William Faulkner – it is clear that she is right. These others are not so 'naive' as she (that is, so purely observant), since they more conspicuously impose their idiosyncracies upon the material, but their moral preferences are unclear, if not chaotic. Carson McCullers had the wit to realize and to profit from this same lack of 'philosophical responsibility'.

The values in her works are buried, waiting to be brought to the surface by future writers. We can say the same of only a few works in Western literature. Her moral neutrality is not at all like Tolstoy's, a neutrality of manner masking Biblical severities. No one is blamed for the malice and frustration in *The Ballad of the Sad Café*. So it is throughout *Reflections in a Golden Eye*, a novel whose plot and characters seem to cry out for the usual awarding of ethical marks. Private Williams is a strange, self-contained creature rather than a fully-conscious man; Leonora Pendleton is a heartless fool, her husband a corrupt, thieving homosexual with a 'sad penchant for becoming enamoured of his wife's lovers',[4] and Major Langdon a childish hedonist. Neither the events leading up to the shooting of Private Williams nor the motives of the characters are in the ordinary sense explained.

In a similar way (though the technique is more dramatic) *The Member of the Wedding* is a record of twelve-year-old Frankie's feelings and elementary doings over an August week-end when 'she belonged to no club and was a member of nothing in the world'.[5] There is no anger or critical comment from the author when, for instance, Berenice, the negro cook, launches into an exposition of negro feelings of entrapment, of being too rigidly a member of a class. 'Everybody', says Berenice, 'is caught one way or another. But they done drawn completely extra bounds around all colored people.'[6] Since Frankie is puzzled by existence itself and particularly by the ways in which people gain some assurance and sense of identity from the groups to which they belong, these remarks illustrate rather than resolve her problem. And to the author herself the novel must have been an artistically rounded examination of certain features of social life which she still, in the 1940s, could not philosophically explain.

As we have seen, Carson McCullers justified this central feature of her work by reference to the present stage of Southern development. Nevertheless she grasped that stage more clearly than her regional contemporaries or predecessors, so that it is chiefly in her writings that it comes to light. But is there more to the matter than that, another aspect that Carson McCullers never discussed, at any rate publicly? I mean that as a woman brought up in Georgia she felt freer than a man of that state to receive impressions of the muddled social scene: there was, perhaps, less duty laid upon her to be something of a lawgiver as well. Of course this clear vision, uncluttered by false or premature ethical judgements, was hers alone, not the property of any and every Georgia woman, but surely the concrete womanly situations of her youth were propitious. She was raised in an easy-going home where her mother, the main influence, assured her (following certain ante-natal oracles) that she would one day be famous.[7] She was caused to grasp her uniqueness, though she was also a normally sociable child. She was firmly in her environment yet not quite of it, somewhat detached and given to fantasy. What confronted the young Carson McCullers (then Lula Carson Smith) was evidently a medley of people and events uncoordinated by fixed or time-honoured principles. The customs seemed arbitrary and borrowed, not closely reflecting the ways in which people lived or desired to live. And as a woman she felt no pressing need to alter this state of affairs. Consequently she wrote innocently, as it were, observing the facts but leaving it to others coming after her to fashion a suitable and to some extent an indigenous code.

However, an interesting point is that Carson McCullers's refusal or inability to preach, though it was related by her to her Georgian milieu, is shared in some degree by other latter-day women writers, some of whom were given in childhood a subtle, comprehensive and authoritative moral scheme. A clear example among American authors is Mary McCarthy whose Roman Catholic boarding-school in Seattle seems to have been as strict and doctrinally all-embracing as that most famous of Catholic schools in literature, James Joyce's Clongowes Wood College. The young Joyce decided not to serve God, but the young Mary McCarthy came to the conclusion that she could not share the Christian faith. The great difference is that Joyce's works retain a sort of priestly authority : everything in them is marvellously interwoven into a grand, indeed a catholic scheme. At the other extreme Mary McCarthy seems to accept a world which is meaningless as a whole : to her ontological and ethical patterns are mildly comic rationalizations by individual characters.

She tells us in *Memories of a Catholic Girlhood* of the time at Forest Ridge Convent when she lost her faith.[8] More precisely, she elected to lose it, hedging her bets in case a public display became too embarrassing. (She was only twelve-years-old.) When the time came she stayed in her pew during the Communion service and in consequence was interviewed by a certain Father Dennis. In the course of the interview her arguments grew clearer and stronger (in fact some of them came to her as she went along) so that in the end she had finally and rationally lost her faith. A little later she found it best for the sake of a quiet life to pretend that her beliefs had returned. It seems from this autobiographical work that in childhood Mary McCarthy already had little use for systems of thought. And of course a clear feature of her adult fiction is the same open-eyed stance. She apparently needs no more than her quick, clear, iconoclastic reactions with which to receive and organize a flux of impressions. She meets the world as if she had no urge to make a scheme, except of a purely narrative or aesthetic nature.

The Group, for instance, is a pure though elaborate story (or a realistically interwoven collection of stories) guided by no object other than truth to life as it might well have been for ex-Vassar girls in New York in the thirties. The novel is remarkably 'pointless', since nothing of note is accomplished, there is no heroine and not even, so far as one can discern, an implied set of values. The political movements of the day are placed on a par with domestic fads, love-affairs, entries into jobs, theatre-life, setting up apartments, and so on. No idea governs the novel and ideas within it are merely characteristic of the individuals uttering them.

> 'I'm burned out on politics,' said Norine. 'Since Munich. My passion's comparative religion. Society is finished if it can't find its way back to God. The problem for people like us is to rediscover faith. It's easy for the masses; they never lost it. But for the elite it's another story.'[9]

This is Norine Schmittlapp talking to the diffident Priss Crockett on a bench in Central Park. Norine has married a Jew and her current 'passion' plainly has something to do with her marriage. But other people's ideas have the same evanescent or rationalizing qualities. Of course Mary McCarthy is satirical, but after the manner of a Chaucer, not of a Swift. Everyone is worthy in her way, and each, however grand or clever, is a little absurd.

But by what criterion are they absurd? It is scarcely a moral criterion in the usual sense, but just the endless play of awareness. At the beginning, in 1933, Kay Strong is married to Harald Petersen at St George's Church, Stuyvesant Square: at the end, in 1940, she is buried at the same church, having killed herself by leaping from her window at the Vassar Club. In the meantime Kay and her friends go their separate but sporadically connected ways. Dottie Renfrew has her sexual initiation, Libbie MacAusland has small adventures in the world of publishing, Helena Davison is mixed up in a strike by hotel waiters, Priss Hartshorn experiences problems with her baby, Polly Andrews becomes a nurse. One of the group, the clever and beautiful Elinor Eastlake, goes off to Paris and we learn little more about her until the account of her return (inserted into the last chapter) with an aristocratic lesbian partner. The novel ends on a quiet note of triumph of women over men, as the Sapphic Elinor discomforts the pretentious and thrusting Harald Peterson.

Although *The Group* is overwhelmingly about young women it is in one key respect the reverse of what is sometimes called a 'woman's book'. That phrase, complimentary or patronizing, implies sentimental notions, while the manner of Mary McCarthy's novel is detached from the emotions of the characters and from the multitudinous daily matters in which they immerse themselves. But in a different and altogether more interesting sense it is emphatically a woman's book because of the author's refusal to impose an ethical framework upon her material. Mary McCarthy's novels generally, like those of Carson McCullers (so different in all other respects), are scarcely didactic or philosophical. Carson McCullers thought that ideas were not yet valid in the South, but it seems that to Mary McCarthy ideas illuminate little beyond the personalities (however sophisticated) of those who utter them.

Here the main issue of this final chapter should be brought into focus. For much of the book we have been chiefly concerned with male authors as 'lawgivers', and have deliberately neglected other aspects of their writings. In the present age, widely regarded in the West as a phase of moral upheaval, a man writes a novel or a play to advocate something or other. I do not maintain that advocacy is his sole intent or that its nature is unambiguous, but as a rule the reader can discern (when he is not plainly told) what sort of changes the author wishes to bring about. For the man is still a lawgiver in a muddled and discordant society : it is not his profession so much as his inescapable nature to assert his views. He sees himself contributing to history in a positive way, seizing strands of the present web and willing a new pattern. This remains true, I think, in the face of any amount of *rational* uncertainty and may include a fair degree of pessimism.

To follow his nature in this way the male author must obviously be selective beyond the demands of aesthetic selection and in that sense untruthful. What is not to his purpose is disregarded or at most carefully arranged in his fiction to give an impression of life's haphazardness. But of course the writer is pretty firmly in control. He knows before he writes, or discovers in the process of writing, what he wishes to maintain and as a rule blithely excludes countervailing possibilities. Sometimes indeed he may give almost equal weight to opposing views (Thomas Mann did this in the twenties and thirties; Saul Bellow has done it in more recent years), but at least they are clear-cut views and the result is not moral confusion. Then again, distinctly different attitudes might reign in different books, though each attitude is held in its day with full conviction.

On the other hand most women writers to-day will not assume this lawgiver's role. They wish instead to find out, to express their feelings or to record multiple, 'senseless' facts. 'A novel', they often seem to say, 'is about some aspects of life and who am I to make a didactic mould?' When, exceptionally in serious fiction, the woman offers laws, she does so with great care but also great *impersonal* confidence (Iris Murdoch), or has embraced and now unhesitatingly asserts an ancient, sanctified dispensation (Muriel Spark). In these noteworthy instances it is understood that the operations of the ethical rules are detected in ordinary society and are manifestations of the Law, beyond human contrivance. But to so many there seems to be no Law, no dispensation, and the woman writer feels it a monstrous conceit to make one from her own stand-point. She may be prepared to offer clear views in another context, say an article or a philosophical essay, but when she turns to her work of fiction the views are abandoned before the sheer flow of life. And this of course is a new situation, for women writers in the past have normally, not exceptionally, been preachers: Jane Austen's beliefs are more conspicuous than Thackeray's, George Eliot's far firmer than those of Meredith.

Partly for this reason it is not certain that the situation will last. Obviously there are those women authors who are now self-indulgently able to throw aside moral discrimination in favour of personal feelings; nevertheless there are many others who do not relish the present disorder but merely face it in a different spirit from a man's. Perhaps we are enduring a phase of fruitful disorder, a period of gestation during which some women are using the opportunity to think things out. They will not rush to judgement in the way of their male counterparts because so much has, honestly, to be taken into account.

We can do no more here than take a tiny number of examples. Among French writers consider Simone de Beauvoir as against Sartre. They are both philosophers, though he is vastly more the philosopher than she. When he writes fiction he supports and illustrates his ideas, in particular the ideas of *Being and Nothingness*. *La Nausée* was of course written before that major philosophical work and anticipates it in small part. The point is, however, that *La Nausée* is probably the only novel in Western literature that is a work both of literature and philosophy. The two are uniquely well fused. Then, the sequence of *Roads to Freedom* is a set of novels about France between 1938 and 1940 and a conspicuous existentialist statement. Characters are defined in terms of their 'projects'; they practise 'bad faith'; they confront 'contingency', and some aspire to change their free and mobile consciousnesses into thing-like structures. No one can have serious doubts about what Sartre is recommending.

On the other hand, Simone de Beauvoir's best work of fiction may well be *The Mandarins* in which her philosophy (which seems to be much the same as Sartre's) is all but submerged. This was done deliberately, as she tells us in *Force of Circumstance*.

> Nor is *The Mandarins,* in my opinion, a novel with a message. Such thesis-novels always impose a certain truth that eclipses all others and calls a halt to the perpetual dance of conflicting points of view; whereas I described certain ways of living after the war, without offering any solution to the problems that were troubling my main characters.[10]

From a reader's point of view it is true that *The Mandarins* has no message, although as we shall see, it is not absolutely the neutral work that is suggested here. Nevertheless it is not a thesis-novel such as Sartre's invariably are, or as men's works commonly manage to be. Furthermore, we know well that when Simone de Beauvoir writes non-fiction she is eager to express her own point of view. In her words reproduced above lies exactly the tendency we are ascribing to so many women writers, a conviction that in fiction solutions are offered at the expense of truth to life. It is as if women cannot now undertake to make fictional worlds which knowingly distort reality, even though they must obviously simplify it.

The Mandarins describes among other matters French intellectual conflicts from 1945 to 1947, or, to be more exact, it pushes into those years the sort of events that took place over a slightly longer period. It deals with the relations betwen two writers, Henri and Dubreuilh (who are usually and rather inexactly identified as Camus and Sartre), and their differing reactions to the news, then reaching Paris, of the existence of Russian labour camps. These two friends quarrel and then make up. At the same time the novel is concerned with Paula, a 'womanly' woman, Dubreuilh's psychiatrist wife, Anne, and the Dubreuilh's plain, promiscuous daughter, Nadine. An important element in the book is a love-affair between Anne and an American writer named Lewis Brogan, conducted largely in Chicago and modelled in some degree upon Simone de Beauvoir's friendship with Nelson Algren.

In other words we have here a picture of an exciting period in recent French history, the period when the grim but exhilarating days of the Resistance were replaced by confused attempts to make decisive changes in French politics. Thus it is in part a political novel, but we are given no idea where the author stands : in that respect it is certainly an objective account. To be precise, politics are woven into the daily lives of the characters, rather than allowed to dictate the actions after the manner of an Orwell or a Koestler. Then, Anne's love-affair is very important and so, for that matter, are Nadine's adventures and Henri's liaison with an actress called Josette. So the novel is really a considerable mixture of elements, yet nicely held together. As Simone de Beauvoir says, there are no solutions.

Nevertheless there are preferences at least one of which is pertinent to our theme. This is the clear superiority of Anne to Paula, and also to Anne's daughter, Nadine. Anne is a woman who, as Simone de Beauvoir might well put it, transcends her femininity. She is open to impressions, healthily variable. Further, she has a recurring sense of her own death, a complete eclipse, awaiting her, and most importantly, she never thinks of her womanhood as a grouping of traits beyond her own responsibility. Paula, on the other hand, sees herself entirely as a woman, which is to say that she assumes quite artificially (though in common fashion) certain roles, weaknesses and occasional strengths. Nadine stands somewhere between these two other women, unable to pose yet equally unable to make satisfactory personal choices. In the portraits of these three there is a sort of thesis, muted yet convincing.

The thesis is in favour of a degree of independence, not crabbed or deliberate but in accordance with nature. Anne loves Lewis Brogan without giving her whole life to him. From time to time she is afraid of losing him but cannot on that account alter her personality or abandon her projects. She will not live through Brogan, as though he were her window on the world. But Paula is and wishes always to be an accessory to Henri. She is constantly in a turmoil over the possibility of losing him and goes mad during the period of his affair with Josette. She would adopt whatever opinion he desired, favour any course, since all her views are provisional and expedient. Nadine, different again, follows independent ways, such as studying Chemistry at the Sorbonne and refusing to ally herself firmly with any man; but she is insecure, sulky, incomplete. These women exhibit three stages of womanhood : total dependence, self-willed independence, and a reasonable, 'masculine' degree of freedom. Despite the general impartiality of the novel this feature is an apt demonstration of certain of the author's views.

It should be stressed that in *The Mandarins* almost everything serves Simone de Beauvoir's purpose of showing behaviour in a particular, influential milieu just after the war. We learn very little of other matters; of places, appearances, prices, fashions and so on. In this way the manner of *The Mandarins* is the reverse of Mary McCarthy's manner in *The Group*. Mary McCarthy in her novel is deliberately, though no doubt congenially, 'womanish' (rigidly excluding her own views, emphasizing exterior detail), while Simone de Beauvoir simply confines her forthright opinions.

In modern fiction there are two striking features of women's writing. On the one hand there are those many novelists who relish both human feelings and random features of the outer world. On the other hand there are a few influential authors (Virginia Woolf, Gertrude Stein, Nathalie Sarraute) whose fictional structures are in some degree paradigmatic. Members of this second group pare away inessential detail, since they regard such detail as misleading or in a sense journalistic. Of course these two ways are directly opposed, yet they have in common a refusal to offer personal moral judgements. The first way treats opinions as largely idiosyncratic, while the second way goes further and tends to invalidate opinions altogether. Thus Nathalie Sarraute seems convinced that the entire spheres of culture and ethics are purely factitious: they are, as it were, 'political' spheres in which assertive people propose views, enlist supporters, alter fashions. Her works imply that the only way for a novelist to undermine these artificial realms is to strip away from fiction many of the usual elements of fiction. In the novel proper, as opposed to Nathalie Sarraute's anti-novels (a phrase coined by Sartre in his preface to *Portrait of a Man Unknown*),[11] characters are, we are made to feel, bogus, plots ludicrously untrue to life, teachings unacceptable. The ordinary novel is part of a cultural game or strategy which ignores the inner reality of any actual person and possibly helps to annihilate that reality.

In a fairly recent work of Nathalie Sarraute, *The Golden Fruits* (1963), an uncertain number of people or mere voices, discuss art in general and a new novel called 'The Golden Fruits' in particular. The animated remarks are sometimes supported by unexpressed thoughts but nowhere is there a single authentic observation. In this novel Nathalie Sarraute aims to show, through a sort of paradigm, how social movements of any kind rise and fall; how positions are adopted, attacked, defended and finally crumble. She satirizes this process as a meaningless sequence to which, never-theless, people give their lives. We are expected to conclude that ordinary novels merely contribute to such charades.

And so perhaps that is all fiction does. Plato thought along these lines and therefore wished to exclude poetry or creative writing of any consequence, from his Republic. But Nathalie Sarraute does not raise up anything resembling Plato's Ideas or Forms to offset the social chicaneries and the mere exterior facts of which she is so contemptuous. It seems, on the contrary, that the truth for her is completely inward and individualistic: in fact there are as many truths as people. Her object is to reveal the falsity of ordinary art, thus presumably leaving us freer to 'be ourselves'.

It is interesting that women seem readier than men to detect the weaknesses in representational art and especially to discern the usual failings on the artist's part of egotism and fantasy-projection. They are quick to see and sometimes to resent what the author is trying to do to them. Moreover, women distrust clear sequences of cause and effect, preferring actually to preserve a sense of the obscure and unmanageable. A contemporary woman writer who affirms that, in life, events and personalities are dark, uncertain or rationally meaningless, is Iris Murdoch. To her a work of art should suggest the inexplicability of life, howevr lucid and well-organized the work itself might be. Literature should not offer us formulae, except the one formula of moral striving: it should not seek to *explain* as science explains.

Iris Murdoch's views are set out in various articles and books, especially 'Against Dryness' ('Encounter', January 1961) and *The Sovereignty of Good* (1970). To summarize and merge some of these ideas we might begin by saying that she finds most literature to be what Plato dismissively said it was. 'Almost all art', she writes, 'is a form of fantasy-consolation and few artists achieve a vision of the real.'[12] But there are a few remarkable and praiseworthy works which show us reality and *thus* (rather than by offering precepts) encourage decent behaviour. For truth, goodness and beauty are all somehow connected, are all perhaps ultimately one transcendent quality. Lesser art, that is nine tenths of art, sets out to console and does so presumably even when its tenor is thoroughly miserable. For even unrelieved misery, a shape of profound grey, is still an obvious harmony and in that sense may be consolatory as compared with the formlessness of life.

Iris Murdoch takes it for granted that while literature is, in all its forms, some sort of comment upon life, this does not necessarily exalt the techniques of realism. For example, it is no good remarking that Iris Murdoch's own novels are not invariably realistic in the narrow sense, since she nevertheless tries to use her imagination to illuminate the real world. Imagination, she believes, has nothing to do with fantasy which, however grim its constituent details in a particular case, is a mode of evasion. On the other hand, the role of imagination proper is to irradiate what is plainly there, before one's eyes. The article, 'Against Dryness', is an attack upon what Iris Murdoch calls 'crystalline' works of fiction, meaning such neatly organized and 'transparent' works as Camus' *The Outsider* and Golding's *Lord of the Flies* (though these examples are mine). She argues that crystalline stories combine aesthetic and didactic clarity but do so by misrepresenting the issues involved. They lack 'imagination' in the healthy sense of that word. For when an author is using his imagination he positively prefers reality to daydreams and this means that he must present people as 'opaque'. We cannot see into other people but must forever make provisional and corrigible judgements of them. This moral procedure is also a realistic way of getting to know a person (an endless activity) through minute, changing and selfless observations.

Iris Murdoch's fiction is consistent with these ideas. From the beginning in *Under the Net* (1954) she has presented heroes and heroines (chiefly the former) whose freedom is based upon mis-readings of actuality. More precisely, there is nothing that absolutely checks their misguided ways of life but they are happier and more truly themselves when they conform to the demands which circumstances, including their own past actions, make upon them. It is necessary to abandon a theory, a notion, an unexamined image of his life which, though it is contradicted by the facts, the hero has entertained for a spell. The net of the title of that first novel refers to an image used by Wittgenstein to describe our tendency to see not reality itself but merely a structure of concepts with which we cover and disfigure reality.[13] In other words, Iris Murdoch was already in the fifties recommending that we look, so far as possible, beneath the net.

In Iris Murdoch's novels the device of casting a net of ideas or fantasy-images over the bare facts is constantly employed by a series of erring figures, but this device brings them misery, not happiness. Illusions are intended to stave off misery but they in fact produce it. Iris Murdoch once wrote that 'Love, and so art and morals, is the discovery of reality'.[14] Everything of value depends upon an efficient perception of reality so that this may lead to love, art, morals and, subjectively, to a sort of bubbling joy or euphoria. At all events it is calculated to lessen pain, Iris Murdoch's heroes and heroines move some of the way towards a discovery of this psychological fact. They discover, in other words, that if they are free, it is only to choose either to make errors of perception and be relatively miserable or to see rightly and be relatively happy – an absurd kind of choice. It is usually clear by the end of a novel what is the correct set of perceptions and indeed the whole novel has led up to this insight. Thus, Jake Donaghue, the narrator-hero of *Under the Net* realizes that he is cut out to be a serious writer and that this role will make him happier than his present 'picaresque' (and 'nervy') way of life; Bill Mor of *The Sandcastle* finds that he should stay with his wife and children rather than run off with a beautiful woman artist; Martin Lynch-Gibbon in *A Severed Head* finally takes up with the severely honest Honor Klein who is, because of her uncompromising nature, suited to some quality at the heart of Martin's own being. These are, of course, early and well-known novels of Iris Murdoch: in more recent years she has followed similar patterns of thought but with greater subtlety. The endings of her novels are no longer quite so obviously 'promising', so cleanly revelatory, but at most suggest difficulties and struggles in the future. For instance, the last chapter of *A Word Child* (1975) leaves the clever hero, Hilary Burde, possibly going to marry his rather simple and childish girl friend, Thomasina, and at the same time he is condemned to picture for the rest of his life two women whose deaths he has been responsible for. In one notable instance, *The Black Prince* (1974), the hero is ignobly hanged for murder and his actual superiority to other characters has all along been hard to define, though discernible.

In such ways as I have roughly indicated Iris Murdoch, unlike the other women whom we have considered, is a moralistic writer. But her moralizing is not a matter of advocating a particular style of life; it is not a romantic preference, still less a satiric attack. She would claim, I am sure, that she is not attempting to impose a set of beliefs which happen to suit her, but merely stressing the urgent and paramount presence of the real world. She praises the 'humble man' who 'because he sees himself as nothing, can see other things as they are'.[15] Insofar as this effort towards self-effacement and reality-perception is part of Iris Murdoch's own motive for writing, it is quite different from the common masculine motive. Her notion of the humble man (who is not of course diffident or meek) is rather like Keats's notion of the man of negative capability. Although she is here concerned with the moral life while Keats was discussing poetry, the two ideas have in common selfless absorption into the real world. As a matter of fact few writers possess much negative capability, or they exercise it for infrequent patches of their writings. For the most part they assert themselves rather than occupy, as Shakespeare effortlessly occupied, the minds of other characters, even the mind of a detestable but lovingly observed villain or fool.

In these ways Iris Murdoch's moralizing rests neither upon personal preferences nor upon traditional canons but upon a prior respect for the world around her: the truth is visible and may be seen by anyone who gives up daydreaming and self-concern. The world is potentially good. To Muriel Spark, on the other hand, the world is a sphere to which we have been banished, a sphere of temptation, vanity and sin. Obviously the writing of fiction can be and usually is a worldly activity in the bad sense, but at their best stories are parabolic. 'Fiction to me', Muriel Spark once wrote, 'is a kind of parable. You have got to make up your mind it's not true. Some kind of truth emerges from it, but it's not fact.'[16] The result of this attitude is that Muriel Spark does not attempt to disguise artifice but rather delights in it. She proclaims, as it were, many events in her novels to be improbable or even absurd, though accurate in their teaching. She takes the defining characteristics of a milieu – say the preoccupations of the elderly people in *Memento Mori* troubled by telephone messages warning them of the approach of death – and causes these to fill the world of the novel. This of course is the common way of satire and it is unashamedly unrealistic. Each of her settings displays, in any event, a concentration of traits which will be found in more diluted or superficially different forms elsewhere. Thus the Peckham of *The Ballad of Peckham Rye* is a defined area where the people merely have their own ways of following the universal practice of evading hard truths.

The important point for us about Muriel Spark is that, unlike Iris Murdoch, she regards the contingent facts of life as insignificant in themselves, though they may be illuminated by truths (ultimately one perfect Truth) which originate elsewhere, beyond the visible universe. Meaning is neither within us nor a property of the things we perceive, but is, as it were, a light shining through us and falling, if we have eyes to see it, upon the objects of our gaze. Those people who prefer their own wills (say Jean Brodie imposing fascism upon her Edinburgh pupils) are wrong, not, as in Iris Murdoch, because they overlook the visible facts but because they are spiritually askew, out of touch with God. Thus Lise in *The Driver's Seat* gives herself up excessively to the external world of office work, department-store shopping, slick encapsulated holidays to the extent that she wills her own death at the hands of a reluctant maniac. However, the important point is that Muriel Spark offers us the zestful though orthodox interpretation of an age-old code : she subverts contemporary society by showing the contemporary style of perennial human flaws.

In our consideration of a small number of latterday women writers there are some features we have signally failed to discover. (We would discover them elsewhere, but as evidence of old-fashioned rather than avant-garde attitudes, whatever the audacity of the author.) First and foremost, we have not found that marked difference from the ways of men, that 'woman's vision' which Virginia Woolf thought was eternal though hitherto pent up. At the most we have come across an admiration for humility (in the best sense) and a preference for a sovereign moral order. It is true that these factors run counter to the egotism which Virginia Woolf tended, in her fiction even more than in her essays, to ascribe to men. All we can honestly say is that women writers seem not to be Luciferian: they may be irreverent towards the Law but do not directly challenge it.

Secondly, the characters of women invented by these women writers do not demonstrate vital personality-differences from men. In the fictional characters there is no uncriticized feminine dependency upon men as a mode of being, no recent equivalents to Virginia Woolf's Mrs Ramsay. On the contrary there is a strong sense that women are or should be primarily individuals in certain social situations and that their characters consist of moment-by-moment transactions with those situations. It seems to be accepted that nature does not assign to women certain important psychological characteristics.

Yet such differentiating characteristics were taken pretty well for granted by some influential thinkers at the turn of the century and are still widely accepted in the sphere of literary criticism. As a pithy example consider Nietzsche's Zarathustra who assures a little old woman that 'Everything about women is a riddle, and everything about woman has one solution: it is called pregnancy.' In a nutshell this is the kind of thinking that we also find in the works of Freud and Jung, and that from the latter especially has spread into literary studies. For Nietzsche presumably meant that a woman is *en rapport* with nature, able above all her other possibilities to gestate and give birth, so that she lives essentially apart from everything purely cultural. She recognizes male 'nonsense' (moral philosophy, for example) for what it is, because she is a basic provider of the human race. Freud thought that boys and girls were much the same sort of creatures up to puberty and then, since pregnancy is an ever-present possibility for the woman and her predestined function, inevitably diverged. Jung of course went much further than this, for differences of male and female inform his entire system. The Jungian archetypes of the unconscious are plainly divided along these lines: the 'anima' as against the 'animus', the 'Wise Old Man' as against the 'Magna Mater'. Jung often speaks of 'masculine' and 'feminine' traits (the man is normally strong, the woman normally sentimental, and so on), and the individual who has grown fully through all the stages of the integration of his personality has brought these opposed elements into a state of fruitful harmony. But are there not grounds for saying that a well-developed person is sceptical about these distinctions anyway, since he or she sees them contradicted at every turn in social life? To recall the chief paragon in literary history, the so-called 'androgyny' of Shakespeare is simply a misleading description of his unrivalled powers of observation and healthy self-effacement. He didn't think 'like a man' but as a human being.

Part of the present problem is that Jungian or other ideas by which we attempt to accommodate within the psyche the supposed wisdom of the ages are very attractive to some literary people. By adopting such notions we are able to be at once non-scientific and explanatory. We are also able to regard literature as an expression of minds alone, of relatively fixed entities which are not radically affected by the social conditions which they encounter. It is easier to think of literature as a body of works very loosely connected with society and history, a vast field of study following its own laws which the expert (and only the expert) has mastered. That this belief is partly true – and is strategically useful – should not cause us to underestimate either the mimetic or the socially dynamic functions of literature. One change that is needed now in literary criticism is for people to treat *historically* the faded myths surrounding sex-distinctions, and in literature itself for all women writers to realize that they too are forming the future, for good or ill, in accordance with their own designs.

Notes and References

The place of publication is London unless otherwise stated.

CHAPTER 1 : CREATIVE MYTHS

1. See Raymond B. Cattell, *The Scientific Analysis of Personality* (Harmondsworth: Penguin, 1965) p. 14.
2. See E. M. W. Tillyard's *The English Epic, and its Background* (Chatto & Windus, 1954) ch. 2.
3. W. H. Auden, 'The Shield of Achilles', *Collected Poems*, Edward Mendelson (ed.) (Faber & Faber, 1976) p. 454.
4. Homer, *Iliad*, bk 24. The translation is by E. V. Rieu in the Penguin Classics edition, 1950.
5. For an exposition of these theories see Sven Armens, *Archetypes of the Family in Literature* (Seattle and London: University of Washington Press, 1966). See also Erich Newmann, *The Great Mother* (New York: Pantheon, 1955).
6. Gilbert Murray, *Aeschylus* (Oxford University Press, 1940) pp. 17f.
7. Herbert Marder, *Feminism and Art: a study of Virginia Woolf* (University of Chicago Press, 1968) p. 105.
8. Sven Armens, *Archetypes of the Family in Literature*, pp. 105f.
9. Karl Vossler, *Mediaeval Culture*, vol. 1 (New York: Frederick Ungar, 1958) p. 299. (Vossler quotes from an article by G. Gröber in the *Deutsche Revue* of December 1902).
10. Charles Williams, *The Figure of Beatrice* (Faber & Faber, 1943) p. 15.
11. Christopher Gillie, *Character in English Literature* (Chatto & Windus, 1967) p. 19.
12. Charles Muscatine, *Chaucer and the French Tradition* (Berkeley: University of California Press, 1957) p. 247.
13. C. S. Lewis, *The Allegory of Love* (Oxford University Press, 1936) pp. 185ff.
14. Chaucer, *Troilus and Criseyde*, bk II, line 450.
15. Juliet Dusinberre, *Shakespeare and the Nature of Women* (Macmillan, 1975).
16. See Gordon S. Haight, *George Eliot* (Oxford University Press, 1968) p. 146.

CHAPTER 2: THE EIGHTEENTH CENTURY

1. See James T. Boulton (ed.), *Daniel Defoe* (Batsford, 1965) p. 32. Compare Dr Johnson's remark: 'Men know that women are an over-match for them, and therefore they choose the weakest or most ignorant. If they did not think so, they could never be afraid of women knowing as much as themselves.' R. W. Chapman (ed.), *Johnson's Journey to the Western Islands of Scotland and Boswell's Journal of a Tour to the Hebrides with Samuel Johnson LLD* (Oxford University Press, 1970) p. 311.
2. Daniel Defoe, *Jure Divino,* bk V.
3. Ibid., bk IV.
4. Ian Watt, *The Rise of the Novel* (Chatto & Windus, 1957) p. 115.
5. Ibid., p. 113.
6. Daniel Defoe, *Moll Flanders* (Oxford University Press, 1971) pp. 273f.
7. Daniel Defoe, *Roxana, the Fortunate Mistress* (Oxford University Press, 1964) pp. 147f.
8. Samuel Richardson, *Sir Charles Grandison* (Oxford University Press, 1972) vol. 1, letter 37, p. 189.
9. Quoted in Morris Golden, *Richardson's Characters* (Ann Arbor: University of Michigan Press, 1963) p. 3.
10. Quoted in T. Duncan Eaves and Ben D. Kimpel, *Samuel Richardson: A Biography* (Oxford University Press, 1971) p. 200.
11. Ibid., pp. 611f.
12. Ibid., p. 205.
13. Samuel Richardson, *Pamela* (Everyman Edition, J. M. Dent, 1974) vol. 1, letter 8.
14. Samuel Richardson, *Clarissa* (Everyman Edition, J. M. Dent, 1968) vol. 2, letter 37, p. 134. Richardson's attitude to power is convincingly analysed in Morris Golden's *Richardson's Characters.*
15. Ibid., vol. 1, letter 5, pp. 22f.
16. See Parts 1 and 2 in particular of Leslie Fiedler, *Love and Death in the American Novel* (New York: Criterion Books, 1960).
17. Henry Fielding, *The History of Tom Jones* (Everyman Edition, J. M. Dent, 1962) bk XVIII, ch. 12.
18. Henry Fielding, *Amelia* (Everyman Edition, J. M. Dent, 1959) bk IX, ch. 5.
19. Henry Fielding, *The History of Tom Jones,* bk IV, ch. 6.

CHAPTER 3: THE EARLY NINETEENTH CENTURY

1. J. G. Tait (ed.), *Journal of Walter Scott,* 1825–6, (Edinburgh, 1939) p. 135 (entry of 14 March 1826). Judith O'Neill (ed.), *Critics on Jane Austen* (Allen & Unwin, 1970) p. 3.
2. The *Edinburgh Review,* vol 76 (January, 1843). O'Neill, *Critics on Jane Austen,* p. 6.
3. *Blackwood's Edinburgh Magazine,* vol. 86 (July, 1859). O'Neill, *Critics on Jane Austen,* p. 8.

4. D. H. Lawrence, 'A Propos of *Lady Chatterley's Lover', Lady Chatterley's Lover* (Heineman, 1961) p. 40.
5. See T. J. Wise and J. A. Symington (ed.), *The Brontës: Their Friendships, Lives and Correspondence* (Blackwell, The Shakespeare Head Brontë, 1932) p. 99.
6. O'Neill, *Critics on Jane Austen,* p. 3.
7. See Harry Levin, *The Power of Blackness* (New York: Alfred A. Knopf, 1958) p. 23.
8. Sigmund Freud, 'Beyond the Pleasure Principle' tr. James Strachey (Hogarth Press, 1960) p. 86. First published in German, 1920.
9. Simone de Beauvoir, *The Second Sex* tr. H. M. Parshley (Harmondsworth: Penguin, 1972) p. 211. (*Le Deuxième Sexe,* first published, 1949).
10. Aristotle in the *Poetics* (section 3 in many editions) claimed that the personages of tragedy are above the common run, while those of comedy are below it, in the sense that we are impressed by tragic figures whatever their faults.
11. Honoré de Balzac, *Cousin Bette* tr. Marion Ayton Crawford (Harmondsworth: Pengin, 1965) pp. 156f.
12. H. Taine, *Essais de critique et d'histoire* (Paris, 1858) p. 96.
13. Balzac, *Cousin Bette,* pp. 38f.
14. W. M. Thackeray, *Vanity Fair,* Kathleen and Geoffrey Tillotson (ed.) (Methuen, 1963) ch. 57.
15. Virginia Woolf, *A Room of One's Own* (Harmondsworth: Penguin, 1945). First edition, Hogarth Press, 1928.
16. Elizabeth Gaskell, *The Life of Charlotte Brontë* (Penguin edition, ed. Alan Shelston, 1975) vol. II, ch. 1, p. 307. First edition, 1857.
17. Charlotte Brontë, *Jane Eyre* (Zodiac Press, Chatto & Windus, 1958) ch. 9.
18. Virginia Woolf, *A Room of One's Own,* pp. 115f.
19. See Chapter 6 of this book.
20. Margaret Lane, *The Brontë Story* (Heinemann, 1953) p. 109.
21. Walter Allen, *The English Novel* (Phoenix House, 1954) p. 188.
22. Emily Brontë, *Wuthering Heights* (Oxford University Press, 1976) ch. 9.
23. Some contemporary reviews of Hawthorne's works are collected in J. Donald Crowley (ed.), *Hawthorne: The Critical Heritage* (Routledge & Kegan Paul, 1970). See especially an article in *Brownson's Quarterly Review* October 1850 and an article in the 'Church Review' of January, 1951.
24. Nathaniel Hawthorne, *The Scarlet Letter* (Everyman Edition, J. M. Dent, 1965) ch. 13.
25. Ibid, ch. 24, 'Conclusion'.

CHAPTER 4: THE LATER NINETEENTH CENTURY

1. The information here is readily accessible in the biographies of Flaubert. I have drawn mainly on Maurice Nadeau, *The Greatness of*

Flaubert, tr. Barbara Bray (The Alcove Press, 1972) and Enid Starkie, *Flaubert: The Making of the Master* (Weidenfeld & Nicholson, 1967).

2. See Maurice Nadeau, *The Greatness of Flaubert,* p. 45.
3. Jean-Paul Sartre, *Search for a Method,* tr. Hazel E. Barnes (New York: Vintage Books and Random Books, 1968) p. 142.
4. Translations are by Alan Russell for the 1950 Penguin edition of *Madame Bovary.*
5. Gustave Flaubert, *Madame Bovary,* tr. Alan Russell (Harmondsworth: Penguin, 1950) part III, ch. 5.
6. Quoted in Sartre, *Search for a Method,* p. 141.
7. George Eliot, *The Mill on the Floss* (The Zodiac Press, Chatto & Windus, 1951) bk fourth, ch. 3.
8. For details see especially Ruby V. Redinger, *George Eliot: The Emergent Self* (Bodley Head, 1975) ch. 2.
9. Ibid., p. 59.
10. Ibid., p. 470.
11. Gordon S. Haight (ed.), *The George Eliot Letters* (Oxford University Press, vol. V, no. 322).
12. George Eliot, *Middlemarch* (The Zodiac Press, Chatto & Windus, 1978) ch. 29.
13. For details of George Eliot's diffidence and Lewes's protectiveness see Gordon S. Haight, *George Eliot: A Biography* (Oxford University Press, 1968) pp. 368f.
14. George Eliot, *Middlemarch,* ch. I.
15. See Henri Troyat, *Tolstoy,* tr. Nancy Amphoux (W. H. Allen, 1968) p. 326 (first published in Paris, 1965).
16. Tatyana Tolstoy, *Tolstoy Remembered,* tr. from the French by Derek Coltman, int. by John Bayley (Michael Joseph, 1977) pp. 154f.
17. Quoted in Cynthia Asquith, *Married to Tolstoy* (Hutchinson, 1960) p. 86.
18. Tatyana Tolstoy, *Tolstoy Remembered,* p. 157.
19. Henri Troyat, *Tolstoy,* p. 369.
20. Tolstoy, *Anna Karenina,* tr. David Magarshack (New York: New American Library, 1961) part 2, ch. 7.
21. Ibid., part 4, ch. 4.
22. Ibid, part 3, ch. 17.
23. Ibid., part 3, ch, 21.
24. Ibid., part 8, ch. 11.
25. F. Nietzsche, *Twilight of the Idols* and *The Anti-Christ,* tr. R. J. Hollingdale (Harmondsworth: Penguin, 1968) p. 110.

CHAPTER 5 : NEW WOMEN

1. Turgenev, *On the Eve* (Penguin Classics Edition, 1950) tr. Gilbert Gardiner, ch. 6, p. 53.
2. Simone de Beauvoir, *The Second Sex,* pp. 381f.

3. Even Hedda Gabler, neurotically wilful Hedda, must be understood as 'saving her soul' when she shoots herself in preference to being blackmailed.
4. See especially Aldous Huxley, *The Perennial Philosophy* (Chatto & Windus, 1946).
5. Robert Gittings, *Young Thomas Hardy* (Heinemann, 1975) pp. 93ff.
6. Florence Emily Hardy, *The Life of Thomas Hardy* (Macmillan, 1962) p. 272.
7. Robert Gittings fairly disposes of this belief and of associated beliefs about Hardy's relationship with his cousin. Gittings, *Young Thomas Hardy*, pp. 92ff.
8. Thomas Hardy, *Jude the Obscure* int. Terry Eagleton (Macmillan, 1974) part 6, ch. III.
9. Ibid., part 3, ch. IV.
10. Ibid.
11. Ibid, part 4, ch. IV.
12. Ibid., part 6, ch. X.
13. The reference here is principally to 'Mind at the End of its Tether' the seventy-first chapter of *A Short History of the World,* revised edition (Harmondsworth: Penguin, 1946).
14. H. G. Wells, *An Experiment in Autobiography,* vol. 2 (Victor Gollancz and The Cresset Press, 1934) p. 470.
15. For relevant details about Bennett's marriage see Margaret Drabble, *Arnold Bennett* (Weidenfeld & Nicolson, 1974) ch. 7.
16. E. M. Forster, *Howards End* (ed.), O. Stallybrass (Abinger Edition, Arnold, 1973) ch. 2.
17. Ibid., ch. 9.
18. Lawrence's 'Study of Thomas Hardy' is most accessible in Edward D. Macdonald (ed.), *Phoenix* (Heinemann, 1936).

CHAPTER 6: VIRGINIA WOOLF AND HER CONTEMPORARIES

1. Virginia Woolf, *A Room of One's Own* (Harmondsworth: Penguin, 1945) p. 82. First edition, Hogarth Press, 1928.
2. Ibid., p. 37.
3. Ibid., p. 45.
4. H. D. F. Kitto, *The Greeks* (Harmondsworth: Penguin, 1951) p. 228.
5. Apart from references and implications in Virginia Woolf's fiction other comments are to be found especially in Virginia Woolf, *Three Guineas* (Hogarth Press, 1938), 'Aurora Leigh', *Collected Essays,* vol. 1, (Hogarth Press, 1966) and 'Women and Fiction', *Granite and Rainbow* (Hogarth Press, 1958).
6. Virginia Woolf, *A Room of One's Own,* p. 77.
7. Ibid., p. 79.
8. Virginia Woolf, *To the Lighthouse* (Hogarth Press, 1960) p. 164. First edition, Hogarth Press, 1927.
9. Not everyone, of course, interprets Lily Briscoe's 'vision' towards the end of *To the Lighthouse* in this way. For a fuller treatment of this

interpretation see K. M. May, 'The Symbol of "Painting" in Virginia Woolf's *To the Lighthouse'*, *A Review of English Literature,* April 1967.

10. Dorothy M. Richardson, *Pilgrimage,* vol. 1, int. Walter Allen (Dent, 1967). Foreword, p. 10.
11. Ibid.
12. Dorothy M. Richardson, *Pilgrimage,* vol. 4, *March Moonlight,* p. 657.
13. Foreword to Dorothy M. Richardson, *Pilgrimage,* p. 11.
14. Ibid., p. 9.
15. Ibid., p. 7.
16. C. K. Stead (ed.), *The Letters and Journals of Katherine Mansfield* (Allen Lane, 1977) pp. 97f (letter of 3 February 1918).
17. Ibid., p. 241 (journal entry of 24 November 1921).
18. Ibid., p. 240.
19. See Gertrude Stein's lecture 'What is English Literature' included in Patricia Meyerowitz (ed.), *Look at Me Now and Here I Am,* int. Elizabeth Sprigge (Harmondsworth: Penguin, 1971).
20. This seems to be the implication of Gertrude Stein's gloss upon 'A Rose is a rose is a rose is a rose' stated one day in 1935 to students at Chicago University. She remarked, 'Now you all have seen hundreds of poems about roses and you know in your bones that the rose is not there.' See James R. Mellow, *Charmed Circle* (Phaidon Press, 1974) p. 404.
21. The lectures chiefly consulted are 'Composition as Explanation', 'What is English Literature' and 'The Gradual Making of *The Making of Americans'*. All included in Patricia Meyerowitz (ed.), *Look at Me Now and Here I Am.*
22. For a full discussion of this point see Robert Denoon Cumming (ed.), *The Philosophy of Jean-Paul Sartre* (New York: Random House, 1965) pp. 3ff.
23. See Virginia Woolf, 'Mr Bennett and Mrs Brown', *Collected Essays,* vol. 1 (Hogarth Press, 1966) p. 320: 'In or about December, 1910 human character changed.'
24. Margaret Mead, *Male and Female* (Victor Gollancz, 1949) p. 373.

CHAPTER 7: CREATIVE EVOLUTION

1. Simone de Beauvoir, *The Second Sex,* p. 741.
2. Carson McCullers, 'How I Began to Write', in Margarita G. Smith (ed.), *The Mortgaged Heart* (Barrie & Jenkins, 1972) p. 251. Originally an article in *Mademoiselle,* September 1948.
3. Carson McCullers, 'The Russian Realists and Southern Literature', *The Mortgaged Heart,* p. 258. Originally an essay in *Decision,* July 1941.
4. Carson McCullers, *Reflections in a Golden Eye* (Cresset Press, 1957) ch. I, p. 16. First published 1942.
5. Carson McCullers, *The Member of the Wedding* (Harmondsworth: Penguin, 1962) part I, p. 7. First published 1946.
6. Ibid., part II, p. 141.

7. This fact is mentioned in Virginia Spenser Carr, *The Lonely Hunter* (New York: Anchor Books, 1976) p. 13. Many other details of Carson McCullers's childhood are given in this book.

8. Mary McCarthy, *Memories of a Catholic Girlhood* (Heinemann, 1957) pp. 87ff.

9. Mary McCarthy, *The Group* (Weidenfeld & Nicolson, 1963) ch. 14.

10. Simone de Beauvoir, *Force of Circumstance,* tr. Richard Howard (Andre Deutsch and Weidenfeld & Nicolson, 1965) p. 270. First published in Paris by Librairie Gallimard, 1963.

11. Jean-Paul Sartre, 'Nathalie Sarraute', *Situations,* tr. Benita Eisher (Hamish Hamilton, 1965) p. 195.

12. Iris Murdoch, *The Sovereignty of Good* (Routledge & Kegan Paul, 1970), p. 64.

13. For a full discussion of this point see A. S. Byatt, *Degrees of Freedom: The Novels of Iris Murdoch* (Chatto & Windus, 1970) pp. 14ff.

14. Iris Murdoch, 'The Sublime and the Good', *Chicago Review,* vol. 13, no. 3 (Autumn 1959).

15. Iris Murdoch, *The Sovereignty of Good*, pp. 103f.

16. Muriel Spark, 'My Conversion', *Twentieth Century,* Autumn 1961, p. 63.

Bibliography

The place of publication is London unless otherwise stated. Novels, plays and poetry referred to in the text are not included here, though where a page reference is required the edition used is mentioned in the Notes and References.

Allen, Walter, *The English Novel* (Harmondsworth: Penguin, 1958).

Armens, Sven, *Archetypes of the Family in Literature* (Seattle and London: University of Washington Press, 1966).

Asquith, Cynthia, *Married to Tolstoy* (Hutchinson, 1960).

Beauvoir, Simone de, *Force of Circumstance,* tr. Richard Howard (André Deutsch and Weidenfeld & Nicolson, 1965).

———— *The Second Sex,* tr. and ed. H. M. Parshley (Harmondsworth: Penguin, 1972).

Boulton, J. T. (ed.), *Daniel Defoe* (Batsford, 1965).

Bowra, C. M., *Landmarks in Greek Literature* (Weidenfeld & Nicolson, 1966).

Brinnin, John Malcolm, *The Third Rose* (Boston and Toronto: Little, Brown, 1959).

Byatt, A. S., *Degrees of Freedom: The Novels of Iris Murdoch* (Chatto & Windus, 1970).

Cargill, Oscar, *The Novels of Henry James* (New York: Macmillan, 1960).

Carr, Virginia Spencer, *The Lonely Hunter* (New York: Anchor Books, 1976).

Crowley, J. Donald (ed.), *Hawthorne: The Critical Heritage* (Routledge & Kegan Paul, 1970).

Drabble, Margaret, *Arnold Bennett: A Biography* (Weidenfeld & Nicolson, 1974).

Dusinberre, Juliet, *Shakespeare and the Nature of Women* (Macmillan, 1975).

Eaves, T. C. Duncan and Kimpel, Ben D., *Samuel Richardson: A Biography* (Oxford University Press, 1971).

Edel, Leon, *Henry James: The Master 1901–1916* (Rupert Hart-Davis, 1972).

Fiedler, Leslie A., *Love and Death in the American Novel* (New York: Criterion Books, 1960).

Gaskell, Elizabeth, *The Life of Charlotte Brontë,* ed. Alan Shelston (Harmondsworth: Penguin, 1975; first edition, 1857).

Gillie, Christopher, *Character in English Literature* (Chatto & Windus, 1967).

Gittings, Robert, *Young Thomas Hardy* (Heinemann, 1975).

Golden, Morris, *Richardson's Characters* (Ann Arbor: University of Michigan Press, 1963).

Gray, Ronald, *Ibsen: A Dissenting View* (Cambridge University Press, 1977).

Higginbotham, John (ed.), *Greek and Latin Literature* (Methuen, 1969).

Kitto, H. D. F., *The Greeks* (Harmondsworth: Penguin, 1951).

Lane, Margaret, *The Brontë Story* (Heinemann, 1953).

Lawrence, D. H., *Phoenix* (ed. Edward D. MacDonald) (Heinemann, 1936).

Levin, Harry, *The Power of Blackness* (New York: Alfred A. Knopf, 1976).

Lewis, C. S., *The Allegory of Love* (Oxford University Press, 1936).

Lucas, F. L., *Greek Drama for the Common Reader* (Chatto & Windus, 1967).

McCarthy, Mary, *Memories of a Catholic Girlhood* (Heinemann, 1957).

McCullers, Carson, *The Mortgaged Heart* (ed. Margarita Smith) (Barrie & Jenkins, 1972).

McKillop, Alan Dugald, *The Early Masters of English Fiction* (University of Kansas Press, 1956; Constable, 1962).

Mansfield, Katherine, *The Letters and Journals of Katherine Mansfield* (ed. C. K. Stead) (Allen Lane, 1977).

Marder, Herbert, *Feminism and Art: A Study of Virginia Woolf* (University of Chicago Press, 1968).

Mellow, James R., *Charmed Circle: Gertrude Stein and Company* (Phaidon Press, 1974).

Meyers, Jeffrey, *Katherine Mansfield: A Biography* (Hamish Hamilton, 1978).

Miller, Robert P., *Chaucer: Sources and Backgrounds* (New York: Oxford University Press, 1977).

Moore, J. R., *Daniel Defoe: Citizen of the Modern World* (University of Chicago Press, 1958).

Murdoch, Iris, 'Against Dryness', *Encounter,* January 1961.

—— *The Sovereignty of Good* (Routledge & Kegan Paul, 1970).

—— 'The Sublime and the Good', *Chicago Review,* vol. 13, Autumn 1959.

Murray, Gilbert, *Aeschylus* (Oxford University Press, 1940).

Muscatine, Charles, *Chaucer and the French Tradition* (Berkeley, Los Angeles, and London: University of California Press, 1957).

Nadeau, Maurice, *The Greatness of Flaubert,* tr. Barbara Bray (Alcove Press, 1972).

Novak, Maximilian E., *Defoe and the Nature of Man* (Oxford University Press, 1963).

Preston, John, *The Created Self* (Heinemann, 1970).

Redinger, Ruby V., *George Eliot: The Emergent Self* (The Bodley Head, 1975).

Rivière, Joan (ed.), *Developments in Psycho-Analysis* (Hogarth Press, 1952).

Sartre, Jean-Paul, *The Philosophy of Jean-Paul Sartre,* ed. and int. Robert Denoon Cumming (New York: Random House, 1965).

—— *Search for a Method,* tr. Hazel E. Barnes (New York: Vintage Books, 1968).

—— *Situations,* tr. Benita Eisher (Hamish Hamilton, 1965).

Spark, Muriel, 'My Conversion', *Twentieth Century,* Autumn 1961.

Starkie, Enid, *Flaubert: The Making of the Master* (Weidenfeld & Nicolson, 1967).

Stein, Gertrude, *Look at Me Now and Here I Am,* ed. Patricia Meyerowitz (Harmondsworth: Penguin, 1967).

Thornton, Agatha, *People and Themes in Homer's Odyssey* (Methuen, 1970).

Tillyard, E. M. W., *The English Epic and its Background* (Chatto & Windus, 1954).

Tolstoy, Tatyana, *Tolstoy Remembered,* tr. Derek Coltman, int. John Bayley (Michael Joseph, 1977).

Troyat, Henri, *Tolstoy* (New York: Doubleday, 1967 W. H. Allen, 1968).

Vossler, Karl, *Mediaeval Culture: An Introduction to Dante and His Time* (New York: Frederick Ungar, 1958).

Watt, Ian, *The Rise of the Novel* (Chatto & Windus, 1957).

Williams, Charles, *The Figure of Beatrice: A Study in Dante* (Faber & Faber, 1943).

Woolf, Virginia;, *A Room of One's Own* (Hogarth Press, 1928; Harmondsworth: Penguin, 1945).

────── *Three Guineas* (Cresset Press, 1938).

Index